THE ECONOMIES OF CHINA AND INDIA
Cooperation and Conflict

Volume 3: Economic Growth, Employment and Inclusivity: The International Environment

THE ECONOMIES OF CHINA AND INDIA
Cooperation and Conflict

Volume 3: Economic Growth, Employment and Inclusivity: The International Environment

Editors

Manmohan Agarwal

Centre for Development Studies, India & Research and Information Systems for Developing Countries, India

John Whalley

University of Western Ontario, Canada & Centre for International Governance Innovation (CIGI), Canada & National Bureau of Economic Research (NBER), USA

World Scientific

NEW JERSEY • LONDON • SINGAPORE • BEIJING • SHANGHAI • HONG KONG • TAIPEI • CHENNAI • TOKYO

Published by

World Scientific Publishing Co. Pte. Ltd.
5 Toh Tuck Link, Singapore 596224
USA office: 27 Warren Street, Suite 401-402, Hackensack, NJ 07601
UK office: 57 Shelton Street, Covent Garden, London WC2H 9HE

Library of Congress Cataloging-in-Publication Data
Names: Whalley, John, editor. | Agarwal, Manmohan, editor. | Wang, Jing, 1974 April 21– editor.
Title: The economies of China and India : cooperation and conflict / editor-in-chief, John Walley; [edited by] Manmohan Agarwal (Centre for Development Studies, India & Research and Information Systems for Developing Countries, India), Jing Wang (University of Western Ontario, Canada)
Description: New Jersey : World Scientific, [2016] Contents: Volume 1. China and India: The International Context and Economic Growth, Manufacturing Performance and Rural Development -- Volume 2. Competitiveness, External Cooperation Strategy, and Income Distribution: Changes in China -- Volume 3. Economic Growth, Employment and Inclusivity: The International Environment.
Identifiers: LCCN 2016006686| ISBN 9789813100398 (hbk : set : alk. paper) | ISBN 9789813100534 (hbk : vol 3 : alk. paper) | ISBN 9789813100527 (hbk : vol 2 : alk. paper) | ISBN 9789813100510 (hbk : vol 1 : alk. paper)
Subjects: LCSH: Economic development--China. | Economic development--India. | China--Economic conditions--1949– | India--Economic conditions--1947– | China--Economic policy--1949– | India--Economic policy--1947– | China--Foreign economic relations. | India--Foreign economic relations.
Classification: LCC HC427.95 .E34135 2016 | DDC 330.951--dc23
LC record available at https://lccn.loc.gov/2016006686

British Library Cataloguing-in-Publication Data
A catalogue record for this book is available from the British Library.

Desk Editors: Herbert Moses/Yu Shan Tay

Typeset by Stallion Press
Email: enquiries@stallionpress.com

Printed in Singapore

Contents

Acknowledgment

The editors would like to acknowledge the support of the China Policy and Research Group (CPRG) at the University of Western Ontario (Canada) for the participation of Chinese researchers in the project. CPRG acknowledges supports from the Ontario Research Fund and Centre for International Governance Innovation (CIGI, Canada). The editors thank the staff at World Scientific Publishing, Herbert Moses, Xiao Qi, R. Raghavarshini, as well as Zvi Ruder for logistical and moral support. Editor Manmohan Agarwal also would like to thank the participants of seminars at the Centre for Development Studies Kerala where some of the papers were presented for helpful comments.

About the Editors

John Whalley is the Professor of Economics and Co-Director of the Centre for the Study of International Economic Relations at Western University; Research Associate at the National Bureau of Economic Research (NBER); Coordinator of Global Economy Group at the CESifo; and Distinguished Fellow at the Centre for Global Governance Innovation (CIGI). Professor Whalley is ranked No.1 in Canada among publishing economists in the RePEc rankings. He won the Hellmuth Prize for Achievement in Research, and also is 2012 Killam Prize Winner.

Manmohan Agarwal is the Reserve Bank Chair at the Centre for Development Studies at Thiruvananthapuram, Kerala, India. Earlier he had retired as a professor from Jawaharlal Nehru University, New Delhi, India where he taught for almost thirty years. Subsequently, he was a senior fellow at the Centre for International Governance Innovation (CIGI) at Waterloo Canada where he worked on issues of the world economy including the G20 and South-South cooperation. He is also a Senior Fellow at Research and Information Systems for Developing Countries, New Delhi and an adjunct senior fellow with the Institute of Chinese Studies. He also worked for a number of years at the World Bank and the International Monetary Fund. His research has been mainly in the area of International Economics and Development Economics.

List of Contributors

Vinoj Abraham
Centre for Development Studies, India

Manmohan Agarwal
RBI Chair Professor, Centre for Development Studies, India
Adjunct Fellow, Research and Information System for Developing Countries (RIS), India

Aritri Chakravarty
Centre for Development Studies, India

Upasak Das
Centre for Development Studies, India

Sunandan Ghosh
Centre for Development Studies, India

Ritesh Jain
Jawaharlal Nehru University, India

Ritika Jain
Center for Development Studies, India

Praveena Kodoth
Center for Development Studies, India

Meeta Keswani Mehra
Jawaharlal Nehru University, India

Rita Pandey
National Institute of Public Finance and Policy, India

Amit S Ray
Centre for Development Studies, India
Jawaharlal Nehru University, India

Introduction

Manmohan Agarwal

The book analyzes major developments in the Indian economy. These developments have been shaped by the economic and social objectives of the government. For instance, India's First Five Year Plan notes that one of the directive principles of the constitution enjoined the government to promote the welfare of the people, which then implied that citizens have the right to an adequate means of livelihood. Improvement of the social conditions of the citizens has been integral to the government's objectives. The role of employment creation and social safety nets has been central to policy debates on how to improve living conditions.

The economy achieved its highest growth rates in the middle of the last decade. This was the culmination of a period of accelerating growth that was accompanied by increasing exports of goods and services. Growth rates of GDP and of exports have declined since the financial crisis of 2008 and the subsequent slowdown of the world economy. A natural question that is explored is the relation between the world economy and Indian economic performance and what changes in the international economic governance architecture would re-ignite growth in India. We also find that this high growth did not translate very well into improvement in living conditions and so the government has adopted a number of social safety nets, but here also the rules of the WTO have affected the ability of the government, as noted in some of the chapters.

The government has also sought to enhance the employment effect of growth, but despite this, employment has increased slowly resulting in substantial emigration, both temporary and permanent. In earlier years, this emigration was viewed negatively as a brain drain. More recently, it has been seen as a source of financial resources, remittances, and also a channel for transfer of technology and skills as workers move to and fro between the home country and the host country. These interrelated issues are analyzed in this volume.

The first section deals with the international system and how this affects developing countries, and also India. A major feature of the international monetary system (IMS) has been the accumulation of foreign exchange reserves by developing countries usually by running current account surpluses. These surpluses are a precautionary measure to obviate the need to borrow from the International Monetary Fund (IMF) in case the country has a current account deficit. Such an accumulation of reserves is a signal of the displeasure of developing countries with the governance of the IMF, the adjustment policies thrust by the IMF on developing countries and the ad hoc nature and so the unreliability of the resources available to help developing countries. The chapter by Agarwal (A1) shows that this accumulation of reserves is beyond any rule of thumb of what an adequate level of reserves should be. Though these reserves enabled developing countries to cope with the 2008 financial crisis, it is not desirable from a systemic point of view. The author argues that such accumulation is a misallocation of resources as in effect the poorer countries are lending to richer countries, mainly the US. Also, the imbalances that have arisen because of the policies adopted by developing countries are held by the G20 to be responsible for the 2008 crisis. The need for reforms is accepted but the agreed reforms have not been implemented.

The Fund has imposed policies that give priority to external balance at the expense of domestic full employment, contrary to the objective of Keynes and White. Also, the lack of sharing of the adjustment burden between deficit and surplus countries, as desired by Keynes, has imparted a deflationary bias to policies.

Developing countries, frustrated by the lack of progress towards reform of the IMF, have also established facilities to provide additional balance of payment (BOP) financing for their members. Though the amounts available under these schemes are substantial they would be insufficient to tackle a full blown exchange crisis. The chapter also argues that the schemes do not indicate any new model of BOP adjustment. Hence, these schemes are no challenge to the hegemony of the IMF. They however are a small beginning and may be a pointer of things to come.

The chapter by Ray and Jain (RJ) discusses another aspect of international governance. The Trade Related Intellectual Property Rights (TRIPs) agreement in the Uruguay Round (UR) had strengthened intellectual property rights provisions. At the commencement of the Doha Round, developing countries were allowed certain flexibilities, particularly in the production and trade in generics. Since then, the developed countries have been incorporating in their bilateral and regional trade agreement provisions that are stricter than the UR agreement, what is called TRIPs plus, and so restricting the flexibilities that were available to developing countries. The RJ paper deals with one aspect that would constrain developing countries. The issue is, what is the basis on which the production and sale of a generic drug is permitted by the authorities? Extensive data on the safety trials for a drug have to be supplied by the producer in order to enable authorities to judge whether it should be allowed in the market. The question is, What should be the process for the approval of a generic drug?

Laws usually allow for a minimum period before the generic could be permitted in the market after the approval to the original producer in order to enable him to benefit from his innovation. A second issue is, what data can the authorities use to see if the generic is safe? If the authorities cannot use the data provided by the original drug producer then the generic drug producer will have to undertake clinical trials which will raise the cost of producing the generic. This obviously has implications for the affordability of drugs. The authors show after detailed analysis of the negotiations in the UR that the TRIPs agreement allowed the authorities to use the information provided by the innovator to pronounce on the safety of the generic drug, but developed countries are trying to close this flexibility. If they succeed then the cost of health care would increase, and it would be more difficult to meet any health goals that the international community may consider desirable such as in the Millennium Development Goals or the more recent Sustainable Development Goals.

Improving the living standards of their people was often a key objective of leaders and policy makers in many newly independent countries of the 1950s and the 1960s. That such a goal was enjoined on Indian policy makers was noted above. The importance of poverty reduction and improvements in other social indicators re-surfaced among the international development community in the 1980s, as the policies adopted to tackle the macro imbalances that had emerged after the hikes in the price of oil in 1973–1974 and the subsequent debt crisis were believed to have had severe deleterious effects on social welfare. A new social consensus was forged and finally accepted at the United Nations in 2000 as the Millennium Development Goals (MDGs). The MDGs recognized that social deprivation is multi-dimensional transcending poverty to include other factors such as malnourishment, high levels of mortality, infant, child and maternal mortality, morbidity because of diseases such as malaria and tuberculosis, lack of adequate education and gender inequalities. It therefore, sought for action to ameliorate standards across a wide spectrum of living conditions.

The chapter by Agarwal (A2) shows that progress in achieving the MDGs is very varied across the different developing regions. However, the regions of Latin America (LAC), East Asia Pacific (EAP) and the Middle East and North Africa (MNA) are likely to achieve most of the MDG goals though they did start off with better social indicators. South Asia (SA) and Sub-Saharan Africa (SSA) that started with the worst indicators are likely to fail in achieving most of the targets. Progress on the MDGs depends on two factors, the rate of growth of GDP and whether the government has specific programmes for the disadvantaged. For instance, progress in EAP has been mainly because of their rapid growth whereas growth has been slower in LAC but the contingent cash transfer programmes have helped in improving social indicators. Social improvements have lagged in countries in SSA because of their low rates of growth of GDP. However, progress has also been slow in SA despite the region having higher rates of growth. When we calculated the response of the social indicators to the growth rate of per capita GDP, we found that these elasticities were much lower in Asia, both East and South.

Even among the South Asian countries, India has a very poor record on the MDGs, despite high rates of growth and a myriad of social programmes. Obviously, the delivery of these programmes has been very poor.

What is the role of the international community in helping improve living standards? Aid has been declining in importance whether measured as a share of GDP or investment. On the other hand, the importance of migration and remittances has increased. A chapter by Agarwal (A3) analyzes the effect of remittances on development. The chapter notes that there have been two periods of extensive migration. One was in the 19th century mainly from Europe to what were the areas of recent settlement, mainly North America, Argentina, Australia and New Zealand. That was permanent migration. Remittances were not substantial. Therefore, the only effect on the origin countries was the labor market effect, and this was to raise wage rates; also migration reduced wage rates in the destination countries. There is little evidence that social conditions improved in the origin countries till much later in the 19th century, almost the end.

A3 does not find any significant link between remittances and development whether at the regional level or the individual country level. This sheds some light on the old question whether emigration is detrimental to the welfare of those left behind in the origin country. It was believed that emigration resulted in a country losing its most skilled people and this 'brain drain' adversely affected its prospects. Furthermore, the country lost the money it had spent on training these people. Schemes were devised to enable countries to recoup their expenditures on training the emigrant. In more recent times, it has been argued that because skilled people can move to and fro between the country of destination and country of origin, their skills are not lost to the country of origin and in fact, they could provide additional technical knowledge, so there is a 'brain gain'. Furthermore, their remittances could lead to increased investment and growth in the country of origin. Our analysis does not find any positive relation between remittances and either investment ratios or ratios of growth of GDP. It seems that the brain drain might be more important than the brain gain.

The second section concentrates on analyzing developments in the Indian economy. Two chapters, those by Ray and Ghosh (RG) and Agarwal and Ghosh (AG), provide an overall macro perspective. The chapter by Das and Chakravarti (DC) deals with the use of information in the agricultural sector. It adds to the analysis of the growth of productivity in the agricultural sector by Agarwal, Lele and Goswami (2015) in an earlier volume in the series which had found that India was lagging in productivity growth relative to Brazil, China and Indonesia, three other large developing countries.

The RG chapter places India integration into the world economy after a turnaround in its policy regime in the 1990s in the context of the evolving domestic and international economic policy environment. The authors seek to see how the shift in the 1990s fits in the evolution of India's development policy framework. The authors also tackle the interesting question. Why did India fail to join the league of 'Asian Miracle' economies that embarked upon a phenomenal growth path during the 1960s, 1970s and 1980s.

Instead of a dichotomous division of India's policy regimes into an inward oriented one and an outward oriented one, the authors propose a fourfold classification. The first phase of the 50s and 60s was marked by a strenuous effort to build a self-reliant economy that could accomplish a complete set of tasks. This involved developing a diversified industrial structure. The choice of an industrialization strategy based on the capital goods industries and the choice of the public sector as an instrument of implementation owed much to the example of the Soviet Union. The second phase of the late 60s and the 70s responded to the changing international environment the wars with Pakistan and the dependence on US for food aid. There was a deepening of the earlier self-reliance model. The Patent Act of 1970 limiting the period of grant of patents and that also only for processes and not products furthered the earlier attempt to foster technological self-reliance. However, there was now greater reliance on the private sector which had grown in the earlier phase though, industrial licensing continued to govern the growth of the private sector. Furthermore, the Foreign Exchange Regulation Act of 1974 sought to reduce the influence of foreign transnationals and the Monopolies Restrictive Trade Practices Act sought to prevent concentration of economic power.

Various inefficiencies bedeviled the industrial sector leading to slow growth of productivity and coupled with the example of the East Asian economies pointed towards the need for a shift in the policy framework. During the third period of the 1980s, there were tentative steps towards liberalization, but these were half-hearted. The authors characterize this period as "There was an attempt to liberalize particular aspects of the control system without affecting the system itself in any fundamental way." This change starting in 1991 saw the emergence of the fourth period where the objective of development policy was to have a low tariff trade regime coupled with far greater reliance on the market to govern resource allocations and for the private sector to play a larger role.

This shift resulted in an increase in the trade to GDP ratio, and RG use the Bai–Perron test to identify two breaks in this series, one in 1992 and the other in 2003. However, RG find two breaks in the GDP series, 1989 and 2000, namely, the increase in growth preceded the increase in trade openness. However, the authors caution against drawing this conclusion as changes in growth rate and increase in trade openness seem to go together. While growth in India approached those in the miracle economies of East Asia, export of labor intensive mass manufactures was not the driver of growth in India.

RG find that India's post-colonial policy thrust on public funded higher education and research in Science & Technology, created a strong base of human capital and technological capability. This allowed for the rapid expansion of technologically sophisticated sectors including modern services. These modern sectors acted as the key drivers of India's economic emergence during the last couple of decades.

The chapter by Agarwal and Ghosh (AG) covers some of the same ground. They take a long-term view of developments in the Indian economy analyzing the behavior of different indicators since the First Plan that started in 1951. AG find a very substantial effect of the shutdown of aid by the World Bank and the US in the mid-60s. This resulted in a severe BOP crisis and a period, of structural adjustment. During this period the rate of growth was substantially lower than the previous three plans. Once the adjustment was over, growth started picking up and there was a gradual acceleration of the growth rate from the mid-70s to the 1991 crisis.

The cut-off of aid had another effect. The development strategy during the second and third plans was based on public investment in the setting up of capital goods industries whose output was demanded by the government for further investment in capital goods industries, but this was financed substantially by foreign aid and the cut-off of aid derailed this strategy. As public investment fell, there was substantial excess capacity in the capital goods industries which resulted in a high capital output ratio. The political differences between the US and India which resulted in the cut-off of aid had very significant results. It brought to a halt the reforms that had been ushered in the mid-60s in the trade regime that relied more on the exchange rate which had been devalued. There had been considerable roll back of high tariffs, reduction in export subsidies and reduction in import quotas. Further significant liberalization did not take place till the 1991 BOP crisis. AG argue that after every crisis the economy recovered very quickly and this together with an accelerating growth rate made the case for liberalization weaker.

Since the reform process started in 1991 statistical analysis confirms that the behavior of a number of indicators has improved and their variability has been reduced, but there seemed to be no significant acceleration of the growth rate of per capita income between the 1980s, the 1990s and the first decade of this century. Furthermore, the authors do not find any significant difference in the growth rates of the manufacturing and services sectors. The backward and forward linkages of the manufacturing sector were larger than that of the services sector. It is hard to support the contention that Indian growth is more service-led than manufacturing-led.

But AG do find a significant increase in exports whether these be of goods or of non-factor services or of factor services in the shape of remittances, corroborating the results of RG.

AG then undertook an analysis of structural changes in the Indian economy. Though most of the crises that had struck the Indian economy were exogenous and externally generated, the authors do not find that breaks in the growth rate of the Indian economy coincide with those of the world economy or in the GDP growth rate of low income countries in the aggregate. AG find breaks in the GDP series in India in 1977–1978, 1986–1987, 2003–2004. None of these correspond to any significant changes in policies, except possibly the 1986–1987 break. This seems to follow the changes in import and industrial licensing policies in 1985–1986, but there is no corresponding break in imports. The break in imports occurs in1984–1985, before the change in policy. The breaks in the manufacturing series usually follow the break in the GDP series suggesting that the constraint facing the manufacturing sector was a demand constraint. In that case, liberalization should help the sector as now the world market represents the demand. Granger causality tests, however, do not support any causality between the growth rates of the manufacturing sector and GDP. AG find that manufacturing growth does depend on imports of non-oil commodities. The dynamic interrelationships underlying the behavior of the Indian economy needs further analysis.

The chapter by DC argues that information is important for decision making in agriculture. Information could be of technology or rainfall or price forecasts. They investigate access to information, how inclusive it is. The inclusiveness of access to information is important to ensure that the benefits of any new technology are widespread, but inclusiveness of access will also determine the effect of any new technology on total agricultural output and thus on the economy, as small holders in India are a substantial proportion of the total agricultural households. The authors note that several studies have found a significant linkage between access to information and agricultural efficiency. The government in India has taken several policy initiatives to provide information to farmers through agricultural extension services and universities. Also several non-government entities have started providing information.

Their chapter attempts to examine the access to information by marginal famers having small land holdings. It also explores if poor and deprived farmers in terms of social group, household headship and consumption expenditure are likely to get the required agricultural information.

Among all the households in the sample, about 44% had accessed information on agricultural issues. The sample of households which have accessed information is dominated by the General caste category and fewer households in the lower groups (scheduled castes (SC) and scheduled tribes (ST)) have accessed information. Also, the more prosperous and bigger farmers access information more. The average land possessed by the farmers, who have accessed information is about 1.9 ha and land possessed by those who did not access information is 1.4 ha. More than 67% of households accessing information possess *pucca* houses. Further, the households which have accessed information on agriculture are found to be significantly poorer that those which have not. For example, among the households who accessed information, 34% belong to the poorest 2 quintiles of MPCE. For households with no information access, this figure is about 45%. Also, expectedly, households with female heads or with illiterate heads access information less.

All these findings reveal that access to information on agriculture has not been inclusive. Clearly, it is found that small and marginal farmers with low income and education lag behind in accessing the much needed information for improving agricultural yield and productivity.

The authors find that government agencies are more inclusive than other private sources of information. They reach more of households residing in *kaccha* houses and those who are worse-off in terms of consumption. Also, land possession is negatively correlated with the probability of households to access information from Government sources. These results are borne out both by regression analysis and non-parametric estimation.

Mehra and Prasad (MP) broadly divide the entire process of developing clean energy from planning to development of complimentary policy instruments into two stages: (i) articulating an energy R&D framework and clearly identifying the barriers faced by different technologies so that policy makers know which technologies to support, and (ii) basic guiding principles in actual design and implementation stage. The authors concentrate on the second.

MP see the necessity for clean energy arising from the need for (i) reduced greenhouse gas (GHGs) emissions, (ii) energy security, (iii) energy access, (iv) lower energy cost, (v) maintenance of international competitiveness and (vi) modernizing national energy systems. While enumerating a variety of market failures that bedevil the search for clean energy, they stress that the most common form of market failure is unpriced social costs of emissions. At the same time inability to appropriate all the benefits and learning-by-doing that leads to decreasing costs can be deterrents to development of clean energy. Major market barriers stem from low interest and awareness of policy makers, producers and consumers with regard to energy concerns, capital market barriers, and distortionary fiscal and regulatory policies. MP stress that apart from identification of specific barriers to renewable energy (RE) technology innovation and diffusion, it is necessary to differentiate the barriers faced by different RE technologies.

They argue that several considerations, with significant overlap among them, determine the choice and design of technology policies. Enhancement of economic efficiency is the primary criterion to rank policy choices. Furthermore, it is important to decide whether to use quantity or price instruments. The choice of appropriate policy instruments will also depend on how optimal are the emissions policies in dealing with GHG emissions reduction and on the availability of many critical factors such as skilled manpower, R&D capability, strong supporting institutions and capacity for developing systems for price discovery. Knowledge about the contribution of specific market failures is also important for making appropriate choices. It is also necessary to ensure consistency between policies enacted at the sub-national/state level with national policies and goals.

The most important aspects of designing complementary fiscal policy instruments are the determination of support level and the duration of support. The policies can be classified into fiscal measures, financial measures, institutional and stricter patent rules to reduce upfront costs and risks of investments. The purpose is to directly target and incentivize the private investment in various stages of technology development and diffusion. As a general rule, technology-push policies such as R&D support, financial incentives, and procurement incentives are more suitable for stimulating commercialization and initial market creation for new technologies. Once a technology is established in the market, further growth can be stimulated by policies such as feed-in-tariffs (FIT), renewable portfolio standards (RPS) and other financial incentives, which are market pull policies.

The authors then analyze three support schemes for more detailed analysis. These are price-based market instruments such as FITs and feed-in-premiums (FITPs), quantity based market instruments called renewable RPSs or quota obligations, and tendering/competitive bidding.

MP conclude that the issue of design and implementation of support measures for renewable energy technologies is complex and requires a nuanced, case-by-case approach.

As noted above, creation of new employment was a major feature of India's plans. The heavy industry industrialization strategy was adopted as it was seen to lead to a higher rate of growth in the long run, but it was recognized that the heavy industries would not create very much employment. Therefore, the handicraft sector which was very labor intensive was to be encouraged to supply the needed consumer goods. In his chapter, Abraham studies discrimination in the labor market. Such discrimination is an expression of inequality as well as perpetuates inequality and inequity. Even though such discrimination is illegal constitutionally, it persists in practice. Discrimination in the labor market occurs through three important modes, one is through barriers to entry into particular labor markets, two is through restrictive occupational mobility within the internal labor markets and third is by way of discriminating on returns to work for the same occupation. While social exclusion from particular labor markets acts as a direct entry barrier into them, wages and earnings discrimination provide a 'premia for tastes' and acts as a signaling mechanism towards discouraging marginalized communities to participate in particular labor markets.

The average daily wages for SC, ST and neo Buddhists, who are very often converted SCs in 1983 were much lower than for 'Others' for both males and females in urban and rural areas. After more than a quarter century, in 2009–2010, the wage discrimination continued to be large. Daily wages among the STs for males, in rural and urban areas and urban females have grown faster than for SCs, though these growth rates lagged behind those for the Others in all categories. This essentially has meant that there is a tendency towards convergence of wages in case of STs, while simultaneously wages of those belonging to the SC are diverging from those of the Others.

In the rural areas, SC wages which were 71% that of Others in 1983, were only 61% in 2009–2010, a widening of the gap, whereas ST wages rose from 72% of Others to 81%. Similarly, in urban areas the relative ST wages rose from 70% to 86%, while for SCs the gap widened as relative wages declined from 65% to 54% during this period. Furthermore, there is a considerable wage gap between males and females within each of these social groups. Male wages were considerably higher than female wages across all social groups. Overall, the gender gap declined as ratio of female wages to male wages rose from 52% in 1983 to 59% in 2009–2010 in rural areas and from 53% to 78% in urban areas.

The government has been following a policy of privatization of public enterprises to improve the efficiency of their operations. However, privatization has been opposed by the trade unions, partly as they fear that privatization will lead to job losses at these erstwhile public enterprises. Jain, in her chapter, notes that since the late 80s, employment in central public sector enterprises (CPSEs) in India has been plummeting. This period overlaps with the inception and evolution of disinvestment since 1991 as a remedial policy tool to improve the performance of the CPSEs. Disinvestment is defined as the transfer of ownership of public sector enterprises from the government to the private sector. She attempts to analyze the effect of privatization on employment by focusing on the employment decisions of all CPSEs (approximately 230) from 1991–1992 to 2011–2012. She uses an instrumental variable approach to analyze this issue. She recognizes the political nature of many decisions regarding public sector enterprises, including that of disinvestment. An important factor in the behavior of CPSEs is the ideology of the government of the state where the enterprise is located. The hypothesis is that ideology not only affects employment directly but also conditions the influence of disinvestment on employee size.

The study finds that, unexpectedly, disinvestment has a strong positive impact on employment. The main reason behind this result is that disinvestment has a positive impact on firm performance through the efficiency channel. This improved firm performance leads to greater output and hence expansion of employment. Furthermore, the impact of disinvestment on employment is conditioned by the ideology of the state where the enterprise operates. Enterprises in right winged states have a stronger impact of disinvestment on employment *vis-à-vis* the left-winged ones. This may be attributed to better labor market conditions in the right-winged states (as compared to the left-winged ones); which strengthens the impact of disinvestment on employment.

The lack of employment opportunities for the unskilled forces migration internally, mainly between the states from the East to the states in the North and West, though migration to the Southern states is increasing as well, and externally mainly to the Gulf countries. Kodoth studies the system, or rather the non-system, which governs the migration of domestic workers from parts of Kerala and Andhra Pradesh, their working conditions and experiences in the Gulf and the rules that govern their working conditions.

Since the 1990s, Indian governments have successively tightened regulations. Potential emigrants with less than 10 years of education require emigration clearance from the Protector of Emigrants (POE) in order to migrate. At present, to be eligible for emigration clearance, domestic workers must be at least 30 years old and must present themselves personally before the POE in possession of a work contract attested by the Indian embassy at the destination, and provision of a security deposit of $2500 by the sponsor-employment. The security deposit would be used by the embassy for repatriation of the worker if necessary. To qualify for a visa, aspirants must pass a medical test, conducted by accredited hospitals in select cities specifically for the Gulf countries, and for emigration clearance they must get a certificate of clearance from the police.

The stronger barriers against the migration of women domestics have failed to stem the flow of domestics from India. Furthermore, it drives aspirants to rely on informal/illegal means to access overseas jobs which renders their employment precarious and worsens their condition.

Their condition is very adversely affected by the *kafala* system which governs their status in the country of employment. Emigrant domestic workers from South India are found in two broad categories of employment in the Middle East, i.e. they have full-time live-in jobs with employers, who have sponsored them as mandated by the system. In case they decide to leave because of mistreatment, they have to seek informal employment that is outside the purview of the system. The regulatory system in the Middle East introduces friction in the relationship between sponsor–employers and domestic workers. The legal obligation of sponsors to pay for the emigration and subsistence of domestic workers imparts a sense of entitlement over the latter and shapes violation of rights. The benefit of this provision, however, is usually absorbed by intermediaries. Thus, South Indian domestic workers invest large sums of money on emigration and are under tremendous pressure to tolerate exploitation and abuse in order to continue employment with the sponsor. In this context, India's emigration policy, which relies on barriers to prevent the flow of domestic workers to the Middle East and denies them support in the destination pushes the latter to depend on informal support networks and heightens their vulnerability in overseas employment. Severe ill treatment by sponsors or aspirations for better jobs could motivate domestics to seek informal employment, which is illegal in the Middle East. The chapter draws attention to how Indian policy undermines the ability of emigrant domestic workers to combat the ill effects of the regulatory framework in the Middle East and induces them instead to make precarious employment choices.

Acknowledgment

We thank all the contributors for their cooperation. We hope that analysts and students will find the book useful. The chapters also point to the many issues that remain unresolved and we hope that researchers will be encouraged to work on these issues.

Part I

International Situation

Chapter 1

International Monetary System: Response of Developing Countries to Its Shortcomings

Manmohan Agarwal

RBI Chair Professor
Centre for Development Studies
Thiruvananthapuram, Kerala, India
manmohan@cds.ac.in

Abstract: Accumulation of reserves by developing countries to avoid borrowing from the IMF with whose governance and policies they are dissatisfied, helped developing countries cope with the 2008 financial crisis. It is argued that it was bad for the world economy. The need for reforms is accepted but the agreed reforms have not been implemented.

The Fund has imposed policies that give priority to external balance at the expense of domestic full employment, contrary to the objective of Keynes and White. Also the lack of sharing of adjustment between deficit and surplus countries, as desired by Keynes, has imparted a deflationary bias to policies.

Developing countries have also established facilities to provide additional Balance of Payments (BOP) financing for their members. Though the amounts available under these schemes are substantial, they would be insufficient. Also the schemes do not indicate any new model of BOP adjustment. These schemes are no challenge to the hegemony of the Bretton Woods Institutions. They however are a small beginning and may be a pointer of things to come.

1 Introduction

The evolution of the world economy and the policies adopted by developing countries after the oil price rise increases in 1973 resulted in a prolonged period of very slow growth. During most of this period, many developing countries faced severe pressure on their external accounts and had extensive dealings with the International Monetary Fund (IMF) and the World Bank, the so-called Bretton Woods Twins. The conditions imposed by these institutions for the loans they granted to developing countries played a prominent part in determining the policies adopted by developing countries. Though the effects of these conditions on growth remain controversial, there is little doubt that growth did not pick up as was expected and also the social situation in these countries deteriorated. Developing countries became increasingly critical of these institutions, particularly the IMF. They were critical of its governance structure, the manner in which its resources are raised and its lending policies. Because of their unhappiness at the conditions imposed by the IMF for its loans, developing countries have tried to follow policies that would obviate the need to borrow from the IMF. A major component of these policies has been the accumulation of foreign exchange reserves. More recently, developing countries have sought to establish institutions to provide balance of payments assistance so that they do not have to approach the IMF.

In Section 2, we discuss the evolution of the world economy, particularly since 1973, noting the worsening performance in many developing countries. This provides the background to the discussion in Section 3 of the unhappiness of developing countries with the IMF, both with its governance and the conditions attached to its balance of payments (BOP) support. In Section 4 we discuss the response of developing countries, in terms of the accumulation of foreign exchange reserves. In Section 5, we discuss the response in terms of institutional innovation and whether this response is adequate. Section 6 contains the conclusions.

2 Evolution of the World Economy

Two features stand out in the post 1973 economic landscape. One, is the slowdown in the world economy and in many regions. Two, is the liberalization of trade and capital flows.

2.1 Economic performance of the world economy

The world economy moved to a permanently lower growth path after the 1973 oil price rise (Table 1). The impact on the growth rate was even more severe in the

Table 1. Growth in per capita GDP (Average annual %).

	1965–1973	1974–1982	1983–1990	1991–2000	2001–2007	2008–2009	2010–2013
World	3.3	0.9	1.9	1.3	2.0	–1.5	1.7
High Income OECD	4.2	1.6	3.1	2.0	1.9	–2.3	1.2
EAP	4.5	4.6	6.2	7.0	8.4	7.2	7.4
LAC	3.3	2.0	–0.4	1.4	2.0	–0.1	2.7
MNA	5.1	1.8	–0.1	1.6	3.1	2.1	0.6
SA	1.3	1.8	3.3	3.3	5.4	4.3	5.4
SSA	2.2	0	–1.2	–0.7	3.4	0.7	1.5

Note: The categories are as defined by the World Bank. EAP is East Asia and Pacific, LAC is Latin America and Caribbean, MNA is Middle East and North Africa, SA is South Asia and SSA is Sub-Saharan Africa.
Source: World Development Indicators (http://data.worldbank.org/data-catalog/world-development-indicators).

Table 2. External balance (% of GDP).

	1965–1973	1974–1982	1983–1990	1991–2000	2001–2007	2008–2009	2010–2013
EAP		0.6	–0.5	1.8	4.7	5.7	2.8
LAC	–0.7	1.6	3.4	–0.9	0.7	–1.0	–1.1
MNA	–0.7	–7.3	–8.1	3.2	3.4	n.a	n.a
SA	–1.6	–4.2	–3.1	–1.7	–2.8	–6.1	–5.9
SSA	–1.6	–4.6	2.3	0.1	0.1	–2.3	–1.5

Source: World Development Indicators (http://data.worldbank.org/data-catalog/world-development-indicators).

shorter run; per capita GDP of the world grew at only 1.4% per year between 1983 and 2000.

Growth rates in Asia, both East and South were hardly impacted by the oil price rises; growth in these economies accelerated for a considerable period of time after the oil price rise. The economies worse affected were those in Latin America (LAC) and Sub-Saharan Africa (SSA). Between 1983 and 2000, per capita GDP in the economies of LAC grew at barely 1% a year, while it declined in SSA by 0.6% a year. There is a substantial increase in growth rates during the period 2001–2007. Despite the post 2007 slowdown, growth rates were higher during 2010–2013 than they had been since 1974.

The external accounts improved after the considerable worsening in the early 1970s because of the oil price rise. They have, however, remained precarious. The external balance of LAC countries improved after the oil price rises (Table 2). It further improved after the debt crisis. A positive balance was necessary to repay loans as very often these were not being rolled over when they fell due.

SSA also had a quick turnaround from the large deficits of the 1974–1982 period. More recently the external balance has again worsened in SSA; but the deficit in the years 2010–2013 was already smaller than in the years 2008–2009. Financing of the external deficits has become easier because of remittances and capital flows. India has a large deficit on goods trade; but that is largely covered by remittances and the surplus on non-factor services trade. It seems that reluctance to borrow from the IMF is also manifesting itself in lower current account deficits.

We now discuss the role of external factors in the performance of developing countries.

2.2 Integration with the world economy

Developing countries reduced tariffs on imports, eliminated substantially quantitative restrictions on trade and liberalized capital flows particularly of foreign direct investment (FDI). The result can be seen in the higher share of exports and FDI in GDP.

The share of exports of goods and services (XGS) in GDP has increased almost consistently for developing country regions throughout the period 1965–2013 (Table 3). The only exceptions are the declines in the share after the 2008 crisis in EAP and LAC. Though, later the share started increasing again in LAC, it continued to decline in EAP. The share of XGS in GDP also declined in SSA in the period 2010–2013.

Capital flows, particularly FDI have been becoming more important as many developing countries have liberalized their capital accounts. First inward flows were liberalized and later outward flows.

Inward flows have increased considerably and have held up well even after the financial crisis (Table 4). Outward flows started much later and have been relatively smaller. These outward flows have increased for EAP and SSA after the financial crisis; they have decreased substantially only in the case of India.

Table 3. Exports of goods and services (% of GDP).

	1965–1973	1974–1982	1983–1990	1991–2000	2001–2007	2008–2009	2010–2013
EAP		13.2	15.6	26.5	38.9	36.6	34
LAC	10.1	14.1	16.5	17.2	22.3	21.7	23.0
MNA	19.7	24.1	18.6	24.9	35.5	n.a.	n.a.
SA	5.1	7.0	7.2	11.7	17.2	20.5	22.3
SSA	23.0	24.4	26.2	27.8	32.2	32.5	30.8

Source: World Development Indicators (http://data.worldbank.org/data-catalog/world-development-indicators).

Table 4. FDI flows (% of GDP).

	1974–1982	1983–1990	1991–2000	2001–2007	2008–2009	2010–2013
A. Inward Flows						
EAP	0.6	0.9	3.5	3.5	3.4	3.9
LAC	0.9	0.7	2.3	2.7	2.4	2.8
MNA	0.2	0.3	0.8	2.5	2.7	1.6
SA	0.1	0.1	0.5	1.3	2.8	1.5
SSA	0.6	0.5	1.5	2.9	3.7	2.4
B. Outward Flows						
EAP				1.1[a]	1.6	1.6
LAC				1.0[a]	0.6	0.7
SA				0.9[a]	0.9	0.3
SSA				0.7[a]	0.3	3.3

Note: [a] Data is for 2005–2007.
Source: World Development Indicators (http://data.worldbank.org/data-catalog/world-development-indicators).

3 Evolution of the IMF[1]

The Fund's role changed substantially after the abandonment finally in 1973 of the system of pegged exchange rates, and the liberalization of financial flows and capital markets that occurred in the 1970s (Williamson, 1977; Cohen, 1977). The liberalization of capital markets implied that, unlike in earlier years, substantial amounts of private BOP financing was available.[2] The 1980s were spent mainly in dealing with the consequences of these developments.

3.1 The fund and exchange rate surveillance

The freeing of the exchange rates was seen as the solution to the problem of the incompatibility of fixed exchange rates, autonomy of monetary policy and free capital flows (Aizenman, 2013).[3] Exchange rates would move to compensate differential inflation rates and so help to maintain the competitiveness of the goods

[1] In this chapter, the underlying model behind the Fund's analysis nor the evolution of this model is discussed.

[2] This was in contrast to the views of Keynes and White noted below, that capital movements should not be free.

[3] Freer exchange rates along with free capital movements were supposed to provide the way of aiming internal balance compatible with external balance (Fleming, 1952; Mundell, 1968).

produced by the higher inflation country, whereas no mechanism existed under the fixed exchange rate system to perform this task.[4]

This raised the question whether the Fund should attempt to influence the major countries to stabilize their rates and coordinate their economic policies (Broughton, 2001). This would be necessary to have a smoothly operating international monetary system (IMS). Alternately, the Fund could concentrate its energies on smaller countries, where its influence was more likely to be felt, but such a strategy would be successful only if the troubles of developing countries were entirely due to their own policies and not caused by policies in the major countries. If their problems were caused by the major countries, then concentrating on smaller countries might be futile. We believe that the Fund failed to analyze the interconnections between the smaller and major countries.

Experience dealt a blow to the belief that market determined exchange rates would be able to manage the BOP. Exchange rates often moved in the wrong direction. For instance, the dollar appreciated in the first half of the 1980s despite the large current account deficit.[5] Also this misalignment persisted over long periods of time (Mussa, 1990).

The IMF was supposed to analyze exchange rate movements to ensure that the movements were not caused by a country's attempt to gain a competitive advantage over other countries, namely, recourse once again to beggar thy neighbor policies. The IMF needed to develop a framework that would enable it to identify excessive intervention in the foreign exchange market. Also the IMF was expected to examine the policies that countries were following in order to ensure that these were compatible with a well-functioning international economy, and all countries were pulling their weight and whether the system of exchange rates was an equilibrium one or even a sustainable one. A framework for such multilateral surveillance would be complex as many policies would affect the exchange rate, but a usable framework was not available nor was one developed.[6]

3.2 Increasing involvement with developing and transition economies

After the adoption of flexible exchange rates, the developed countries no longer required assistance from the IMF until the current eurozone crisis as exchange

---

[4] Devaluations when substantial imbalances had been built did provide a corrective, but this corrective was periodic and did not prevent substantial problems in the meantime.

[5] The movement in the wrong direction was not just short lived. Also, models which explained one anomaly did not explain other anomalies that cropped up in future periods (De Grauwe, 2000).

[6] There were disputes particularly between the US on one side and the European and Japanese governments, as to the policies that the different governments should adopt to get the economies out of the stagflationary situation in the late 1970s and the dollar overvaluation of the early 1980s.

rates were supposed to move to manage the BOP, and when there were current account deficits developed countries borrowed from international capital markets rather than the Fund. Recourse to the capital markets meant that government policies were now geared towards sustaining the confidence of the capital markets.

The last borrowings by a developed country from the IMF before the current eurozone crisis were the borrowing by Italy in 1974–1975 and by the UK in 1976.[7] Previously, IMF conditionality had applied equally to developed and developing countries when they borrowed from the IMF. Now, the IMF became almost exclusively a lender to first the developing countries and then, in addition, to the transition economies. This change in the nature of the borrower changed the politics of the functioning of the Fund and its lending policies (Polak, 1981). The developed countries determined the conditions imposed by the Fund and these conditions were imposed on developing and transition countries. This asymmetry did not lead to harmonious relations. The increasing involvement with these economies had mainly two aspects. One was expansion of the facilities of the IMF to help these economies deal with normal balance of payments deficits. This included much greater involvement with the debt problems of developing countries. The second was to deal with currency crises.

3.2.1 *Establishment of new facilities*

The IMF has sought to respond to the balance of payments difficulties confronting many developing countries, particularly the poorest. The managing director (MD) of the Fund at the time of the oil price rises in 1973–1974, Johannes de Witteveen, got agreement to set up a supplementary financing facility (SFF)[8] to provide additional financing to countries with severe BOP problems that could not be tackled by normal level borrowings from the Fund. Furthermore, in August 1975, the Executive Board subsidized borrowings through a subsidy account for the most seriously affected members using the oil facility (https://www.imf.org/external/np/exr/chron/chron.asp). The SFF operated from June 1974 and lent $6.9 billion in 156 transactions.

The IMF responded to the balance of payments difficulties confronting many poor countries by providing concessional financing. In May 1977, a Trust Fund was established with profits from the sale of part of its gold and between 1977 and 1981 about $3.8 billion was disbursed (Ghatak and Sánchez-Fung, 2007).

Then beginning in March 1986, concessional financing was provided through the structural adjustment facility (SAF), and then through the enhanced structural adjustment facility (ESAF) beginning in December 1987. Between March 1986

[7] The happenings in the UK and the consequences of the IMF loan are examined in Hickson (2005).

[8] See https://www.imf.org/external/np/exr/chron/chron.asp.

and December 1987, SDR 1.8 billion (about $2.4 billion) was disbursed. Between December 1987 and November 1999, SDR 7.6 billion (about $10.7 billion) was disbursed under 90 ESAF arrangements to 52 countries (https://www.imf.org/external/np/exr/facts/esaf.htm). Loans under the ESAF carried an annual interest rate of 0.5%, with repayments made semiannually, beginning 5½ years and ending 10 years after the disbursement.

ESAF operations were financed mainly through contributions from a broad cross-section of IMF member countries in the form of loans and grants to the ESAF Trust, which was administered by the IMF.

In December 1993, the ESAF was enlarged and extended. In September 1996, the ESAF was made a permanent (rather than a temporary) facility, but in 1999 the ESAF was replaced by the poverty reduction and growth facility (PRGF). It was intended that the PRGF approach would result in policies that integrated better, the poverty reduction and macroeconomic elements of IMF programmes, and also encourage greater participation by civil society.

The IMF had also the systemic transformation facility (STF) to provide funds and advice to help the transition economies to move towards a market oriented framework.

The extended fund facility (EFF) was established for countries experiencing serious payments imbalances or serious structural imbalances that resulted in low growth (http://www.imf.org/external/np/exr/facts/pdf/eff.pdf). Given that structural reforms to correct deep rooted weaknesses often take time to implement and bear fruit, the EFF allowed for loans for longer period of up to 3 years with possible extension to a fourth year and for longer repayment periods of 10 years. This was to accommodate the argument of developing countries that their balance of payments problems could not be resolved within the time frame allowed under the usual Fund schemes. The EFF stressed structural adjustment, namely, reforms to address institutional or economic weaknesses in addition to the usual policies needed to be implemented for macroeconomic stability. Normally a country could borrow till 200% of quota in a year so that over a three period it could borrow 600% of quota. In exceptional circumstances it could borrow more.

3.2.2 *Quotas and international money*

At the commencement of the IMF international money consisted of convertible currencies, the US dollar and the Pound Sterling, gold and IMF quotas. Sterling soon fell out of fashion and the role of gold was eliminated in the 70s. So, international money came to consist only of US dollars and IMF quotas.[9]

---

[9] Countries also held limited amounts of other currencies such as the German mark and the Japanese yen, which would also be considered international moneys. But their share of the total was very small.

If there is currently no quota increase, a country can increase its foreign currency reserves only by running a BOP surplus. If the surplus is with other countries, then the existing supply of international money would be merely re-allocated. If the surplus is with the US, then the world supply of dollars would increase, namely international money supply would increase. Therefore, for the supply of dollars to increase for the whole world the US must run a current account deficit. This depends mainly on US policies.

IMF quotas are periodically reviewed and if the members agree, can be increased. If quotas are not increased countries would have to increase their holdings of dollars as trade increases, and this implies that countries are essentially extending a low interest loan to the US. Thus, the US has a vested interest in preventing an increase in IMF quotas. Since the US has over 17% of the IMF's voting rights and a quota increase requires an 85% vote in favor, the US can block a quota increase. There is a moral hazard problem as the US that gains from quotas not increasing can block any quota increase. As can be expected, quota increases have not kept up with the growth in world trade or capital flows. Whereas, trade in goods has increased by a factor of almost 150 between 1950 and 2010, IMF quotas would increase by a factor of just over 80 if the latest quota increases are ratified. With lagging increases in quotas, countries can only increase their reserves in proportion to their increase in trade by running current account surpluses.

In brief, the supply of international money is beyond the control of almost all countries.

3.2.3 *IMF and structural adjustment*

Increasingly, the BOP payments problems of developing countries were seen as the result of structural weaknesses and rigidities. The Fund accepted the idea that the BOP difficulties of developing countries were caused by structural factors, but developed its own framework for dealing with these issues. It believed that the rigidities arose mainly from government interference in the working of the market. Therefore, conditionality was extended from monetary and fiscal policies to manage aggregate demand, to all aspects of the economy that were felt to be a market interference, and so preventing a supply response. The case for extending market oriented reforms was further strengthened as the central planning countries began their move to market economies. There was no limit to the scope for conditionality. Conditionality was even extended to the contingency and compensatory funding facility (CCFF) which had been a low conditionality facility. As a result, countries stopped borrowing under that facility.

The conditionality on loans was very far reaching as the IMF sought to eliminate the bottlenecks that prevented a supply response in the export industries, but ultimately this approach proved inadequate and a substantial amount of debt had to be forgiven or written off. This happened with debt in mainly the middle income Latin American countries though the Brady Plan (Cline, 1995).[10] The debt problems of the low income countries resulted in the initiative to deal with highly indebted poor countries (HIPC). The HIPC initiative involved strong conditions that countries had to fulfill before the debt would be forgiven. The IMF sought to develop general principles to deal with debt restructurings, but most debt is still treated on a case by case basis.

The IMF provided financing, sought to convince banks to continue lending, and also helped in debt rescheduling. This involvement increased further in the 1990s as many of the countries mainly in SSA who had received soft multilateral and bilateral loans found that they could not service their debts. The debt problems raised the question, "What conditions should be imposed on these loans in order to return to a stable growth path". In addition, in the case particularly of the Latin American countries the issue was what should be the relative roles of official and private financing in meeting the debt crisis.

The availability of private financing raised other questions about IMF policies. Should the IMF borrow from private sources? That has not happened as yet. Should the Fund seek to influence the behavior of providers of private BOP finance? Usually in providing assistance to countries in BOP difficulties with substantial private borrowing, the IMF has insisted on agreement with private finance to ensure that they contribute so that the assistance does not merely help repayment of private obligations.

3.2.4 *Outcomes of structural adjustment*

There are so many factors that influence the behavior of an economy that it is difficult to analyze the effect of the structural adjustment programmes (SAPs). It depends on the basis of the comparison, namely what is the counter factual that is used for the comparison (Moseley *et al.*, 1991).

There is a very fundamental question as to what was the basis for the judgment that what was needed was diminution of the role of the government and a shift towards more market determined allocations. Two different views have been advanced for the rationale for the shift (Toye, 1987; Bruton, 1998). Both raise serious questions about the rationale for the shift. Bruton notes that the results of the import substitution policies adopted in the 1950s, 1960s and 1970s had been mixed with some successes, increases in growth rates and in savings rates and some failures, repeated BOP problems and slow increases in employment. He then

---

[10] The earlier Baker Plan had proved to be inadequate.

argues that in such a situation the existing policies required fine-tuning rather than a complete rejection. He goes on to argue that even on its own terms the success of the SAP required greater attention on how to increase exports rather than a belief that the market would bring it about automatically. The inadequate attention to these aspects resulted in the policies failing as growth remained low (Table 1) and BOP problems persisted because of slow growth of exports.

Toye (1987) on the other hand argues that the shift in policy was guided more by political considerations and notes that at the same time similar shifts were occurring in the US and the UK under President Reagan and Prime Minister Thatcher. He along with colleagues also more formally undertook an evaluation of the SAP (Mosle *et al.*, 1991). They found that structural adjustment was successful in leading to an improved current account position, but this was more because of falls in imports because of income declines than increases in exports. Also bringing down inflation and the government budget deficit was more difficult.[11] A major role for the IMF became its involvement in debt renegotiations starting in 1982 as servicing the debt and the stoppage of new loans by commercial banks resulted in large balance of payments deficits.[12]

3.2.5 *IMF dealing with currency crises*

The debt crises of the 1980s and 1990s had serious consequences on the economic performance of the affected countries. It also resulted in a shrinking of commercial bank lending to governments in developing countries. New forms of lending were used. Commercial banks began lending directly to enterprises in developing countries. Governments issued more bonds to raise money in the major capital markets of the world, but the 1990s saw a series of currency crises. The first was in Mexico in 1994 followed by the Asian crisis in 1997, crises in Brazil during 1998–1999, in Russia in 1998 and in Argentina in 2001.[13] In most cases, except finally in Argentina and in Russia, the IMF stepped in with special funding to deal with the currency crises. This funding was often arranged outside the normal operations of the IMF. Therefore, the stability of the world economy depended on ad hoc and

---

[11] A lesson being repeated in the Eurozone as countries there follow policies that are essentially similar to the SAP. They are less bedeviled by inflation as the euro has not been devalued.

[12] These problems were initially mainly in the middle income countries who had borrowed from banks to fund their deficits arising from the increase in their oil bills (Sachs, 1991). The crisis was set off by Mexico's inability to service its debt because even though it was an oil exporter it had borrowed extensively in anticipation of large oil revenues.

[13] See Sachs *et al.* (1996) for an analysis of the Mexican crisis, Radelet and Jeffrey (1998) (for the Asian crisis, Desai (2003) and Kharas *et al.* (2001) for the Russian crisis, Goretti (2005) for the Brazilian crisis and Mulraine (2005) for the Argentine crisis.

short-term increases in the Fund's resources and on a spaghetti ball of bilateral or regional safety net agreements, some of them out of sight beneath the table, their aggregate stabilizing effects unknown (Broughton, 2001). Ad hoc funding arrangements were also accompanied by conditions that seemed to have little to do with the crisis.[14] While there were calls for a new financial architecture after the Asian crisis, not much was accomplished.

The crises in the 1990s saw a further shift in how developing countries accessed private capital. Countries liberalized their FDI policies and FDI became the main component of capital inflows that financed current account deficits.

Models that sought to understand how crises occur gradually became more complex as each crisis could not be predicted on the basis of existing models. The initial model (Krugman, 1979) showed that a government budget deficit would inevitable lead to a crisis if there was a fixed exchange rate.[15] The simple policy advice was that the budget should be balanced, but later crises such as in the European Monetary System (ERS) in 1992–1993 and in Asia in 1997–1998 occurred even when there was no deficit in the government budget. So, second generation and third generation models were developed. In these, for instance, there might be multiple equilibria and an event could shift people's expectations and require a large change in the equilibrium exchange rate and this would be accomplished through a crisis, or the behavior of the private sector could lead to crises (Calvo and Mendoza, 2000). The more complex models did not lead to any simple policy rules.

One consequence of the Asian financial crisis was to establish a programme, the Financial Sector Assessment Program, run jointly by the IMF and the World Bank. Under this programme, the financial systems of countries were examined to see whether they were complying with international standards in banking, auditing, stock market operations, etc. The financial systems were also analyzed from the viewpoint of their ability to withstand various shocks, but the general belief was that the problem of weak financial systems was one in developing countries. The US refused to have its system examined though it was systemically more important than most developing countries.

3.2.6 *Capital account liberalization and the IMF*

Many of the above crises occurred because of fixed exchange rates. Fixed exchange rates are incompatible with free capital flows and monetary autonomy.

---

[14] For instance, in the case of Korea during the Asian crisis the IMF called for privatization when the crisis was not caused by excessive government borrowing or large budget deficits but by excessive private sector borrowing itself caused by liberalization of capital flows.

[15] This came to be called the problem of the twin deficits. A deficit in the budget resulted in a BOP deficit.

The crises have often occurred as capital flows were being liberalized, a process the IMF encouraged; that capital flows would create problems for the Bretton Woods System had been recognized earlier.

A major feature of the debate about the establishment of the IMF was the role of capital movements. The orthodox position held by most bankers was that capital movements should be free. Throughout the inter-war period they had pushed for balanced budgets, independent central banks, free capital movements and the gold standard. They believed that speculative capital movements occurred only when governments followed incorrect policies so that capital movements would force governments to adopt proper policies. Also, of course, bankers would profit from capital movements. The Keynes/White combination accepted that movements of productive capital were good but not movements of speculative capital.[16] The experience of the 1930s had revealed the limitations of the orthodox view and had also showed the conflicts that arose when national governments gave higher priority to domestic employment. So the final IMF agreement was based on the premise that capital movements should be controlled.[17] The issue of the impossible trilemma, namely the incompatibility of fixed exchange rates, free capital movements and autonomy of monetary policy, was to be solved by restricting capital movements.[18]

No agreement could be reached either on the question of capital controls or on measures to regulate the euro–dollar market. Under these circumstances, the new parities agreed to in 1971 turned out to be only a stop gap measure. The new fixed exchange rates turned out to be unsustainable. Negotiations to come to a new agreement failed and most developed countries adopted a floating rate (Williamson, 1977).

One or another country objected to the imposition of capital controls or to regulating the euro–dollar market. In particular, the UK and the US objected to capital controls as these might jeopardize their importance as international financial markets. The Bank of England also objected to regulation of the euro-dollar market as it sought to strengthen the position of the UK in international financial affairs. They only supported capital controls when they were themselves subject to speculation against their currencies.

---

[16] The US accepted the need for restrictions on capital movements. For a detailed discussion of the debate see (Helleiner, 1994). Also see Ruggie (1982) and de Vries and Horsefield (1969).

[17] For instance, Keynes (1980) said of the IMF agreement that "not merely as a feature of the transition, but as a permanent arrangement, the plan accords to every member government the explicit right to control all capital movements."

[18] The bankers were successful in diluting some of the proposals. The final version allowed countries to cooperate in enforcing capital controls instead of requiring them to. Keynes/White believed that controls would be more effective if they were monitored at both ends. Also governments were no longer required to submit a list of all assets held in their country by foreigners.

The US objected to measures to control capital flows when proposed by the British in response to their exchange rate crisis in 1976. This crisis was caused by capital outflows even though the current account was improving and the rate of inflation was falling. The Germans and the Japanese, in particular, would not support capital controls when proposed somewhat half-heartedly by the US in 1978 when it was faced with a dollar crisis (Helleiner, 1994).

In both cases the governments were forced to undertake significant fiscal and monetary contractions which meant the abandonment of the earlier policy of maintaining full-employment policies and seeking to manage the balance of payments through other policies including policies to finance the capital flow. Also for the longer term there was a move to adopt more market friendly policies, and in particular to adopt monetary and fiscal policies geared towards gaining the confidence of financial markets. The US moved away from its earlier position of recognizing that capital flows could be destabilizing and may need to be controlled towards pushing for capital liberalization both domestically and abroad. It increasingly argued about the benefits from freer capital flows and excessive capital flows were a sign of policy mistakes in the country, and so were a signal to correct the policy mistakes. The US pressed for a fully liberal capital flow regime.

US authorities believed that freer capital flows would free the US of any restraints in its domestic policy making. Large deficits and dollar availability would lead to the dollar depreciating and there would be no need to engage in contentious negotiations with Europeans and Japanese about appropriate exchange rates.[19] A more liberal financial regime would preserve US policy autonomy even in the longer run given the size and strength of the New York market.[20] This move on capital flows was part of a broader move to more liberal market oriented policies in the US starting in the early 1970s. Other countries also liberalized their capital flow policies in order to maintain the competitiveness of their financial systems. Also a culture favoring more liberal policies had grown up nurtured in part through the frequent meetings of financial officials at the Bank of International Settlements and the Working Party Number 3 of the OECD.[21]

The US vetoed attempts to recycle the surpluses of the oil exporters through the IMF, arguing instead to let private markets largely handle the financing of the

---

[19] Changes in exchange rates and subsequent macro policies to offset the demand reducing effect of lower exports resulted in the elimination of the current account deficit of the US without the US having to take any policy action.

[20] This was the result of the analysis by Fleming (1952) and Mundell (1963) who showed how capital flows could result in policies that achieved both full employment and a balanced external position.

[21] The Fund appears to be inadequately equipped to face such a situation. It became clear that the technical staff of this institution needs to fine-tune its knowledge of financial markets (Mantega, 2007).

deficits. The large surpluses of the oil exporting countries were recycled to the oil importing countries mainly through the US banks.

4 Unhappiness of Developing Countries with the IMF

Developing countries have been unhappy mainly with the governance of the IMF, the response of the IMF to various international developments and the conditions attached to its loans.

4.1 Governance of the IMF

By convention, the MD of the IMF has always been a European. In addition, of the 24 members on the executive board of the IMF 8 are from Europe and 1 each from the US, Canada and Australia. Also, the developed countries have more than 50% of the voting rights, but their decision making power is even greater as major decisions currently require 85% of votes. The US alone with about 17% of voting rights wields a veto power. It has held the veto power over the entire period of operation of the Fund as when its voting share has fallen the voting percentage required for major decisions has been increased. A small group of European countries could also wield the veto.[22]

The second in command, who was initially the Deputy Managing Director and since 1994 the First Deputy Managing Director, as the number of deputy directors was increased to three, is a US citizen.

The developed countries hold the majority of the voting powers in the IMF, and as noted above important countries have a veto power on important decisions. A result of such a requirement can be seen in the implementation of the 2010 agreement which had two components, a quota increase and board reform which would reduce the number of European directors. Acceptance by three-fifths of the Fund's 188 members (or 113 members) having 85% of the Fund's total voting power is required for reforming the Executive Board.[23] As of May 8, 2015, 147 members having 77.25% of total voting power had accepted the amendment. For the quota increases under the 14th General Review of Quotas to become effective, the consent by members having not less than 70% of total quotas (as of November 5, 2010) is required, but the US has linked the two so

[22] A group of developing countries could also wield the veto, but this would require a relatively large group.

[23] Acceptances of the Proposed Amendment of the Articles of Agreement on Reform of the Executive Board and Consents to 2010 Quota Increase. Last Updated: June 30, 2016. http://www.imf.org/external/np/sec/misc/consents.htm

the implementation of the quota increase requires the entry into force of the proposed amendment to reform the Executive Board. Therefore, though 164 members having 80.34% of total quota had consented by May 8, 2015, the quota increase could not be implemented.

The G20 had agreed to a shift in voting rights to developing countries,[24] reform of the governance structure of the IMF with European representation at the Board reduced and that of African countries increased, and that the selection of the MD would be made more democratic. We have seen above that the voting and Board reforms have not been implemented yet. When Mr. Strauss-Kahn resigned as MD of the IMF in 2011, despite the acceptance of the need for a more democratic process, the Europeans jumped in and proposed Ms. Lagarde as the MD arguing essentially that only a European could understand European problems which were at the center of the IMF's concerns at that time.

In brief, despite all the talk and agreement at various formal venues, little progress in reforming the IMF is seen on the ground.

4.2 IMF responses to developments; its conditionalities

A number of major developments took place in the post, 1973 international system that affected the relation of developing countries with the IMF. Two important developments that have been discussed above were the oil price rises in 1973–1974, repeated at the end of the 1970s and 1980s, that increased hugely the current account deficits of many developing countries and the gradual liberalization of capital movements. A number of countries borrowed from private banks to finance the deficits. When interest rates skyrocketed in the early 1980s as the Federal Reserve in the US sought to control inflation, these countries became unable to meet the huge interest payments leading to a debt crisis. These countries approached the IMF for financing. The IMF sought to place these countries on a permanently more sound macroeconomic path. The conditions imposed as a package by the IMF came to be known as structural adjustment. They are also often referred to as the "Washington Consensus" reflecting the agreement for their need by the IMF, the World Bank and the US Treasury (Williamson, 1990). These structural adjustment policies were not able to return these economies to a high growth path, as we saw above, and their social costs were considerable.

Meanwhile, the high rates of inflation resulting from the oil price rises were very dissimilar among the developed countries resulting in changes in their international competitiveness and current account imbalances among them. As we saw above, this resulted in the final collapse of the Bretton Woods System of fixed

[24] This reform would still leave the share of developing countries at less than 5%.

exchange rates and the adoption of floating rates by most developed countries. Soon after the command economies of eastern Europe and the Former Soviet Union (FSU) collapsed, the IMF was called upon to help their transition to market economies. The policies that the IMF sought to get implemented may be considered an extreme form of structural adjustment in the sense that the scale of adjustment in the organization of their economies was immense and change was sought to be implemented very quickly leading to considerable hardship to the populations. Developing countries saw the similarity between the social costs of their own structural adjustment and that which accompanied the transition. They contrasted this with the smoother and slower transition in China which did not seem to have huge social costs. This led to a general unhappiness with the policies recommended by the IMF.

This unhappiness was compounded in Asia by what was perceived to be slow response of the IMF, the intellectual inadequacy of the response and the irrelevance of some of the conditions. These countries contrasted the very rapid response of the IMF to the Mexican crisis in 1994, to the very slow and prolonged negotiations they went through.[25] The intellectual inadequacy was shown by the neglect by the IMF of the effect of the programme in one country on its neighbors, so the combined effect of the programmes was severely contractionary and this was completely misjudged by the IMF, as it later admitted.[26] An example of an irrelevance of a condition is that of insisting on privatization in Korea. The crisis in Korea was caused by unregulated foreign borrowing by the private, and which had not been hedged against. So the private sector was severely hit when the devaluation of the Korean won raised the debt servicing costs of many firms forcing them into bankruptcy. It was not clear how privatization would resolve this issue.

Developing countries have expressed their unhappiness in the form of reluctance to borrow from the IMF. Many countries prepaid their loans so that the

---

[25] In the case of Indonesia there was a suspicion that this was deliberate to bring about a regime change (Khan, 2011). Krugman (2015), has argued similarly in the case of Greece: Breaking Greece "So what is happening? Is the goal to break Syriza? Is it to force Greece into a presumably disastrous default, to encourage the others? At this point it's time to stop talking about "Graccident"; if Grexit happens it will be because the creditors, or at least the IMF, wanted it to happen." Also note. When crises broke out in Latin America and Asia, the IMF promptly came up with a standard package of recommendations without any hesitation and dictated policies though many were subsequently shown to be mistaken or questionable. Now, (2007), the epicenter of the crisis is in the US, and for the time being, has affected primarily US and European financial markets. The Fund had little to say that was practical. It has been excessively cautious in its recommendations." Mantega (2007).

[26] It was somewhat amazing that an international organization set up to prevent adoption of beggar-my-neighbor policies and so to take account of interactions completely failed to do so.

interest income of the IMF fell. The losses forced the IMF to retrench before the 2008 crisis. Developing countries have also responded to their unhappiness with Fund conditionality by increasing their reserves so that they do not have to approach the Fund for balance of payments support and developing alternate sources of financing.

5 Response of Developing Countries: Accumulation of Reserves

Earlier, the rule of thumb was to hold three months of imports as reserves.[27] Later, Guidotti, former Argentinian Finance Minister and Greenspan a former Chairman of the Federal Reserve in the US suggested that countries should keep reserves equal to their short term liabilities to meet any withdrawal of credit facilities (Olivier and Rancière, 2006).

Developing countries have been increasing their reserve holdings beyond such previous rules of thumb. The major countries have increased the level of reserves whether measured as a percentage of GDP (Table 5) or of imports (Table 6). All the 11 countries that are members of the G20, but may be considered as not fully

Table 5. Reserves (as % of GDP).

	1997	1999	2001	2003	2005	2007	2008	2009	2010	2011	R1	R2
Argentina	7.7	9.3	5.4	10.9	15.3	17.7	14.2	15.6	14.2	10.4	2.3	0.6
Brazil	5.9	6.2	6.5	8.9	6.1	13.2	11.7	14.7	13.5	14.2	2.2	1.1
China	15.4	14.9	16.6	25.4	36.8	44.2	43.5	49.1	49.1	44.5	2.9	1.1
India	6.7	7.8	10.0	16.8	16.5	22.3	21.0	20.9	17.6	16.0	3.3	0.7
Indonesia	8.11	19.5	17.5	15.4	12.1	13.1	10.1	12.2	13.6	13.0	1.6	1.0
Korea	4.0	16.6	20.4	24.2	24.9	25.0	21.6	32.4	28.8	27.5	6.3	1.1
Mexico	7.2	6.6	7.2	8.4	8.7	8.4	8.7	11.4	11.6	12.9	1.2	1.5
Russia	4.3	6.3	11.8	18.2	23.9	36.8	25.7	35.9	32.2	26.8	8.5	0.7
S Africa	4.0	5.6	6.4	4.8	8.3	11.5	12.4	14.0	12.0	11.9	2.9	1.0
S Arabia	9.8	11.4	10.3	11.4	49.9	80.4	94.8	111.8	101.9	96.5	8.2	1.2
Turkey	10.4	9.8	10.2	11.7	10.9	11.8	10.1	12.2	11.8	11.4	1.1	1.0

Note: R1 is ratio of 1997– 2007 and R2 is ratio of 2007–2011.

[27] Countries with greater variability in export earnings or import payments might find it prudent to keep larger reserves. But this necessity lessened after the establishment of the compensatory finance facility at the IMF in 1963 to enable a member to borrow to meet a temporary shortfall in foreign exchange earnings due to circumstances beyond its control. It was extended in 1981 to cover sudden higher costs of cereal imports.

Table 6. Reserves (as % of imports of goods and services).

	1997	1999	2001	2003	2005	2007	2008	2009	2010	2011	R1	R2
Argentina	59.9	80.6	53.1	76.9	79.9	87.0	68.8	97.7	76.9	53.1	1.5	0.6
Brazil	65.8	57.3	48.0	73.9	52.9	111.5	87.0	132.1	113.1	112.6	1.7	1.0
China	89.1	85.0	81.1	92.7	116.8	149.4	159.5	220.3	184.0	162.9	1.7	1.1
India	57.2	58.7	75.2	109.1	75.0	91.3	73.4	82.0	66.8	52.6	1.6	0.6
Indonesia	28.8	71.2	56.9	66.7	40.6	51.9	35.2	57.4	59.2	52.2	1.8	1.0
Korea	12.0	51.4	60.9	73.0	68.2	61.9	39.9	70.4	57.9	50.8	5.2	0.8
Mexico	23.7	20.4	24.2	31.4	30.6	28.5	28.8	38.9	36.9	39.2	1.2	1.4
Russia	19.3	24.0	48.9	76.3	110.9	171.0	116.3	175.3	148.7	120.1	8.9	0.7
S Africa	17.1	24.8	24.7	19.0	30.0	33.6	32.0	49.5	43.8	40.6	2.0	1.2
S Arabia	37.5	48.9	42.8	47.4	179.4	212.9	255.4	259.8	263.7	314.9	5.7	1.5
Turkey	34.2	50.7	43.6	48.8	42.9	43.0	35.6	49.9	43.9	34.8	1.3	0.8

Note: R1 is ratio of 1997–2007 and R2 is ratio of 2007–2011.

developed, increased the level of reserves as percentage of GDP and of imports between 1997 and 2007. While China had a high level of reserves it did not have the highest level of reserves. As a percentage of GDP, it had the second highest level of reserves, and as a percentage of imports it had the third highest level. Nor did it have the fastest rate of increase in these percentages.

Five countries increased the share of reserves as a percentage of GDP more than China did. Also, five countries increased reserves as a percentage of imports more than China did (Table 6). Even after the financial crisis only three countries, Argentina, India and Russia saw a decline in the ratio of reserves to GDP; in addition to these three another two countries, Korea and Turkey, saw a fall in their reserves to imports ratio.

These 11 countries have also increased their reserves as a percent of short-term debt. As short-term loans borrowed by developing countries might not be rolled over or could be withdrawn, the Greenspan–Guidotti rule was enunciated that countries should hold reserves equal to their short-term liabilities, but these large economies have been reducing their level of short-term debt as a percentage of reserves and reserves are considerably larger than their short-term debt (Table 7).

The ratio comfortably meets the Greenspan–Guidotti rule even after the financial crisis except for India and Turkey. A few countries have short-term debts slightly greater than reserves, a ratio of 1.1, and surprisingly China is included in that group.

Why are these large economies holding such large reserves whether measured in terms of GDP or imports or short-term debt? One possible explanation is that

Table 7. Short-term debt (as % of reserves).

	1997	1999	2001	2003	2005	2007	2008	2009	2010	2011	R1	R2
Argentina	143	112	137	158	124	42	43	41	27	36	0.3	0.9
Brazil	67	80	79	50	45	22	19	17	19	12	0.3	0.6
China	22	9	2	21	18	13	10	10	12	15	0.6	1.1
India	18	11	6	6	6	13	17	16	19	26	0.7	2.0
Indonesia	188	73	71	54	32	33	40	36	34	35	0.2	1.1
Mexico	97	76	33	39	30	31	30	28	32	34	0.3	1.1
Russia	34	128	52	39	15	21	17	12	13	14	0.6	0.7
S Africa	183	144	110	101	69	73	75	54	50	39	0.4	0.5
Turkey	91	96	82	65	73	56	72	66	91	95	0.6	1.7

Note: R1 is ratio of 1997–2007 and R2 is ratio of 2007–2011.

Table 8. Reserves (as % of M2).

	1997	1999	2001	2003	2005	2007	2008	2009	2010	2011	R1	R2
Argentina	28.9	29.6	20.0	36.3	48.8	57.5	54.3	56.6	48.6	36.0	2.0	0.6
Brazil	15.8	14.2	13.2	18.0	11.2	21.3	18.3	21.2	19.6	19.1	1.3	1.9
China	13.2	11.0	11.6	16.3	24.1	29.2	28.7	27.4	27.2	24.7	2.2	0.8
India	14.4	15.4	17.5	27.0	25.6	31.4	27.8	26.8	23.1	20.8	2.2	0.9
Indonesia	14.5	33.4	34.3	32.6	28.1	31.5	26.4	32.1	35.4	33.5	2.2	1.1
Korea	9.6	26.8	28.4	33.5	38.0	41.1	32.3	44.7	38.1	35.2	4.3	0.9
Mexico	20.3	19.4	23.5	31.1	31.8	31.9	32.6	37.2	37.2	41.2	1.6	1.3
Russia	22.1	30.6	49.5	60.8	71.5	86.0	65.1	73.0	61.2	50.8	3.9	0.6
S Africa	7.4	9.8	11.0	7.7	11.9	13.9	14.7	17.2	15.4	15.7	1.9	1.1
S Arabia	22.3	22.8	21.4	22.3	107.3	145.8	180.5	151.9	157.6	168.6	6.5	1.2
Turkey	28.0	25.0	22.3	33.3	26.8	27.0	20.8	22.3	20.9	20.7	1.0	0.8

Note: R1 is ratio of 1997–2007 and R2 is ratio of 2007–2011.

outflow of short-term loans is not the only danger that developing countries face. With the significant capital account liberalization that has occurred, domestic individuals and companies can convert their liquid assets into foreign currency and transfer them out of the country. M2 is a measure of liquid assets. So adequacy of reserves should be measured against M2 as M2 maybe a good first approximation as to what can be converted into foreign exchange and transferred.

On this measure, China has one of the lowest ratios — it has the eighth smallest ratio (Table 8). Further, capital account liberalization may require China to increase its reserve holdings.

One of the consequences of IMF conditionality and the reluctance of countries to borrow from the Fund has been the building up of their reserves as a precautionary measure. As Brazilian Finance Minister Guido Mantega (2007) said of the consequences of a failure to reform the Fund: "*We will seek self-insurance by building up high levels of international reserves and regional monetary institutions, and we will participate in regional reserve-sharing pools. The fragmentation of the multilateral financial system, which is already emerging, will accelerate.*"

Such reserve accumulation by poor countries implies lending by poor countries to the much richer US which is a misallocation of resources. This also reduces the incentive for the US to change the system. The increase in reserves by almost all developing countries and not only China has meant that the US can and has run large deficits.[28] This pattern of current account balances is held by the G20 leaders to have been a cause of the crisis and its elimination is considered essential for restoring the world economy to stable and balanced growth.

Developing countries have increased their reserves whether measured against their imports, or short term debts or GDP or M2 as a precautionary measure (Aizenman and Lee, 2005). There is a sharp increase in these ratios after the 1997 Asian financial crisis. During the Asian crisis borrowed reserves were promptly withdrawn so that many countries will only feel comfortable if the reserves are accumulated by current account surpluses (Williamson, 2010). About half of the total reserve accumulation has been the result of developing countries running current account surpluses (Williamson, 1992).

5.1 Institutional innovation

Developing countries have also undertaken new initiatives to provide additional BOP financing. Two of the main initiatives are the Chiang Mai Initiative Multilateralized (CMIM) and the Contingent Reserve Arrangement (CRA). The CMIM was originally established as a bilateral swap arrangement among East Asian countries in the wake of the Asian financial crisis of 1997–1998. It was later multilateralized and the amounts under the scheme were increased. The CRA is a swap arrangement among the BRICS countries.

The CMIM has the characteristics of its origin as a network of bilateral swaps. Its membership is limited to the original members, China, Japan, Korea and the ASEAN countries, with no provision in its articles for new members. The reserves

[28] Detailed analysis shows that of the 11 non-developed countries in the G20, namely those other than the G7 and Australia, China is usually in the middle in the extent and speed of its reserve accumulation (Agarwal, 2013).

continue to be owned by the countries and would only be available if another country makes a request. Also a country can opt out of meeting a request; there seem to be no conditions specified under which a country can opt out.[29] At the time of the Asian financial crisis undoubtedly Korea would have opted. Many analysts believe that only China and Japan would be in a position to meet any request that was made.

A macro surveillance unit has been set up under the CMIM to analyze the macro policies of the countries and determine whether a country's policy can maintain external balance and, particularly, whether they are sufficient to return it to BOP sustainability (Siregar and Chabchitrchaidol, 2013), but no analysis of its work seems to be available.[30] It is not clear what macro framework is used for any analysis and whether it differs from that used by the Fund. Nor has the advice proffered, if any, been revealed and whether the countries have been receptive to that advice.

Since the inception of the CMIM in 2000 the amounts available under the Initiative have been increased, currently the total available is US$ 240 billion (Siregar and Chabchitrchaidol, 2013). Also the amount that can be borrowed without a Fund programme has been increased to 30% of a country's drawing and is to further increase to 40% in 2014, but the conditions that would be attached to the loan to ensure its repayments have still not been determined.

Countries are limited to the amounts they can borrow under the Multilateralized Chiang Mai Initiative and the time for which they can borrow which may have prevented any borrowing from it as yet. Korea and Singapore preferred to activate their bilateral swap programme with the Federal Reserve of the US at the time of the 2008 crisis rather than borrow under the CMI and Indonesia asked the World Bank for financial assistance.

The CRA was created at the Sixth BRICS summit held at Fortaliza, Brazil in August 2014 "to forestall short-term balance of payments pressures, provide mutual support and further strengthen financial stability".[31] It seeks to achieve this provision of "liquidity and precautionary instruments in response to actual or

---

[29] Countries can opt out of meeting a funding request by the IMF if their BOP position is not comfortable.

[30] In particular, it is not known whether the members are more heedful of the advice of the macro unit than they are of the IMF.

[31] Article 3bi gives the GC the power to admit new members, but lays no conditions for who can be a new member. This is in contrast to the New Development bank which was set up at the same meeting. Any UN member is eligible to become a member of the Bank with a minimum subscription of 41,00,000 and a maximum subscription of 7% of the total capital. Available at http://brics.itamaraty.gov.br/media2/press-releases/220-treaty-for-the-establishment-of-a-brics-contingent-reserve-arrangement-fortaleza-july-15. Accessed on August 1, 2015.

potential BOP pressures". The BRICS have established the CRA with $100 billion to which China will contribute $41 billion, Brazil, India and Russia each $18 billion and South Africa $5 billion. The procedures for drawing on the facility and the conditions have yet to be determined.

5.1.1 *Governance structure of the CRA*

The governance structure consists of a Governing Council (GC) and a Standing Committee (SC). Each member country will be represented on both. Though the GC can approve the entry of new countries, it is not specifically stated whether the new members will be represented on the GC or the SC, nor is any criteria specified as to who is eligible to apply for membership. Presumably the GC will also decide on the contribution of any new entrant. Unlike in the case of the NDB where many of these matters are explicitly dealt with in the agreement, this is not the case for the CRA.

The party that chairs the BRICS shall act as the coordinator of the GC and the SC, which implies that the coordinators' positions will be short-term ones. All decisions of the GC will be by consensus. Also all decisions of the SC will be on the basis of consensus except those related to the use of the resources of the CRA. These will be by a simple majority of the weighted voting power.[32]

The CRA will come into force 30 days after the deposit of the fifth instrument of accession.

5.1.2 *Resources of the CRA*

The amount that each country can borrow is a variable multiple of their contribution: the multiple is 0.5 for China, 1 for Brazil, India and Russia and 2 for South Africa. So China can borrow up to $20.5 billion, Brazil, India and Russia can each borrow $18 billion while South Africa can borrow $10 billion.

For the request to be considered the party shall not be in arrears with other BRICS countries or their public financial institutions, nor must it be in arrears to any other multilateral or regional financial institution and it must be in compliance with surveillance and provision of information obligations to the IMF. About 30% of the eligible amount is de-linked from the IMF. So, China would be able to borrow $6 billion and South Africa $3 billion while the other countries would be able to borrow about US $5 billion. To access the other 70% the country must provide evidence that it is on an "on track arrangement with the IMF that involves a

[32] 5% of the votes will be divided equally among the members. The rest will be apportioned according to their contributions.

commitment by the IMF to provide financing to the requesting country". Another country can opt out of supplying the requested amounts if this is justified by the BOP and reserve position of the country.[33]

The amounts that the countries can borrow from the CRA can be compared to what they can borrow from the IMF. China's quota at the IMF is about 13.4 billion, that of India and Russia is just over 8 billion while that of Brazil is about 6 billion and that of South Africa is 2.6 billion.[34] Countries can borrow up to twice their quota in any year and cumulatively up to two times their quota under the extended fund facility (EFF). So in any year China could borrow almost 27 billion, India and Russia about 16 billion, Brazil about 12 billion and South Africa about 5 billion. The amounts these countries can borrow from the CRA while not inconsiderable is about what they can borrow from the IMF in any year, though they can borrow much more cumulatively from the IMF. The ability to borrow from the CRA is particularly substantial for South Africa as it can borrow twice as much from the CRA as it can borrow in a year from the IMF. However, countries also can borrow from the IMF under other programmes. Under the Precautionary and Liquidity Line (PLL) they can normally borrow up to 250% of their quota, but this can be increased to 500% of their quota if they are faced by a particularly severe BOP situation. Under the PLL for a two year programme they could borrow 10 times their quota. Obviously, these amounts are considerably larger than what they can borrow from the CRA.

The amounts they can borrow from the CRA can also be compared to their current account deficits (CADs) in recent years. The CAD that Brazil, India or South Africa are currently running are much larger. The CAD of Brazil averaged about $50 billion during the years 2010–2012, that of India averaged almost $7 billion during these years and that of South Africa averaged $12 billion.

The amounts available from the CRA can also be compared to some recent IMF programmes. The IMF approved lending to Russia of $38 billion (SDR 24.786 billion) in the 1990s. In 2002 alone, the IMF approved a standby programme for Brazil of $30 billion. These amounts should also be compared to the 50 billion package for Mexico in 1994, 21 billion for Thailand, 23 billion for Indonesia and over 58 billion for Korea. Since then, international capital movements have increased further so that the required bailouts may be larger.

The period for which countries can borrow from the CRA is only three years, much shorter than the period for which they can borrow from the Fund.

---

[33] A country can also opt out by an event of force majeure such as war or natural disaster.

[34] The quotas are expressed in terms of SDR and the value of the SDR is determined in terms of a basket of currencies and so its value fluctuates with respect to any currency. The above dollar values for the quotas are based on the dollar value of the SDR in September 2014.

5.2 New institutions and the IMS

MCMI and CRA provide countries with an additional source of funding, but they cannot ensure that adjustment is undertaken by both deficit and surplus countries. The asymmetry can only be removed through a multilateral system which requires both surplus and deficit countries to adjust. Without a proper multilateral system the asymmetry between deficit and surplus countries will continue. Deficit countries usually adjust by adopting deflationary policies and this will impart an overall deflationary effect on the world economy.[35] This deflationary impact may not have mattered in the 1950s and 1960s, during which period the world economy grew at unprecedented rates, and which some authors have called the 'golden age of capitalism' (Marglin and Schor, 1990). Since the 1973 oil price rise, the world economy and most regions in it have grown at much lower rates (Agarwal, 2008) and Fund policies may have contributed to the slowdown, though this hypothesis has not been examined.[36]

Furthermore, new international money that can respond to the needs of the world economy and those of developing countries, in particular, is created by either of the two schemes. While the schemes would increase the amounts that would be available to their member countries to meet any BOP crisis, the amounts available are unlikely to be sufficient to meet a serious crisis.

A second important issue is that of adjustment and this is not replicated at the national level. Every economy will not always be in BOP equilibrium where earnings of foreign exchange equal expenditures of foreign exchange. How is a situation of an imbalance handled? If a country's BOP had always to be in balance, the only way to ensure such a balance would be to license expenditures so that they equaled earnings. So, if earnings were less, then expenditures on foreign goods and services would have to be reduced, and if earnings exceeded expenditures then expenditures would have to be increased. It would be like if for an individual expenditures always had to equal income. This would create considerable volatility in expenditures and since a country's expenditures are its partner countries' earnings, the earnings of the other countries would be very volatile. Individuals avoid such volatility by using savings to bridge the gap between incomes and expenditures or use borrowings to bridge the gap. So one must analyze what possibilities

---

[35] The lower income would reduce demand which, in turn, would lower the demand for imports and so help to improve the current account. In a sense the system was operating like the pre-World War I gold standard where there was no domestic policy objective of maintaining full employment and all that mattered was to achieve external balance.

[36] Economists such as Krugman and Stiglitz have criticized such policies as being inappropriate. Though the Fund admitted at that time that its policies had been too restrictive it has continued to champion fiscal adjustment even in the current crisis as shown by its World Economic Outlook and the conditions on loans to countries such as Greece.

exist in the international system to smooth expenditures, but in the longer run a country cannot continue to have expenditures and earnings be unequal, particularly it cannot spend on foreign goods and services more than the foreign exchange it earns by selling goods and services to foreigners. So the question is of financing imbalances in the short run and adjusting them in the longer run.

A serious shortcoming of the current schemes is that they do not incorporate any new model of BOP adjustment. Historically there have been two broad modes of adjustment to a BOP deficit. One is to reduce demand and output in the economy and so demand for imports. This is how the gold standard operated for most countries. The other is through changes in the exchange rate. The members of CRA or CMIM have not indicated what their preferred mode of adjustment is, or whether they have an entirely different adjustment mechanism in mind.[37] The CRA has not yet set up any macro analysis unit as has been done by the CMIM.

The establishment of the CMIM and CRA are, however, small beginning to break the monopoly of the Bretton Woods institutions. It may be a signal that the developed countries should be more serious about reforms at these organizations. However, the developed countries are unlikely to be serious about the reform of the Bretton Woods institutions unless they believe that the BRICS or other groups of developing countries are mounting a serious challenge to the hegemony of the Bretton Woods institutions. Presumably, the loans to countries requiring BOP financing will be in convertible currencies, mainly the dollar, and will be repaid in those currencies.[38] Since no new international money is created, the member countries will have no control over the supply of international money. This also implies that though an additional source of BOP financing is now available the burden of adjustment will remain on the deficit countries. Surplus countries will be under no pressure to adjust.

Furthermore, there are no rapid response procedures to handle a fast developing emergency. Some analysts believe that it would be difficult to actually release funds as these can only be released subject to surveillance and conditionalities and as yet even though an implementing agency has been set up there are no institutional mechanisms for surveillance or to monitor conditionality.

6 Conclusions

Developing countries, dissatisfied with the governance and policies of the IMF have been running BOP surpluses in order to accumulate reserves as a precautionary measure. The reserve accumulation policies adopted by developing countries have

[37] Since exports are important for all the members, devaluation may be frowned upon as it might be considered a beggar-thy-neighbor policy.

[38] This is explicitly stated in the CRA agreement.

helped them cope with the 2008 financial crisis and its aftermath; but it is ironic that the accumulation of reserves has meant that developing countries have been lending to the richer countries, particularly the US, rather than the richer countries lending to the poorer countries to raise their investment levels. A proper monetary system that would help the international allocation of savings is still needed. Too often private capital flows have flown into the housing sector leading to real estate bubbles whether in Thailand or Spain or Ireland, with ultimately a crash with disastrous effects of the affected country's growth rate and the welfare of its citizens.

Discussion of the reform of the IMF has centered on altering its governance arrangements. The changes proposed have included eliminating the convention that the head of the IMF should be a European. It has also been argued that the number of chairs occupied by Europeans should be reduced and more representation given to African countries on the IMF's Board. In the same vein, it has been proposed that the voting percentages of developing countries should be increased. One of the measures to do this that has been suggested is that the number of basic votes that each member gets should be increased. Basic votes as a proportion of total votes were a much higher percentage at the founding of the IMF and over the years they have shrunk. There is agreement on many of these reforms at the G20 or other bodies, but these reforms have not been implemented.

A more fundamental question about the IMF is its function. What are the objectives that the IMF should serve and how can it achieve its objectives? Keynes and White had sought to build a system where external constraints would not prevent countries from achieving and maintaining full employment. Keynes had also sought to create an international money and an authority able to adjust the money supply to maintain a high level of activity in the world economy. He had also sought to craft a system where the burden of adjustment would be shared by deficit and surplus countries.

However, the IMF has supported orthodox policies, balanced budgets and free flow of capital. It has moved away from the earlier reliance on fixed exchange rates. The conditions have amounted to giving priority to external balance at the expense of domestic full employment. The system has become very similar to the GS, except where governments fear a popular backlash some of the policies may be ameliorated at the edges mainly through adjustment of the exchange rate, but unlike in the theoretical GS, adjustment has not been symmetric. The pressure to adjust has been on the deficit countries. Where the exchange rate cannot be depreciated as in the countries in the eurozone, the policies are very reminiscent of those adopted during the great depression, particularly in the gold bloc countries. Such policies have resulted in imparting a deflationary bias to policies in deficit countries with no pressure on surplus countries to adjust. The amount of international money and therefore the state of the world economy depends largely on the policies of the US, the key currency country. There is no actor at the international level to play the role of the central bank in a national system, and the international monetary system remains a half-built house.[39]

Developing countries have also established facilities such as the CMIM and the CRA to provide additional BOP financing for their members. Though the amounts available under these schemes is large compared to their quotas at the IMF, they are small compared to the amounts that have had to be mobilized to meet the different BOP crisis over the past couple of decades. Also the schemes do not indicate any new model of BOP adjustment. The onus would also continue to remain on deficit countries.

These schemes are no challenge to the hegemony of the Bretton woods institutions. They however are a small beginning and may be a pointer of things to come.

Acknowledgment

I would like to thank my colleague Sunandan Ghosh for comments on an earlier draft of the paper. I would also like to thank the participants at a seminar at the Centre where it was presented.

References

Agarwal, M. (2008), The BRICSAM Countries and Changing World Economic Power: Scenarios to 2050, Working Paper No. 39, Waterloo, Canada. Centre for *International Governance Innovation.*

Agarwal, M. (2013), South-South Economic Cooperation: Emerging Trends and Future Challenges, Background Research Paper Submitted to the High Level Panel on the Post-2015 Development Agenda, May 2013, UN, New York.

Aizenman, J. (2013), The impossible Trinity — from the Policy Trilemma to the Policy Quadrilemma, *Global Journal of Economics*, 02:01.

Aizenman, J. and Jaewoo, L. (2005), International Reserves: Precautionary vs. Mercantilist Views, Theory and Evidence. IMF Working Paper No. WP/05/198, Washington DC: IMF.

Balance of Payments Adjustment, 1945 to 1986: The IMF Experience, Page 29.

Broughton, M. (2001), *Silent Revolution: The International Monetary Fund, 1979–89*, IMF, Washington DC.

Bruton, H. (1998), A Reconsideration of Import Substitution, *Journal of Economic Literature*, 36(2).

---

[39] See Paul de Grauwe International Money, for a discussion of the evolution of national monetary and monetary control systems and a comparison of developments in the international monetary system with these national developments.

Calvo, G.A. and E.G. Mendoza (2000), Contagion, Globalization, and the Volatility of Capital Flows in Edwards, S. (eds.) *Capital Flows and the Emerging Economies: Theory, Evidence, and Controversies*, Chicago: University of Chicago Press.

Cline, W.R. (1995), *International Debt Reexamined.* Peterson Institute for International Economics, Washington DC.

Cohen, B.J. (1977), *Organizing the World's Money: The Political Economy of International Monetary Relations.* The Political Economy of International Relations Series, New York, Basic Books.

de Vries, M. and K. Horsefield (1969), *International Monetary Cooperation*, Volume I: Chronicle; Volume II: Analysis, with collaboration of others; Volume III: Documents. International Monetary Fund, Washington, DC.

De Grauwe, P. (2000), *International Money: Postwar Trends and Theories.* Second Edition, Oxford University Press, Oxford.

Desai, P. (2003), *Financial Crisis, Contagion, and Containment: From Asia to Argentina.* Princeton University Press, Princeton.

Fleming, J.M. (1952), Domestic Financial Policies Under Fixed and Floating Exchange Rates. *IMF Staff Papers*, 9: 369–379. Reprinted in Cooper, R.N. (Eds.) (1969). *International Finance*, New York: Penguin Books.

Ghatak, S. and J.R. Sánchez-Fung (2007), *Monetary Economics in Developing Countries*, Available from: (Online) http://www.imf.org/external/np/exr/facts/esaf.htm.

Goretti, M. (2005), The Brazilian Currency Turmoil of 2002: A Nonlinear Analysis, *International Journal of Finance & Economics*, 10(4), 289–306.

Helleiner (1994), States and the Re-Emergence of Global Finance: From Bretton Woods to the 1990s. Cornell University Press, Cornell.

Hickson, K. (2005), *The IMF Crisis of 1976 and British Politics: Keynesian Social Democracy*. I. B. London: Tauris Publishers.

Keynes, J.M. (1980), The Collected Works, Vol. 25, Activities 1940–1944, The Clearing Union, Moggridge, D. (Eds.), Cambridge University Press, Cambridge.

Khan, M. (2011), Stepping up from Regional Influence to a Global Role. *East Asia Forum Quarterly*.

Kharas, H., B. Pinto and S. Ulatov (2001), An Analysis of Russia's 1998 Meltdown: Fundamentals and Market Signals, *Brookings Papers on Economic Activity*, 1, 1–68.

Krugman, P. (1979), A Model of Balance-of-Payments Crises. *Journal of Money, Credit and Banking*, 11, 311–325.

Krugman, P. (2015), June 25, 2015 Available from: http://krugman.blogs.nytimes.com/.

Mantega, G. (2007), Statement to International Monetary and Financial Committee Sixteenth Meeting October 20, 2007 by Minister of Finance, Brazil On behalf of Brazil, Colombia, Dominican Republic, Ecuador, Guyana, Haiti, Panama, Suriname, Trinidad and Tobago accessed at https://www.imf.org/External/AM/2007/imfc/statement/eng/bra.pdf

Marglin, S. and Juliet, S. (Eds.) (1990), *The Golden Age of Capitalism: Reinterpreting the Postwar Experience*. Clarendon Press, Oxford.

Moseley, P., J. Hartigan and J. Toye (1991), *Aid and Power: The World Bank amd Policy Based Lending*, Volume 1. Routledge, London.

Mulraine M.L.B. (2005), An Analysis of the 2002 Argentine Currency Crisis. Available from: http://homes.chass.utoronto.ca/~mulraine/arg.pdf.

Mundell, R.A. (1963), Capital Mobility and Stabilization Policy Under Fixed and Flexible Exchange Rates. *Canadian Journal of Economic and Political Science*, 29(4): 475–485 Reprinted in Mundell, R. A. (1968) *International Economics*, Macmillan, New York.

Mussa, M. (1990), Exchange rates in theory and in reality, *Essays in International Finance No. 179*, Princeton, NJ: Princeton University.

Olivier, J. and R. Rancière (2006), The Optimal Level of International Reserves for Emerging Market Countries: Formulas and Applications International Monetary Fund, *IMF Working Paper No. WP/06/229.*

Polak, J.J. (1981), The Changing Nature of IMF Conditionality Essays in International Finance, No. 184.

Radelet, S. and Jeffrey, S. (1998), The Onset of the East Asian Crisis. *Brookings papers in Economic Activity*, 1, 1–68.

Ruggie, J. (1982), Transactions, and Change: Embedded. Liberalism in the Postwar Economic System. *International Organization*, 36(2).

Sachs, J. (Ed) (1991), Developing Country Debt and Economic Performance, Volume 1: *The International Financial System* (National Bureau of Economic Research Project Report) University of Chicago Press, Chicago.

Sachs, J., A. Tornell, A. Velasco (1996), The Mexican Peso Crisis: Sudden Death or Death Foretold. *Journal of International Economics*, 41, 265–283.

Siregar, R. and Akkharaphol, C. (2013), Enhancing the effectiveness of CMIM and AMRO: Selected Immediate Challenges and Tasks. *ADBI Working Paper Series No 403*, Manila: Asian Development Bank Institute.

Toye, J. (1987), *Dilemmas of Development: Reflections on the Counter-Revolution in Development Theory and Policy*. Basil Blackwell, Oxford.

Williamson, J. (1977), *The Failure of World Monetary Reform, 1971–74*, New York University Press, New York.

Williamson, J. (1990), *Latin American Adjustment : How Much Has Happened?* Institute for International Economics, Washington D.C.

Williamson, J. (1992), *International Monetary Reform and the Prospects for Economic Development Finance: Rethinking the International Monetary System.* FONDAD, The Hague.

Williamson, J. (2009), Understanding Special Drawing Rights (SDRs) Peterson Institute for International Economics, Policy Brief No. PB 09-11, Washington DC.

Chapter 2

Data Exclusivity in Trade Agreements: An Indian Perspective*

Amit S Ray[†,‡,§] and Ritesh Jain[‡]

[†]*Centre for Development Studies, Thiruvananthapuram, Kerala, India*

[‡]*Jawaharlal Nehru University, New Delhi, India*

[§]*asray@cds.edu*

Abstract: Newer dimensions of IPR are being brought into the agenda under trade agreements with the sole objective of restricting diffusion of pharmaceutical innovation and preventing the spread of generics. One such issue pertains to protection of test data for products which require marketing approval, especially pharmaceuticals. This chapter is an attempt to discuss how policies on data protection/exclusivity are being brought into trade agreements. We outline the logic and scope of data exclusivity,its impact on developing countries and present an Indian perspective on the issue. Three broad conclusions emerge from this paper. First, TRIPS does not mandate data exclusivity in the US/EU sense. Second, there are serious adverse implications of data exclusivity for developing nations, posing serious public health concerns by circumventing all flexibilities that were extracted by the coalition of developing countries on the TRIPS agreement towards achieving developmental goals. Finally, the Indian position on the issue of data exclusivity has been characterized by a dual and contradictory position taken by the administrative leadership and the political leadership. Fortunately, so far, the political position has prevailed over the administrative position and India has not succumbed to the international pressure lobby to introduce data exclusivity in its legal framework working through the route of trade agreements. However, the administrative position reflected in the Reddy Committee Report is a matter of concern as it always hangs as a threat to sustaining India's political position.

*We gratefully acknowledge a research grant received from ANRS, France (Project No. 12213) for this research.

In fact, the response of countries like India with substantial manufacturing capacities for generic production, would decide the fate of future of access to affordable medicine for the entire developing world. It is, therefore, crucially important for India to get rid of any confusing administrative signals and posit a consistent position against data exclusivity.

1 Introduction

India, in its quest for self-reliance in the 1970s and 1980s, was quite successful in creating a unique policy space for its pharmaceutical industry to flourish and emerge as a major global supplier of generics. In a recent paper, Ray and Bhaduri (2014) have "shown how endogenously determined homegrown policy models have helped this industry to become self-reliant, not only in manufacturing but also in technology, and eventually compete successfully in global markets through technological capability." Unfortunately, developments in the world economic order driven by neo-liberal institutions like the WTO, for instance, during the last couple of decades have reduced this space for endogenous policy making by national governments. One area that deserves a special mention in this regard is the institution of intellectual property rights (IPRs) which got linked to trade during the Uruguay Round of multilateral trade negotiations. The inclusion of TRIPS in the WTO agreement, despite strong opposition from developing countries, marked the beginning of a new institutional arrangement to homogenize IPR regimes across the world.

Patent is a key dimension of IPR policy that has attracted significant scholarly attention. Patent policy has very significant implications for technological learning and technological capability accumulation in developing countries (Lall, 2001; CIPR, 2002; Dutfield and Sutharsanan, 2005). Despite the strong belief that a weak patent regime, facilitating diffusion and learning, could prove to be most important for technological catch-up in developing countries and they are likely to lose out under strong patent regimes due to shrinking opportunities of imitative R&D (Helpman, 1993; Lall, 2001; Maskus, 2000), a uniformly strong and homogenous patent regime across the world has been imposed, erasing the endogenous policy space for nations.[1]

The issue of patents becomes particularly contentious in case of the pharmaceutical sector, where monopoly pricing of pharmaceutical inventions can prove to be detrimental for access to medicines in poor countries, by throttling the production of cheaper generic versions of patented drugs for the

[1] Dutfield and Sutharsanan (2005), for instance, documents "numerous instances of how today's developed countries often ensured they had weaker IP regimes than those of the technologically more advanced countries with which they were seeking to catch up".

entire patent duration. Especially for diseases like HIV-AIDS or cancer, where non-innovating developing/emerging economies bear a significant disease burden, patents may have serious public health implications in these countries. It is with this perspective that developing countries could form a powerful coalition during the Doha rounds of WTO negotiations to introduce some flexibilities in the TRIPS agreement (especially with respect to patents' policy) to address these developmental concerns.

However, newer dimensions of IPR are being brought into the agenda with the key objective of restricting diffusion of pharmaceutical innovation and preventing the spread of generics. One such recently discussed issue pertains to protection of test data for products which require marketing approval, especially pharmaceuticals. This paper is an attempt to discuss how policies on data protection/exclusivity are being brought into trade agreements and how they may impinge on public health in developing countries. Our objective is to present an Indian perspective on this issue.

The paper is structured as follows. Section 2 discusses data protection/data exclusivity as an IPR instrument. Section 3 brings out the historical origins of data exclusivity rooted in US/EU legislation, linking it with the objectives of the Hatch–Waxman Act and associated political economy forces. Section 4 presents how data exclusivity featured in multilateral (TRIPS) and bilateral/regional trade agreements. Section 5 discusses the implications of data exclusivity from the perspective of developing countries. Section 6 outlines India's position on data exclusivity and the losses which India could incur if it accepts data exclusivity.

2 Protection of Undisclosed Information — Rights on Test Data

A pharmaceutical product, whether patented or otherwise, requires marketing approval by a regulatory agency to certify its safety, efficacy and quality. The producer, as a precondition for this approval, has to submit to the approval authority all data generated by him during clinical trials to test for the safety, efficacy and quality of the drug. This data is often referred to as 'clinical trial data'. The regulatory agency based on this data grants marketing approval for a new drug application, only if it satisfies all stipulated conditions and norms. Since this data is submitted to the public authorities for approval, it entails the possibility of a third party[2] using this data for its own commercial advantage, which may not be fair. Hence, this data needs to be protected from disclosure to others. Such protection may not prevent the use of this data by the public authority itself. This is required

[2]Third party here refers to the second entrant commonly generic producers.

when they grant marketing approval to third parties for generic versions based on the data submitted by the original innovator. The issue of data exclusivity is centered on closing this particular loophole. While the indirect use of test data by the public authorities facilitates early entry of cheap generics into the market, the large pharmaceutical industry lobby argues that it places the innovating drug manufacturers at a serious commercial disadvantage and hence the incentives to innovate are weakened (IFPMA, 2011). This argument brings us back to the classic problem of trade-off between the twin goals of innovation and diffusion in the context of strong vs. weak patent protection.

In the case of data protection, a policy regime that only prevents the unauthorized use of test data by third parties but allows the use of test data by public authorities for granting marketing approval of generics may be considered as a weak regime that facilitates early generic entry but reduces incentives to innovate. It is argued that generic producers effectively then free ride on the clinical data generated by the original producer at substantial costs, both in terms of time and money. Due to this, the originator is put to a severe commercial disadvantage and it may be that there is no incentive for the originator to develop and market new drugs. The argument is based on the estimates of time and money which go into the generation of test data and consequent marketing approval. According to the International Federation of Pharmaceutical Manufacturers Association (IFPMA), it takes 15 years and costs on an average US$500 million for a new drug to be marketed. According to IFPMA, out of the total expenses incurred on R&D, 40% go for preclinical, 30% for phase I, II, III trials. Accordingly, 70% of total R&D expenditure is spent on obtaining regulatory approvals. According to DeMasi and (2014), 'the estimated average pre-tax industry cost per new prescription drug approval (inclusive of failures and capital costs) is US$2,558 million.[3] By contrast, a generic manufacturer has to incur only US$1million to introduce the same drug in the market, as long as they do not have to replicate the test data for safety, efficacy and quality. It is in this context that the developed countries, under the pressure from their domestic pharmaceutical industry, are demanding a form of data exclusivity for a fixed period of time which will prohibit the use of clinical trials data even by the regulatory authorities for marketing approval of generic versions. Data exclusivity, thus, stresses on the proprietary rights of the original innovator over the test data submitted to the regulatory authorities.

---

[3] These estimates are contestable. However, the enormity of resource requirement for new drug development cannot be brushed under the carpet.

3 Historical Origins of Data Exclusivity — USA and EU

3.1 Hatch–Waxman Act 1984, USA

Data exclusivity emerged as a form of IPR in response to the introduction of stringent requirements and norms for obtaining marketing approval of pharmaceutical products from the national drug regulatory authorities. Norms were not so stringent in the early days. Prior to 1962, new drugs were approved in the US on the basis of clinical tests for safety only. For introduction of generics, the generic producer only had to prove bioequivalence with the original product already in the market. In 1962, the US Federal Food, Drug and Cosmetic Act was amended to mandate pharmaceutical manufacturers to demonstrate that their new drug was both safe and effective. This condition was a result of the Kefauver–Harris Act 1962 (Scherer F.M. (2009)).

The new legislation required submission of clinical trial data based on which the USFDA would grant 'marketing approval' for new drug applications. The act was, however, silent on any specific guidelines for the approval of generics. Generic manufacturers were therefore compelled to file a New Drug Application (NDA) and to submit evidence proving that the generic drug was safe and effective, even if their product was chemically identical and bioequivalent to the original drug already approved for marketing. However there were certain exceptions to this requirement, namely, pre-1962 drugs and special regime for antibiotics. These were exempted from the regular process of NDA and were allowed a process called Abbreviated New Drug Application (ANDA), where bioequivalence was enough for regulatory approval.

The act of 1962 created strong barriers to the entry of low-cost generics into the market and thus provided a favorable incentive structure for innovating firms. From the public policy point of view, there was a felt need to strike a balance between the two objectives, namely, encouraging new innovation as well facilitating entry of low cost generics. To achieve these twin goals, a major pharmaceutical legislation was enacted in 1984, called the Drug price Competition and Patent Restoration Act (also known as the **Hatch–Waxman Act, 1984**). The act had far reaching implications for the pharmaceutical industry. This act extended the exemptions in the 1962 amendment that existed for antibiotics (and pre-1962 drugs) to all generic drugs, allowing generic manufacturers to gain USFDA marketing approval by filing ANDA, based on the safety and efficacy data from original NDA, so long as the generic drug was bioequivalent with the originator's drug. This naturally reduced the barriers to entry for generic producers considerably.[4]

[4] For various provisions facilitating entry of generics, see Mehl (2006).

To facilitate generic entry even further, certain exceptions to the patent provision were introduced which allowed experimental manufacturing of patented drugs for further research. This came to be popularly known as the 'Bolar exception'. Facilitation of generic entry was seen as independent of patent protection and it was felt that generics should be able to hit the market the very next day after the patent expires.

This, of course, was strongly opposed by the big pharmaceutical lobby as they felt that the incentive to innovate contained in patent protection was being diluted. As it is, the innovator loses considerable time after the patent grant during the period of regulatory marketing approvals. Therefore, to incentivize innovation, the patent period was extended to 20 years in order to compensate for the time lost in the process of obtaining regulatory approvals.

The Hatch–Waxman act also introduced several non-patent market exclusivities, which include the new product data exclusivity or simply data exclusivity.[5] As discussed earlier, data exclusivity prevents the national regulatory authority from relying on the originator's test data to approve subsequent applications during a specific period of time. The New Drug Product Exclusivity is regulated in Section 355 of the Federal Food, Drug and Cosmetic Act and it provides

(1) ***5-year data exclusivity*** — This provides 5-year period of data exclusivity from the date of the FDA approval granted to new pharmaceutical products containing new chemical entities.
(2) ***3-year data exclusivity*** — A 3-year period of marketing exclusivity from the date of the FDA approval is granted to new uses/indications of pharmaceutical products containing an active moiety that has been previously approved, for which the originator has conducted or sponsored new clinical investigations that were essential for the approval.

It should be noted that data exclusivity as provided in the US law is only applicable for *new chemical entities* and it excludes *new biological entities*.[6]

In summary, the logic of the Hatch–Waxman Act of 1984 was to hasten the entry of generic products into the market by relying only on bioequivalence tests for generic approvals, but at the same time encouraging and incentivizing new drug development by extending the patent duration from 14 to 20 years and introducing data exclusivity for 5 years and 3 years, respectively.

---

[5] Other marketing exclusivities include orphan drug exclusivity, pediatric drug exclusivity, generic drug exclusivity, drugs approved between 1982 and 1984, and medical devices exclusivity.

[6] The inclusion of pharmaceutical products which are biologicals in the realm of data exclusivity is the matter of current debate on the DE in US.

3.2 Data exclusivity in EU

The first European Community pharmaceutical directive was issued in 1965 in response to the Thalidomide tragedy, in which thousands of babies with limb deformities were born to mothers taking thalidomide as a sedative during pregnancy in the early 1960s. This directive provided for compulsory testing and authorization before pharmaceuticals could be marketed in a Member State.

Article 3 of the Directive mandated that no proprietary medicinal product could be placed on the market in a Member State unless an authorization had been issued by the competent authority of that state. Article 4 outlined what materials must accompany an application for authorization. However, the issue of data exclusivity was not addressed. According to Article 4(8)(a)(ii), when a new proprietary product with ingredients that are identical with that of a known proprietary product with an established use is introduced, rather than supplying test results, the manufacturer may substitute a list of published references. These references should relate to the pharmacological tests, toxicological tests and clinical trials. There was no minimum time limit for the original product to have been marketed before the product with "identical" ingredients could rely on its data.

It was in 1986 that the 1965 directive was amended by Directive (EC) 87/21/EEC of December 22, 1986. As a result, Article 4(8)(a)(ii) of Directive 65/65 required that a product be in use for not less than six years and be marketed in the Member State for which application is made before a second product can take advantage of the "similar constituent" provisions. The time period of protection was extended to ten years in the case of high technology medical products, or to all products marketed in the territory of a Member State if that State considered it necessary in the interest of public health.

Due the provisions on the time period of data exclusivity, some countries adopted 10 years of data exclusivity and some countries adopted 6 years of data exclusivity. Belgium, France, Germany, Italy, the UK, Luxemburg, the Netherlands and Sweden were the countries which had 10 years of data exclusivity regime for all medicinal products. On the other hand, Austria, Denmark, Finland, Ireland, Greece, Spain, Portugal, Poland, Czech Republic, Hungary, Lithuania, Latvia, Slovenia, Slovakia, Malta, Estonia, Cyprus and also Norway, Lichtenstein and Iceland were the countries which adopted 6 years of data exclusivity regime for medicinal product.

In 2004 Directive 2001/83/EC (as amended by Directive 2004/27/EC) provide a harmonized data exclusivity period for all Member States. As per amended Article 127b, Article 3 of the Directive, Member States were required to bring into force the laws, regulations and administrative provisions necessary to comply with this Directive no later than October 30, 2005. As a result of this Directive,

data exclusivity is now provided for a period of "8+2+1" years. According to this formula, new pharmaceutical products, including both new chemical entities and new biological entities, would be entitled to 8 years of data exclusivity, 2 years of marketing exclusivity (in which generic companies would be allowed to rely on the data of the original product, i.e. submit bio-equivalence tests, but not market their generic substitute) and an additional year of protection for new indications of existing products. It should be noted that the Bolar exception works only after 8 years i.e. within the 2 years in the '8+2+1' formula. It is important to note that the data exclusivity regime in the EU is stricter than in the US.

The history of data exclusivity and the current regimes of data exclusivity in the USA and the EU highlight the degree of protection provided by their laws to the large and innovative pharmaceutical firms. These provisions, however, are absent in many other nations, especially in the developing and in the emerging worlds. It is therefore of interest to explore how such provisions are sought to be built into trade agreements, both multilateral and bilateral, with a view to bringing their laws in line with that of the interest of large pharmaceutical companies in the developed world.

4 Data Exclusivity and Trade Agreements

4.1 TRIPS under the WTO regime

The World Trade Organization has brought a comprehensive multilateral trade agreement binding all states to align their trade policies as well as other economic policies with the diktats of the WTO with the stated objective of creating an environment to foster free trade. The TRIPS agreement builds in an intellectual property regime within this multilateral trading arrangement. The issue of data protection/data exclusivity remains one of the most contentious clauses in the TRIPS agreement. As discussed in Section 1, the debate surrounding right to test data essentially boils down to whether the regulatory authority may use clinical test data supplied by the original innovator to provide marketing approval for subsequent generic substitutes. It is, therefore, very important to understand the scope of data protection as provided by TRIPS contained in Article 39.3 under the heading of Protection of Undisclosed Information. The original text of Article 39.3 of TRIPS which determines the basis for data protection is: "*Members, when requiring, as a condition of approving the marketing of pharmaceutical or of agricultural chemical products which utilize new chemical entities, the submission of undisclosed test or other data, the origination of which involves a considerable effort, shall protect such data against unfair commercial use. In addition,*

Members shall protect such data against disclosure, except where necessary to protect the public, or unless steps are taken to ensure that the data are protected against unfair commercial use."

The meaning and scope of this article has been analyzed by several authors and organizations, both in the developed and developing worlds.[7] Unfortunately, there are sharp differences in interpretations of Article 39.3. While some argue that Article 39.3 provides for data exclusivity and prohibits the reliance of regulatory authorities, others contend that Article 39.3 only provides for protection of undisclosed information against unfair commercial use. A close reading of the text, however, clearly brings out the scope of data protection provided by TRIPS Article 39.3.

In principal there can be two types of data protection regimes the first one acknowledges the use of undisclosed information by third parties as an unfair commercial advantage and demands protection from such acts. But the reliance on this data by the public authorities for granting marketing approval of generic substitutes is not considered as use by a third party for unfair commercial advantage. In short, data protection in this frame only prohibits direct use of data by the third party but allows its indirect use. The second regime acknowledges both the direct and indirect use of the data as an unfair commercial use and hence demands a form of exclusivity that prohibits direct as well as indirect use of clinical trials data.

Since Article 39.3 does not define the terms 'new', 'considerable effort', 'unfair commercial use', it gives the member countries the flexibility to define these terms in accordance with their norms, cultures and domestic laws. For example, in light of the above discussion, the term unfair may include the reliance of regulatory authorities on test data bringing about an exclusivity approach to data protection. Likewise, this reliance may not even be considered as unfair by others, leading to the adoption of the first kind of data exclusivity regime where data protection does not prevent the use of test data by regulatory authorities for granting generic approval. Similarly, reliance by the government may not be considered as "commercial use" since the use by the government is only to test the toxicity and safety which in itself is not a commercial use, although it may have commercial consequences.

Given that TRIPS is a minimum binding agreement and sets only the baseline, all kinds of data protection regimes are compatible with TRIPS among which data exclusivity is the strongest of all.[8] Data exclusivity in US/EU is as much TRIPS compliant as it is so in a regime that allows drug regulatory authorities to use the

[7] Correa (2002a), CIPR (2002), CIPIH (2006), Satwant Reddy report, Dhar and Gopakumar (2006).
[8] See Correa (2002a) for the types of regimes compatible with Article 39.3 of TRIPS.

test data submitted by an original innovator for granting marketing approval of generic substitutes, since the use by government may not be construed *as unfair commercial use*. This is the position that has been adopted by international experts and has been highlighted in various reports and commissions. Correa (2002a), for instance, argues in a detailed analysis of Article 39.3:

> *"But these positions are not well grounded in either the text or negotiating history of TRIPS. TRIPS negotiators specifically considered and rejected language requiring grants of exclusive rights to test data"*

Developed countries, however, have constantly argued that Article 39.3 should be interpreted as nothing less than data exclusivity. The Office of the United States Trade Representative has interpreted Article 39.3 of the TRIPS Agreement to mean that:

> *"the data will not be used to support, clear or otherwise review other applications for marketing approval for a set amount of time unless authorized by the original submitter of the data. Any other definition of this term would be inconsistent with logic and the negotiating history of the provision".*

Similarly, EU argues that Article 39.3 established an exclusivity obligation. According to the EU, all that is left to member countries is the determination of the duration thereof:

> *"the only way to guarantee that no "unfair commercial use" within the meaning of Article 39.3 shall be made is to provide that regulatory authorities should not rely on these data for a reasonable period of time, the determination of what is a reasonable period of time being left to the discretion of the Members".*

It is interesting to note that the Committee headed by Mrs. Satwant Reddy, which was set up in 2004 by the Government of India to suggest the obligations for data exclusivity under TRIPS, has categorically acknowledged the fact that TRIPS does not demand data exclusivity and at the same time holds that it does prohibit approval of generics based on bioequivalence tests in any way.

This conflict can be well understood by looking into the negotiating history of the TRIPS agreement. The bracketed text under consideration at the Brussels Ministerial Meeting and the text which appeared finally i.e. Article 39.3 clearly convey the roots of the controversy explained above. The former read as follows:

> *"[Parties, when requiring, as a condition of approving the marketing of new pharmaceutical products or of a new agricultural chemical product, the submission of*

undisclosed test or other data, the originator of which involves a considerable effort, shall protect such data against unfair commercial use.

Unless the person submitting the information agrees, the data may not be relied upon for the approval of competing products for a reasonable time, generally no less than five years, commensurate with the efforts involved in the origination of the data, their nature, and the expenditure involved in their preparation. In addition, Parties shall protect such data against disclosure, except where necessary to protect the public]."

It should be noted that this text clearly includes the word 'reliance', making data exclusivity inevitable, however, the text which appeared finally was silent on this and as explained earlier it is open to all kinds of interpretations. It can be inferred that it was the public health concern of the developing countries which rejected the earlier draft in favor of Article 39.3. This clearly points out to the fact that the TRIPS agreement does not require data exclusivity. Data exclusivity is clearly a TRIPS Plus Provision.[9]

Indeed, this position is vindicated by the explicit inclusion of data exclusivity in different bilateral/regional trade agreements being signed by the USA and the EU. Had it been covered by the TRIPS agreement, this would not have been required.

4.2 Bilateral/regional trade agreements and data exclusivity

The rejection of the exclusivity approach to data protection by developing countries in TRIPS led the developed world, especially the USA, to pursue bilateral and regional trading agreements through which they are able to achieve what was not possible at the multilateral levels Roffe and Spennemann (2006). This refers to the circumventing the flexibilities of TRIPS, gained by developing countries during the multilateral negotiations, by introducing TRIPS Plus provisions in bilateral/ regional trade agreements. These include[10]:

(a) Data exclusivity for 5 years: US–Singapore/Chile/Australia/Dominican Republic-CAFTA (Central American Free Trade Agreement)/Bahrain.
(b) Data exclusivity for 5 years and additional 3 years for new indication as in US law: US–Morocco.

[9] A TRIPS PLUS provision is a clause which is not a part of the TRIPS agreement and undermines the flexibilities provided in TRIPS: See Roffe and Spennemann (2006) and CIPIH Study 4C.
[10] See Table 2 in Fink and Reichenmiller (2005).

(c) Data exclusivity beyond national territories: In this, the domestic regulatory agencies cannot rely on the regulatory approval granted in a foreign country unless the consent of the originator of the data is obtained. The US–Singapore FTA prevents only recognition but not reliance. But the FTAs with Australia, DR-CAFTA and Bahrain do not allow even reliance. In other words, the US type data exclusivity is applicable for approvals given in foreign territories as well.
(d) Chemical entities covered: As discussed earlier, data protection is given only to drugs containing 'New chemical entities', however, some FTAs have broadened this definition by providing data protection to all new products, US–Singapore and US–Australia.
(e) Linkage between patent status and drug marketing approval: In principle, patent law and law on regulatory approval are independent. But some FTAs have linked these two by requiring the prohibition of marketing approval of a generic drug without the consent of the patent holder during the life time of the patent. This essentially extends the period of data exclusivity to the life time of the patent for patented drugs. Except US-Vietnam FTA, all other FTAs mentioned above contain this provision.

The stark implication of all these provisions is to slow down the entry of generic substitutes with serious adverse impact on access to affordable medicines, especially in the developing world. We shall discuss these adverse effects in the following section. But we note here that the reason why countries are willing to give up at the bilateral level what was considered to be important at the multilateral level is the market access these FTAs provide to developing countries in exchange for stronger IPR regimes. Fink (2007) notes that *"Their (TRIPS Plus Standards) acceptance by developing countries cannot be explained by expected economic benefits, but has to be understood as a quid pro quo for preferential market access in developed country markets for agricultural and manufactured goods"*. It is for this reason that it is easy for the developed world to break the coalition formed at the multilateral negotiating stage very easily through bilateral negotiations.

5 Implications of Data Exclusivity for Developing Countries

The major concern of developing countries about the TRIPS agreement, voiced especially during the Doha rounds, is that trade and business interests should not come in the way of addressing public health concerns of developing countries.

In the context of pharmaceuticals, the objective is to ensure timely availability of cheap and affordable generics, especially for AIDS, Cancer, and Malaria that constitute a significant disease burden in developing countries. It is for this reason that several countries kept the pharmaceutical sector outside the purview of intellectual property rights.[11] However, the TRIPS agreement obliges the developing countries to provide IPR in all fields of technology which includes pharmaceuticals.

To ensure that these provisions do not become an obstacle to the pursuance of public health objectives, TRIPS contained several flexibilities that allowed governments to set aside IPR obligations in situations deemed necessary to address public health issue. These flexibilities were further highlighted in the Doha Declaration on the TRIPS and public Health (Correa, 2002b). Two important flexibilities provided within TRIPS allow national governments to (1) define the scope of patentable subject matter, according to their developmental needs and (2) to issue compulsory licenses for non-commercial government use in situations of national interest. A third flexibility relates to the provision of data protection allowing regulatory authorities to use original test data for generics approval. The circumvention of this flexibility forms the basis of discussion in this section.

It is very important to distinguish between two situations while discussing the implications of data exclusivity — (1) when the subject matter is patentable and (2) when the subject matter is non-patentable.

In the former case, according to global standards, the minimum duration of patents is 20 years from the date of filing the application. If the drug is launched in the market in the next say 12 years, then a 5-year data exclusivity regime will not mean anything as it will be covered under patents anyway. Only in a case when the drug is marketed in the 17th or 18th year of its patent life will a 5-year data exclusivity regime extend the marketing exclusivity period over and above the patent term. The problem becomes more acute if we are taking the EU regime of 10 years ('8+2+1') of data exclusivity. However, from the developing countries point of view, the issue which commands attention is the ability to invoke **compulsory licenses**. Compulsory license refers to the right of the government to override the market exclusivity granted by patents in situations deemed as emergencies. When a government uses this provision it allows the generic production of a patented product in order to make available cheaper generic substitutes of a patented drug to address public health concerns. Note that the use of compulsory license makes sense only for the cases when products are patented. In this case, a

---

[11] At the time of initial negotiations on the TRIPS Agreement, some 50 countries did not provide patent protection to pharmaceuticals products.

compulsory license even if issued would not allow cheap manufacture of generic production since in the presence of data exclusivity regime the costs for generic producers become exorbitant due to the requirement of producing all test data afresh for obtaining a marketing approval.

In the second case, the subject matter under data exclusivity is non-patentable in a particular nation. As discussed earlier, the TRIPS agreement only lays down minimum standards to be followed by member countries and leaves various provisions to be defined by the member countries in consonance with their domestic laws and customs. In respect of patentable subject matter, TRIPS leaves it open for the member countries to define the scope of patentability i.e. to define the terms 'novelty', 'inventiveness' and 'industrial applicability'. For instance, the Indian Patents Act 2005 does not allow for patents for various products including plant varieties, biotechnological products and new indication of existing drugs or new dosage forms. One of the objectives to have a broad definition is to prevent the problem of *ever-greening* of patents. The introduction of data exclusivity in such cases will introduce a patent like protection against the entry of cheaper substitutes, even though the drug is deliberately left outside the scope of patent protection.

Keeping this distinction in mind, we now focus on the two areas in which data exclusivity will have serious implications, namely, compulsory licensing and *'patent-like'* monopoly protection over non-patentable products.

5.1 Data exclusivity and compulsory licenses

The significance of compulsory license lies in its use as a bargaining tool to induce the innovating drug manufacturer to offer a discounted/reduced price for its patented drug in situations of health emergencies as perceived by a national government. The mere presence of compulsory license in IPR law has an effect on the actual behavior of the patent holder. Even a threat of issuing a compulsory license, if credible, rather an actual use license, disciplines the owner of the patented product. This could explain why in reality few compulsory licenses are actually invoked.[12] For instance, Roche offered a 40% price reduction on its AIDS drug, Viracept, to Brazil after the Brazilian government publicly announced in 2001 that it would issue a compulsory license to a local laboratory (Fink, 2006). Compulsory license will be a credible threat only if the country has the capacity to either buy or produce the drugs at a lower cost. Salama and Benoliel (2010) examine the

[12] CIPIH (2006) and Fink (2006).

political economy factors underlying the Brazilian strategy of Compulsory License as a credible and aggressive threat.

Introduction of data exclusivity will render the compulsory licenses ineffective by increasing the costs of regulatory approvals. As a matter of fact, the threat of a compulsory license will also become non-viable or non-credible. The impact will be different for two types of countries:

(A) Countries with substantial capacity to produce generic drugs domestically,
(B) Countries lacking domestic production capacity and relying on import of generic medicines.

The former group of countries will be affected by the fact that the costs of generic production will increase which will undermine the use of the compulsory license itself. The problem becomes more acute for the latter group of countries. The reason for this asymmetric effect lies in the fact that countries with large domestic markets will be better able to absorb the increased cost due to data exclusivity. The countries, which lack domestic capacity to produce due to small markets and lack of technical capacity, can use compulsory licensing as a bargaining tool only if they are allowed to import generics through the route of parallel imports where the compulsory license is issued to a generic producer in some other country with manufacturing capacity. In that case, the country producing the drug under compulsory license will do so exclusively for exports and data exclusivity will act as a major disincentive to this generic company which may not be willing to make substantial investments needed to duplicate the tests for marketing approval. Thus, data exclusivity undermines the threat of issuing a compulsory license and puts the developing countries in a weaker position on the bargaining table with the big pharmaceutical companies producing patented drugs.

5.2 Data exclusivity on non-patentable products

Although the TRIPS agreement demands uniform patent protection in all fields of technology, Article 27.1 does not define the patentability criteria and leaves the terms 'novelty', 'inventiveness' and 'industrial applicability' to be defined by member countries according their own priorities. From the public health point of view, minor innovations over a patented product should not be eligible for patents, as it creates "ever-greening" of pharmaceutical patents. Moreover, new indications and new dosage forms of existing patented drugs are not patentable in countries like India. Apart from this, biological and biotechnological products are not patentable. The issue of data exclusivity becomes extremely important in all these cases, since data exclusivity extends patent-like protection to these non-patentable products. This point is highlighted in the Satwant Reddy Committee report as well:

> *"A growing commercial significance of data protection is being realized for products that are not under patent protection due either to the new chemical entities not meeting the novelty test for a patent or there may be new uses of products, whose patents have expired... The issue of data protection becomes especially relevant for off-patent products as well as for products such as biologicals that are often difficult to patent"*

The fact that certain innovations do not satisfy the criterion of patentability and hence represent a built-in safeguard for public health, data exclusivity, by increasing the cost for generic substitutes, extends a monopoly right to the original producers although the products do not satisfy patentability criteria. This completely undermines the flexibility in TRIPS to exclude certain non-innovative products from the scope of patentability.

In summary then, data exclusivity will undermine all the safeguards and flexibilities provided in the TRIPS agreement and which were clarified and upheld in the Doha Declaration 2001.[13] Given the importance given to public health in the Doha declaration over TRIPS, data exclusivity runs counter to the spirit and provision of the Doha Declaration. To highlight the importance of the issue of Public health in the context of the TRIPS agreement, the Doha Declaration notes that *"the TRIPS Agreement does not and should not prevent members from taking measures to protect public health... The agreement can and should be interpreted and implemented in a manner supportive of WTO members right to protect public health and to promote access to medicines to all."*

Interpreting the scope of the Doha declaration, Correa (2002b) argues that this declaration implicitly includes data exclusivity also and therefore public health objectives should not be compromised for data exclusivity.

6 India's Stand on Data Exclusivity

It is now well acknowledged that the Indian generic industry has carved a niche for itself in the production of cheap generic products across the world (Ray and Bhaduri, 2014). Data exclusivity, if introduced in India, will increase the costs for generic manufacturers and put them under a serious disadvantage. It is in this context that the position of the Indian government has to be viewed.

---

[13] See Correa (2002b) for an interpretation of Doha declaration.

India is characterized by the presence of a strong manufacturing capacity for generics that is not only capable of supplying to the entire domestic market but also capable of exporting affordable generic to the world market. Indeed, India is called the 'pharmacy of the developing world'. Moreover, the Indian Patents Act 2005 follows a strict patentability criterion, excluding minor/incremental innovations from the ambit of patents. Given these two parameters, based on our discussion in the previous section, data exclusivity will have serious adverse implications on both counts — limiting the use of compulsory license and extending patent-like protection to non-patentable products. The countries which rely on India's exports will also suffer as the data exclusivity regime, if adopted in India, will increase the cost of Indian generic drugs and consequently undermine the credibility of threats of compulsory license for this set of countries. It is for this reason that the proposed India–EU FTA, which included a data exclusivity provision in its early versions, was seen as a threat to the cause of public health not only for India but also for the entire developing world, as it would have severally limited the access to affordable drugs.[14] Therefore, India's stand on data exclusivity is not only important for India but equally crucial for the future of public health in the developing world. Keeping the public health effects in mind, the Government of India in 2003 issued a statement:

> *"The Government does not have a position on data exclusivity at the moment. But it is clear that we have no obligation under TRIPS (trade-related aspects of intellectual property rights) to have provisions for the same in the country."* Also, a Government official reportedly stated that *"TRIPS only requires us to protect test data against unfair use under Article 39.3, but there is nothing that says that we have to provide marketing exclusivity. Interpretations vary depending on which side you are on. It is only when a case comes up at the Appellate Authority at WTO can there be clarity...... Under the existing circumstances, it is highly unlikely that marketing exclusivity would be provided for any period of time. It would be possible only if TRIPS is modified, which one cannot see happening. With new products not coming to the market, new uses are being found for the existing ones. While patents would not cover these, data protection is being seen by American companies as a new form of intellectual property right to effectively extend patent life."*

It is then clear that the Government of India had acknowledged the inbuilt flexibility provided by Article 39.3 with respect to data exclusivity. However, in 2004, the Government of India set up the Satwant Reddy Committee to assess its stand on data exclusivity and to suggest measures to be adopted in the context of

[14] There is a perception that the India generic industry caters to nearly 80% of the demand for drugs in the LDCs.

data protection provisions outlined in Article 39.3 of TRIPS. It has been alleged in popular discourse that the Reddy Committee was set up amidst international pressures on India to incorporate data exclusivity, a TRIPS Plus provision, in its legal framework. The major recommendations of this committee were to provide data exclusivity for ayurvedic medicines and agricultural products. However, the Committee failed to take a clear stand on the issue of data exclusivity for pharmaceuticals. It acknowledged that data exclusivity is not demanded by TRIPS Article 39.3. However, for pharmaceutical products, the Committee recommended that a data exclusivity regime that would provide a five year data exclusivity from the date of first approval of the product anywhere in the world, subject to various safeguards, may be considered in the near future. It is interesting to note that the Reddy Committee Report faced severe public criticism in the media and in academic discourses. Even the Parliamentary Standing Committee on Commerce, in their 88th Report on Patents and Trademarks Systems in India submitted to the Rajya Sabha Secretariat in October 2008, came out with a strong rejection of the regime of data exclusivity mulled by the Reddy Committee Report:

> "5.47 *As a condition for registering pharmaceutical and agro-chemical products, national authorities normally require the applicant to submit data relating to quality, safety and efficacy of the product. The Committee were informed that the MNCs are demanding 'Data Exclusivity' on their data, so that its use could be prevented for allowing generic manufacturers to take marketing approval. The Committee is aware of the fact that there is considerable pressure on the Government to accede to this demand. The Committee feel that conceding to demand for Data Exclusivity would amount to agreeing to TRIPS plus provisions. Once such a demand is agreed at bilateral forum, there will be additional demands, which may relate to higher level of intellectual property right, such as extension of patent period, restriction on compulsory licenses, restriction on parallel imports, and may be on R&D activity on patented subject matter. Data Exclusivity may result in delay in ensuring role of domestic enterprises through compulsory licensing system, and in preventing other parties from developing similar data.*
>
> 5.48 *Since the consequences of Data Exclusivity are quite serious, the Committee strongly recommends that the Government should not fall prey to such demands of MNCs. The Government must thwart such attempts, being made at the behest of certain vested interests. It should also guard against moves to enter into FTA with USA, as the developed countries, particularly the USA, are trying to bring in certain TRIPS Plus measures through Bilateral and Regional Agreements.*"

The concerns highlighted above by the parliamentary committee clearly points to the issues discussed earlier in the paper. Recently, discussions on the issue of data exclusivity in India resurfaced with the proposal for an India-EU FTA. According to the recent position based on the statements issued by Anand Sharma in March and April 2011 it becomes clear that India's stand on data exclusivity continues to be tough. This is reflected in his statements:

> *"India does not provide data exclusivity for pharmaceuticals and agro-chemicals which is in the paramount interest of our generic pharmaceutical industry as grant of data exclusivity would have considerable impact in delaying the entry into the market of cheaper generic drugs" (March 2011)*

> *"There is no question that we will accept data exclusivity in any (free trade) agreement with any country. On intellectual property rights (IPR) issue, whatever is discussed has to be in compliance with the TRIPS commitment (under the WTO)," (April 2011)*

The above depiction of India's stand on data exclusivity might appear to be somewhat layered. There are strong domestic lobbies against data exclusivity, including civil society upholding the cause of public health and the domestic pharmaceutical industry protecting their position in generics. Naturally, the political leadership finds it difficult to subvert these interests and ends up with an unequivocally strong position against data exclusivity. However, the global pharmaceutical giants lobbying for data exclusivity have also been rather active through their national governments as well as through their own channels and initiatives to create a favorable public opinion about data exclusivity in India. No wonder, we see a clear divergence in the administrative position on data exclusivity in India as reflected in the Reddy Committee Report, from that of the political position. Although the report acknowledges all pitfalls of data exclusivity, it goes on to recommend one for India. Fortunately, the power of democratic politics perhaps made India's political class take cognizance of national interest and they adopted a clear and tough stand against data exclusivity.

6.1 Concluding observations

This paper has attempted to outline the logic and scope of data exclusivity and its possible impact on developing countries. Three broad conclusions emerge from this paper.

First, TRIPS does not mandate data exclusivity in the US/EU sense.

Second, there are serious adverse implications of data exclusivity for developing nations, posing serious public health concerns by circumventing the in-built flexibilities contained in the TRIPS agreement.

Finally, the Indian position on the issue of data exclusivity has been characterized by a dual and contradictory position taken by the administrative leadership and the political leadership. Fortunately, so far the political position has prevailed over the administrative position and India has not succumbed to the international pressure lobby to introduce data exclusivity in its legal framework working through the route of trade agreements. However, the administrative position reflected in the Reddy Committee Report is a matter of concern as it always hangs as a threat to sustaining India's political position.

When developing countries tend to accede to the pressure and demand from developed nations for introducing data exclusivity, it undermines all the flexibilities that were extracted by the coalition of developing countries on the TRIPS agreement towards achieving developmental goals. In fact, the response of countries like India with substantial manufacturing capacities for generic production would decide the fate of the future of access to affordable medicine for the entire developing world. It is, therefore, crucially important for India to get rid of any confusing administrative signals and posit a consistent position against data exclusivity.

References

CIPR (2002), *Integrating Intellectual Property Rights and Development Policy*, Report of the Commission on Intellectual Property Rights (CIPR), London.

CIPIH (2006), *Public Health, Innovation and Intellectual Property Rights*, Report of the Commission on Intellectual Property Rights, Innovation and Public Health (CIPIH), World Health Organization: Geneva.

Correa, C.M. (2002a), *Protection of Data submitted for the Registration of Pharmaceuticals: Implementing the Standards of TRIPS Agreement*, South Centre: Geneva.

Correa, C.M. (2002b), *Implications of the Doha Declaration on the TRIPS Agreement and Public Health*, World Health Organization: Geneva.

Dhar, B. and K.M. Gopakumar (2006), Data Exclusivity in Pharmaceuticals: Little Basis, False Claims, *Economic and Political Weekly*, 41(49), 5073–5079.

DiMasi, J.A, H.G. Grabowski and R.W. Hansen (2014), *Innovation in the Pharmaceutical Industry: New Estimates of R&D Costs*, Briefing: Cost of Developing a New Drug, Tufts Center for the Study of Drug Development, Tufts University, November 2014.

Dutfield, G. and U. Sutharsanan (2005), Harmonisation or Differentiation in Intellectual Property Protection? The Lessons of History, *Prometheus*, 23(2), 131–147.

Fink, C. (2006), Intellectual property and public health: The WTO's August 2003 Decision in perspective' in Newfarmer, R. (ed.), *Trade, Doha and Development: A Window into the Issues*, Washington DC: The World Bank.

Fink, C. and P. Reichenmiller (2005), *Tightening TRIPS: The Intellectual Property Provisions of Recent US Free Trade Agreements*, Trade Note 20, International Trade Department, Washington DC: The World Bank Group.

Helpman, E (1993), Innovation, Imitation and Intellectual Property Rights, *Econometrica*, 61, 1247–1280.

IFPMA (2011), *Data Exclusivity: Encouraging Development of New Medicines*, Geneva. International Federation of Pharmaceuticals Manufacturers and Associations.

Lall, S. (2001), *Indicators of the Relative Importance of IPRs in Developing Countries*, Draft Report for UNCTAD.

Maskus, K. (2000), *Intellectual Property Rights in the Global Economy*, Washington DC: Institute for International Economics, Available from: www.iie.com/publications/.

Mehl, A.B. (2006), The Hatch–Waxman Act and Market Exclusivity for Generic Drug Manufacturers: An Entitlement or an Incentive, *Chicago Kent Law Review*, 81(2), 649–677.

Ray, A.S. and S. Bhaduri (2014), The Indian Pharmaceutical Industry: Policy Space that fosters Technological Capability, in D. Drache and L. Jacobs (Eds.): *Linking Global Trade and Human Rights: New Policy Spaces in Hard Economic Times*, New York: Cambridge University Press.

Roffe, P. and C. Spennemann (2006), The Impact of FTAs on Public Health Policies and TRIPS Flexibilities, *International Journal Intellectual Property Management*, 1(1/2), 75–93.

Salama, B.M. and D. Benoliel (2010), Pharmaceutical Patent Bargains: The Brazilian Experience, *Cardozo Journal of International and Comparative Law*, 18(3).

Scherer, F.M. (2009), The Political Economy of Patent Policy Reform in the United States, *Journal on Telecommunications and High Technology Law*, 7.

Chapter 3

India and the MDGs in the Context of Developing Countries Particularly in South Asia

Manmohan Agarwal*
RBI Chair Professor
Centre for Development Studies
Thiruvananthapuram, Kerala, India
Adjunct Fellow
RIS, New Delhi, India
**manmohan@cds.ac.in*

Abstract: The chapter analyzes the progress of developing countries towards achieving the millennium development goals (MDGs). We look at the performance of different regions. East Asia, Latin America and the Middle East and North Africa are on the way to achieve most of the MDGs. Sub-Saharan Africa and South Asia which lagged behind the other regions in their social indicators have made the least progress. Progress has depended either on rapid growth or on having special social programmes. The acceptance of the MDGs by the UN had a positive effect as it led to faster improvement in social indicators. The responsiveness of social progress to economic growth also improved after the acceptance of the MDG goals. Within South Asia, India has tended to lag in meeting the MDGs.

1 Introduction

Improving the living standards of their people was often a key objective of leaders and policy makers in many newly independent countries of the 1950s and the 1960s.

For instance, India's First Five Year Plan notes that one of the directive principles of the constitution was 'the State shall strive to promote the welfare of the people' and one of the implications of this was that 'the citizens, men and women equally, have the right to an adequate means of livelihood' (Government of India, First Five year Plan, 1952). The Plan went on to say that the Plan sought to fulfill this commitment which was reiterated in the declared objective of the government to promote a rapid rise in the standard of living of the people. The importance of raising living standards and reducing poverty was reiterated by the Prime Minister in his Preface to the First Five Year Plan. The importance of poverty reduction and improvements in other social indicators re-surfaced in the 1980s as the policies adopted to tackle the macro imbalances that had emerged after the hikes in the price of oil in 1973–1974 were believed to have had severe deleterious effects on social welfare (Cornia *et al.*, 1988; Hulme, 2009; Hulme and Fukuda-Parr, 2009). A new social consensus was forged and finally accepted at the United Nations in 2000 as the Millennium development Goals (MDGs) (Agarwal, 2013). It is recognized that social deprivation is multidimensional. Therefore, the MDGs transcend poverty reduction to other objectives such as reducing malnourishment, improving health by reducing mortality, infant, child and maternal mortality, by reducing incidence of diseases such as malaria and tuberculosis, improving access to immunization, by providing for universal primary education and reducing the gender disparity in education.[1]

This chapter tries to examine the success in achieving some of these MDGs in India; it compares the progress made in India with that in other developing countries.

In Section 2, we briefly review the genesis of the MDGs. In Section 3, we examine the progress in the different regions in reducing poverty; but we look also at malnourishment. In Section 4, we discuss the reductions in mortality rates, infant, child and maternal mortality rates that have been reached in the different regions. Then in Section 5, we calculate the elasticity of reduction in these with respect to growth in per capita GDP and find that these elasticities vary considerably among the regions, being much lower in Asia than the other regions.

We find that adoption of goals such as the MDGs seems to have a beneficial effect on social progress. The rate of improvement is higher after the adoption of the MDGs by the United Nations (UN) in 2000. This improvement is partly because of faster growth but the growth has a greater beneficial effect on social indicators either because the nature of growth has changed or countries are paying more attention to social progress.

We conclude that an increase in growth of GDP would be sufficient to achieve the goals in Latin America, East Asia and the Middle East; however, the effect of

[1] For a full list of the objectives and the indicators to measure the success in reaching the objectives, see the United Nations' Secretary-General's Road Map towards the Implementation of the MDGs, http://www.un.org/documents/ga/docs/56/a56326.pdf.

the 2008 financial crisis has been to reduce growth rates and has resulted in a serious setback to social progress. The problem is more acute in South Asia (SA) and in Sub-Saharan Africa (SSA). The problem in SA is of a very low rate of improvement in these social indicators as income grows, so more effective social programmes are needed; in SSA the problem is of low rates of growth.

Then, in Section 6 we discuss the performance of the South Asian nations and in particular India in achieving the MDGs. In Section 7 we discuss the role of health expenditures in achieving MDGs; what is true of health expenditures is generally true of other social expenditures also. We close in Section 8 with some final observations.

2 The Genesis of the MDGs

Many strands came together in the formation of the MDGs at the UN in 2001.[2] The debt crisis affecting many developing countries, particularly the middle income ones, had started in 1982 and had persisted through the 1980s with deleterious social consequences.[3] The attention of policy makers and international agencies such as the International Monetary Fund (IMF) and the World Bank (WB) was concentrated on achieving macro stability which was considered necessary for growth,[4] but the 1980s and 1990s saw a stagnation in the economies of LAC and SSA as per capita incomes grew by only 0.7% a year between 1982 and 2000 in LAC while they declined by 0.8% a year in SSA. Already by the end of the 1980s dissatisfaction with these policies was growing as they were held to lead to a deterioration in education and health outcomes and also other public services and, consequently, there were calls for adjustment with a human face (Cornia *et al.*, 1988).[5] Such analysts believed that it was necessary to shift attention back from macro stabilization to policies for improving the human condition (Desai, 2007). Furthermore, even the concept of macro stability is not well defined. For instance, between 1965 and 1973 East Asia and the Pacific (EAP) had the highest inflation rate among all developing country regions and grew the fastest, and in the period 1974–1982 EAP had the second highest inflation rate and again grew the fastest (Manmohan Agarwal, 2008). In particular, through much of the 1960s and 1970s Korea had a higher rate of inflation than India but grew faster.

---

[2] For a more detailed discussion see Agarwal (2013).

[3] For a discussion of the causes of the crisis and its consequences see Sachs (1989).

[4] Macro stability and fiscal management were part of the Washington consensus which expressed the conditions which needed to be established for growth to occur (Williamson, 1989).

[5] The interplay of growth and poverty as objectives of policy has a fascinating history. The UN stressed that Growth was an instrument for reducing poverty; a sentiment echoed by Prime Minister Nehru in the preface to India's First Five Year Plan. See also Bhagwati (1966).

In the meantime, the UNDP had published the first HDR in 1990 in which countries were ranked according to their level of social development (UNDP 1990; Hulme, 2009). The measurement of human development was based on welfare concepts developed by Amartya Sen (1980, 1985, 1989). The WB's World Development Report (WDR) for 1990 also concentrated on the theme of poverty, returning to it after many years (Hulme, 2009).[6] The UN had also throughout the 1990s organized many international conferences to analyze various aspects of social achievement and to recommend policies to improve the conditions in that particular area (Hulme, 2009).[7] The recommendations from these conferences were refined in the Development Assistance Committee (DAC) of the Organisation for Economic Co-operation and Development (OECD) to become the International Development Goals (IDGs).[8] Later, there were further negotiations as the IDGs of the OECD became the MDGs of the entire world including both donors and countries getting aid (Bradford, 2002; Hulme and Fukuda-Parr, 2009).[9]

Another contributing factor was bureaucratic competition. Ministers and bureaucrats dealing with development who found themselves increasingly marginalized as aid declined (Hulme, 2009) sought to regain the initiative. At the international level the WB and the UNDP took the lead, particularly the latter sought to recover the prominent role of the UN in earlier debates about development

---

[6] McNamara had established poverty reduction as a major goal for the WB in his speech at the annual meetings of 1974 held at Nairobi. This was the first time that poverty reduction was given priority by the BW institutions. But it had slipped into the background before being resurrected in the 1990 WDR (Yusuf, 2009).

[7] In 1990, there was the UN World Summit for children which became a model for future summits as it resulted in commitments by governments to improve the condition of children as well as provide greater financial resources (Bradford year). In 1990, there was also a conference on education for all and an United Nations Conference on Trade And Development (UNCTAD) conference on the Least Developed Countries. In 1992, a conference on food and nutrition was held in Rome; in 1993, there was a conference on human rights in Vienna; in 1994, there was a conference in Cairo on population and development and on environment in Rio de Janeiro; in 1995, a world summit on social development in Copenhagen and a conference on women in Beijing; in 1996, a Habitat conference in Istanbul and a food summit in Rome.[7] International non-governmental organizations (NGOs) played an important role in these UN summits. For instance, the International Coalition on Women's Health played an important role in mobilizing support at the Cairo conference on Population and Development.

[8] See Hulme (2009) for a discussion of the process by which some of the goals espoused by the conferences were included in the IDGs, and which were relegated to either an inferior status or ignored altogether.

[9] The US was ambivalent to many of the goals adopted in the IDGs and the MDGs. Many NGOs believed that important aspects of the social condition had been neglected in the adopted goals and developing countries were lukewarm in their acceptance of the MDGs. Also see Hulme (2009), for details of the negotiation process.

and which had taken a back seat in the 1980s.[10] Achieving the MDGs would require greater involvement of the UN agencies, for example, those dealing with education, health, children's welfare, etc.

The MDG declaration was, therefore, the result of a number of different forces — the failure of structural adjustment polices to generate growth and in particular, their unfavorable effects on social conditions, the elaboration of new concepts of welfare, the work of UN conferences in providing concepts, targets and policies for achieving social objectives and bureaucratic interests at both the national and international level.

The different components of the social condition accepted in the MDG declaration and the indicators chosen to represent the conditions were the result of, at one level, the analytical recognition that poverty was a multi-dimensional concept and not merely income deprivation (Hulme and Fukuda-Parr, 2009), and on the other hand, negotiations first at the OECD level and then at the UN as to which of the recommendations of the various UN conferences should be included (Hulme and Fukuda-Parr, 2009). It was necessary that the dimensions chosen have indicators that could be monitored.[11] They share a common vision of material well-being, freedom and equity (Fukuda-Parr, 2004a). They were also an instrument for mobilizing support and resources (Fukuda-Parr, 2004b; Desai, 2007). The eighth goal talks of a commitment to a global partnership and this includes provision of aid to help achieve the goals, but this is a weak commitment in that the developed countries will try their best to achieve the stated aid target and there are no quantified and time-bound indicators (Fukuda-Parr, 2004b).

The purpose of development is to improve people's lives; progress towards meeting the MDGs is one indicator of the extent to which people's lives have been improved. We, therefore, examine the progress made in achieving the MDGs.

3 Progress in Reducing Poverty and Malnourishment

Substantial progress has been made over the past two decades in reducing poverty. At the aggregate level, taking all regions together the target of reducing

[10] The UN agencies had been in the forefront of development policy debates in the 1950s particularly, Prebisch's work on the declining terms of trade for primary commodities and therefore the need for industrialization done when he was at the Economic Commission for Latin America. The UN agencies had also been active in developing the tools for development planning. In the 1970s United Nations Conference for Trade and Development (UNCTAD) had been in the forefront of debates about a New International Economic Order (Bhagwati and Ruggie, 1984).

[11] They reflect a general trend towards accountability and selection of monitorable goals of aid. However, this created a conflict in that aspects of development that are not quantifiable are neglected.

Table 1. Regional poverty (% of population).

					Annual rate of decline			
	1990	2000	2005	2010	1990–2000	2000–2005	2005–2010	1990–2010
EAP*	57	36	17	10	4.5	13.9	10.1	9.3
LAC	12	11	7	5	0.9	8.6	6.5	4.3
MNA	6	5	3	2	1.8	9.2	7.8	5.3
SA	54	48	39	29	1.8	2.8	5.8	3.1
SSA	57	59	53	48	–0.4	2.1	2.0	0.8

Note: The regions are as defined by the World Bank.
Source: World Bank (2003, 2008, 2012). UN (2015) The Millennium Development Goals Report, World Bank and IMF (2013), Global Monitoring Report 2013, Rural–Urban Dynamics and the Millennium Development Goals.
*This region as used by the World Bank covers East Asia, and South East Asia.

poverty by half will be met, but this is fundamentally because of the great progress in EAP (Table 1).

LAC and MNA also had already met the target of halving poverty by 2015 in 2010, though the decline in poverty in these regions was less than in EAP. EAP, LAC and MNA saw a considerable acceleration in the decline of the poverty rate after the acceptance of the Millennium development goals by the UN in 2000. This might indicate the importance of the international community specifying development goals as it seems to energize governments and other actors. Though the rate of poverty decline also accelerated in SA and SSA the acceleration in those regions was considerably less. However, SA seems to be well on the way to achieving the poverty target as the poverty rate had to decline by merely a further 2% points in the remaining five years. The only region which will be far from achieving the target would be SSA. This would be partly because the region experienced an increase in poverty during the 1990s as growth of per capita income was negative mainly because of the poor performance of the agricultural sector partly because of declining terms of trade (United Nations, 2010).

We now examine the decrease in rates of malnourishment in the different regions.

LAC and EAP regions have experienced the fastest decreases in malnutrition (Table 2). As a consequence, malnutrition levels in these two regions are negligible. MNA also has low levels of malnutrition though the decline was at a slower pace than in the other two regions. These three regions have malnourishment rates almost comparable to those in the developed countries. Unfortunately, the two regions with the highest levels of malnutrition experienced the slowest decreases in malnutrition. Furthermore, SA had a low rate of decrease of malnutrition

Table 2. Regional prevalence of malnourishment.

	Rate of malnourishment					Annual rate of decline				
	1990	**2000**	**2005**	**2010**	**2013**	**1990–2000**	**2000–2005**	**2005–2010**	**2010–2013**	**1990–2013**
EAP	20	11	8	6	5	5.8	6.2	5.6	5.9	5.8
LAC	8	5	3	2		4.6	9.7	7.8		6.7*
MNA	12	9	8	7	6	2.8	2.3	2.6	5.0	3.0
SA	52	43	39	35	32	1.9	1.9	2.1	2.9	2.1
SSA	39	25	24	22	21	1.5	0.8	1.7	0.5	1.4

*Average is for 1990-2000.

Source: World Bank (2003, 2008, 2012). UN (2015) The Millennium Development Goals Report, World Bank and IMF (2013), Global Monitoring Report 2013, Rural–Urban Dynamics and the Millennium Development Goals.

despite these economies growing rapidly, but once again there is an acceleration in the rate of improvement after the announcement of the MDGs.

4 Mortality Rates

The goals for mortality rates are to reduce infant and child mortality by two-thirds and maternal mortality by three-fourths.

Between 1990 and 2015, the world has made substantial progress in reducing the infant mortality rate, reducing the rate 49%, from 90 deaths per 1,000 live births in 1990 to 46 in 2013. (http://www.un.org/millenniumgoals/childhealth.shtml). The declines in mortality rates for infants and children are greatest for EAP, LAC and MNA where the rates were low even in the base year, 1990 (Tables 3 and 4). The infant mortality rate at under-five for the developed countries is still lower than that in the developing country regions.

In 2013, the under-five mortality rate in low-income countries was 76 deaths per 1,000 live births — more than 12 times the average rate of 6 in high-income countries. (Levels & Trends in Child Mortality Report 2014, Estimates developed by the UN Inter-agency Group of WHO, UNICEF, WB, UN, 2014).

While EAP and LAC have achieved maternal mortality rates comparable to those in the developed countries, where they average 16, their rates of infant and child mortality are still considerably higher than in the developed countries. Again the two regions with the highest mortality rates, SA and SSA, saw smaller decreases in mortality rates. However, the pattern is different for declines in maternal mortality (Table 5). The greatest decline was in SA, but SSA again lagged behind other regions.

Again the rate of improvement increased after the 2000 acceptance of the MDGs. The only exceptions were LAC, where the improvement in all the three

Table 3. Infant mortality rates by regions.

	Mortality rates					Annual rates of decline				
	1990	2000	2005	2010	2013	1990–2000	2000–2005	2005–2010	2010–2013	1990–2013
EAP	45	33	25	19	16	2.8	5.4	5.3	5.6	4.3
LAC	44	27	21	18	16	5.0	4.9	3.0	3.9	4.4
MNA	52	36	29	23	21	3.6	5.6	3.2	3.0	3.9
SA	92	69	58	50	45	2.9	3.4	2.9	3.5	3.1
SSA	107	95	80	67	61	1.2	3.4	3.5	3.1	2.4

Source: Levels & Trends in Child Mortality Report 2014, Estimates developed by the UN Inter-agency Group of WHO, UNICEF, WB, UN, 2014.

Table 4. Child mortality rates by regions.

	Mortality rates					Annual rates of decline				
	1990	2000	2005	2010	2013	1990–2000	2000–2005	2005–2010	2010–2013	1990–2013
EAP	59	42	30	23	20	3.9	6.5	5.2	4.6	4.1
LAC	55	33	25	23	18	5.0	5.4	1.7	7.8	4.7
MNA	67	43	36	28	26	3.9	4.4	4.9	2.4	4.0
SA	129	94	77	64	57	3.1	3.9	3.6	3.8	3.5
SSA	179	156	129	103	92	1.4	3.7	4.4	3.7	2.9

Source: http://www.un.org/millenniumgoals/childhealth.shtml.

Table 5. Maternal mortality rates by regions.

	Mortality rates					Annual rates of decline				
	1990	2000	2005	2010	2013	1990–2000	2000–2005	2005–2010	2010–2013	1990–2013
EAP	170	130	110	82	75	2.6	3.3	5.7	2.9	3.5
LAC	150	110	97	90	87	3.5	2.8	1.5	1.1	2.3
MNA	160	110	97	83	78	3.7	2.5	3.1	2.0	3.1
SA	550	370	280	220	190	3.9	5.4	4.7	4.8	4.5
SSA	990	830	680	560	510	1.7	3.9	3.8	3.1	2.8

Source: Trends in maternal mortality: 1990–2013, Estimates by WHO, UNICEF, UNFPA, The World Bank and the United Nations Population Division.

indicators of mortality slowed after 2000 and MNA, where the improvement in maternal mortality declined after 2000. Another important feature is that the improvement in maternal mortality was considerably greater in SA than in infant and child mortality in contrast to the other regions. Overall, as women have gained access to family planning and skilled birth attendance with backup emergency obstetric care, the global maternal mortality ratio has fallen from 380 maternal deaths per 100,000 live births in 1990 to 210 deaths per 100,000 live births in 2013, a 45% decline

(http://www.unfpa.org/maternal-health). This has resulted in many countries halving their maternal death rates. At a country level, India (19% or 56,000) and Nigeria (14% or 40,000) accounted for roughly one-third of the maternal deaths in 2010. Furthermore, Afghanistan, Bangladesh, Democratic Republic of the Congo, Ethiopia, Indonesia, Pakistan, Sudan and the United Republic of Tanzania each accounted for 3–5% of maternal deaths. Together these 10 countries accounted for about 60% of all maternal deaths.[12]

Generally, it is held easier to reduce infant and child mortality as a few specific actions can lower mortality significantly. On the other hand, maternal deaths can take place due to a number of reasons and general improvement in the health delivery system is required rather than a few specific interventions.

5 Responsiveness of Social Indicators to Income Growth

We calculated the change in the social indicator relative to the rate of growth of per capita income for the different regions, namely the elasticities of reduction. The calculation of the elasticities reveals a number of interesting facets of the nature of the growth process in the different regions.

1. The elasticities are usually less than 1 in Asia, particularly East Asia, whereas they are greater than one in LAC and SSA and usually substantially greater than 1 (Table 6).
2. The elasticities for reduction of poverty are usually greater for the entire period 1990–2010, than for 1990–2000, implying that the elasticities are greater for the period after the MDGs had been accepted than the period before. The acceptance of the MDGs meant faster social progress, not only because faster growth was achieved but also greater responsiveness to growth in per capita income. This could be because the nature of the growth process had changed or that it was now accompanied by more or better special social programmes.
3. This greater responsiveness is, however, not true for reduction in malnourishment. Here, except for LAC the elasticities are smaller in the second period (Table 6).

[12] For a detailed analysis, see the report prepared jointly by the WHO, UNICEF, UNFPA, and the World Bank. Available at http://www.un.org/millennium/declaration/ares552e.htm.

Table 6. Elasticity of reduction with respect to growth in per capita income.

	Poverty rate		Malnourishment	
	1990–2000	1990–2010	1990–2000	1990–2013
EAP	0.7	1.1	0.9	0.8
LAC	0.8	2.9	4.1	4.3
SA	0.6	0.7	0.6	0.5
SSA*	0.5	1.0	–2.0	1.7

*Per capita income declined in SSA during the years 1990–2000. In the case of poverty, the poverty ratio increased as per capita income declined, but in the case of malnourishment, its extent declined despite falling per capita income.

Source: Author's calculations based on the above data and data on growth of per capita income from World Bank (2003, 2008, 2012).

Table 7. Elasticity of reduction of mortality rates with respect to growth of per capita income.

	Infant mortality		Child mortality		Maternal mortality	
	1990–2000	1990–2013	1990–2000	1990–2013	1990–2000	1990–2013
EAP	0.4	0.6	0.5	0.6	0.4	0.5
LAC	4.4	2.8	4.4	3.1	2.7	5.1
SA	0.9	0.7	1.0	0.8	1.2	1.1
SSA	–1.6	2.9	–1.8	3.4	–2.4	3.4

Source: Author's calculations based on the above data and data on growth of per capita income from World Bank (2003, 2008, 2012).

4. That growth in incomes is not necessary for social improvement is borne out by most social indicators improving in SSA during the period 1990–2000, despite declining per capita income.

The picture for reductions in mortality rates is more varied than that for reduction in poverty and malnourishment. It must again be noted that the elasticity for SSA for the period 1990–2000 is of the opposite sign than all the other elasticities, as mortality rates declined despite falling per capita incomes. Also elasticities, in Asia both East and South are lower than in the other two regions (Table 7), but there is no uniformity in the behavior of the elasticities in the two periods. Whereas, the elasticities are higher in the second period for EAP, they are lower in LAC and SA.

6 Social Progress in South Asia

We now analyze the progress in some South Asian countries towards achieving the MDGs.

We first consider reductions in poverty rates and in malnourishment.

The rate of decline in poverty accelerated in the second period, 2000–2010, as compared to the first period, 1990–2000 (Table 8). This was because the growth in per capita income accelerated and also the effect of growth on poverty reduction increased as the elasticity of poverty reduction increased in the countries.

The reduction in the malnourishment rate follows a different pattern. Despite the growth acceleration, the rate of decline in malnourishment decelerated in the countries except for Pakistan (Table 9). There was a substantial decline in the effectiveness of growth in reducing malnourishment.

Table 8. Reduction in poverty.

	Annual rates of decline in poverty ratio		Elasticity w.r.t. to per capita GDP	
	1990–2000	1990–2010	1990–2000	1990–2010
Bangladesh	1.2	2.4	0.4	0.5
India	1.4	3.8	0.3	0.6
Pakistan	10.0	11.5	2.0	2.6
Sri Lanka	0.4	6.0	0.1	1.5

Source: World Bank (2003, 2008, 2012). UN (2015) The Millennium Development Goals Report, World Bank and IMF (2013) Global Monitoring Report 2013 Rural–Urban Dynamics and the Millennium Development Goals.

Table 9. Reduction in malnourishment.

	Annual rates of decline in malnourishment		Elasticity w.r.t. per capita GDP	
	Period 1	Period 2	Period 1	Period 2
Bangladesh	3.7	2.8	0.8	0.5
India	1.9	1.1	0.3	0.2
Pakistan	0.4	2.6	0.1	0.6
Sri Lanka	2.2	1.2	0.6	0.3

Source: World Bank (2003, 2008, 2012). UN (2015) The Millennium Development Goals Report, World Bank and IMF (2013) Global Monitoring Report 2013 Rural–Urban Dynamics and the Millennium Development Goals.

Table 10. Annual rate of decline in mortality.

	Infant mortality		Child mortality		Maternal mortality	
	Period 1	Period 2	Period 1	Period 2	Period 1	Period 2
Bangladesh	4.4	4.7	4.8	5.3	4.7	5.0
India	2.7	3.3	3.2	3.7	4.1	4.6
Nepal	4.9	4.8	5.9	5.4	5.9	6.5
Pakistan	1.8	1.8	2.0	2.1	3.5	3.7
Sri Lanka	3.2	3.0	4.2	3.2	2.9	4.4

Source: Trends in maternal mortality:1990–2013. Estimates by WHO, UNICEF, UNFPA, The World Bank and the United Nations Population Division, Levels & Trends in Child Mortality Report 2014, Estimates Developed by the UN Inter-agency Group for Child Mortality Estimation, World Bank and IMF (2013) Global Monitoring Report 2013 Rural–Urban Dynamics and the Millennium Development Goals.

Table 11. Elasticity of decline of mortality w.r.t. GDP per capita.

	Infant mortality		Child mortality		Maternal mortality	
	Period 1	Period 2	Period 1	Period 2	Period 1	Period 2
Bangladesh	0.9	0.9	1.0	1.0	1.0	0.9
India	0.5	0.5	0.6	0.6	0.7	0.7
Nepal	0.9	0.9	1.0	1.0	1.1	1.2
Pakistan	0.4	0.4	0.4	0.5	0.7	0.8
Sri Lanka	0.8	0.7	1.1	0.8	0.7	1.1

Source: Author's calculations.

There is, in general an acceleration in the rate of reduction of mortality rates with the second period showing greater improvement than the first (Table 10). Furthermore, Bangladesh and Nepal show greater improvement than do India, Pakistan and Sri Lanka.

When we calculate the elasticities of decline of mortality rates with respect to the growth of per capita incomes, we find that Bangladesh, Nepal and Sri Lanka have much higher elasticities than do India and Pakistan. There is no overall tendency for elasticities to be higher in the second period than in the first.

7 Health Expenditures

We now analyze regional health expenditures in order to see how far they can explain the variations in mortality outcomes in particular Asian countries. Both

Table 12. Health expenditures (% of GDP).

	1990–1997		2003		2005		2008		2010	
	Total	Public	Total	Public	Total	Public	Total	Public	Total	Public
EAP	3.6	1.8	5.0	1.9	4.3	1.8	4.2	2.0	4.7	2.5
LAC	6.3	2.6	6.8	3.3	7.1	3.3	7.2	3.6	7.8	3.9
MNA	4.7	2.3	5.6	2.7	5.8	3.0	5.0	3.6	4.7	2.4
SA	5.0	0.8	4.4	1.1	4.5	0.9	4.0	1.3	3.8	1.1
SSA	2.7	1.7	6.1	2.4	6.1	2.6	6.1	2.6	6.5	2.9

Source: World Bank, World Development Indicators (2003, 2008, 2012).

Table 13. Health expenditures in some south Asian countries (% of GDP).

	1990–1997		2003		2005		2008		2010	
	Total	Public	Total	Public	Total	Public	Total	Public	Total	Public
Bangladesh	2.4	1.2	3.4	1.1	2.8	0.8	3.3	1.0	4.7	2.5
India	5.6	0.7	4.8	1.2	5.0	1.0	4.2	1.4	7.8	3.9
Nepal	5.0	1.2	5.3	1.5	5.8	1.6	6.0	2.0	4.7	2.4
Pakistan	3.5	0.8	2.4	0.7	2.1	0.4	2.6	0.8	3.8	1.1
Sri Lanka	1.9	1.4	3.5	1.6	4.1	1.9	4.1	1.8	2.6	6.5

Source: World Bank, World Development Indicators (2003, 2008, 2012).

EAP and SA, spend much less on health than countries in the other regions (Table 12). Furthermore, health expenditures as percentage of GDP have been rising in all the regions except SA.

In addition, public expenditures on health are much lower in SA than the other regions, and have been stagnant whereas they have been increasing in the other regions.

Health expenditures have been increasing in these South Asian economies. Public expenditures on health have also been increasing.[13] Public expenditures have been increasing the most rapidly in Sri Lanka and India. Among South Asian countries health expenditures in India tend to be higher than in other South Asian economies, though Sri Lanka has the highest level of public expenditures on health. The lack of adequate improvement in health indicators for India despite these expenditures suggest a very poor delivery system for health services.

[13] It is difficult to reconcile these individual figures with the figures for the region as a whole.

8 Regional Dimensions of Social Progress from MDGs to SDGs

We now discuss what the past experience with the MDGs may foretell about likely progress in the SDGs.

(A) Latin America

The experience of Latin America is that social indicators have improved, despite slow growth. The region had met before the terminal year its targets for reduction of poverty, malnourishment and infant and child mortality. This reduction has been helped by the decline in the extent of inequality (Birdsall *et al.*, 2011),[14] but much of this reduction has occurred because of the special cash transfer programmes which result in high elasticities with respect to income growth. To achieve the proposed sustainable development goals (SDGs), it is imperative that the slowdown in growth since the financial crisis is reversed. Furthermore, the nature of growth strategy needs to be changed. This is so particularly in agriculture where strategy has to shift from growth based on higher productivity on large farms to one that stresses development of small holders. The trend of declining value added in the non-agricultural sector needs to be reversed. Even if this trend is reversed it is unlikely that growth would be based on labor intensive manufactures as wage rates are much higher in Latin America than in much of Asia or SSA. Consequently, as wages are high and these countries are not competitive in labor intensive industries strategies have to be based on enabling their industries to move up the value chain.

Progress towards achieving the SDGs will require special programmes of two kinds. One is expansion of the safety nets, namely the conditional cash transfer programmes, but these will need to be supplemented by measures to protect the population from what are expected by more volatile food prices because of environmental factors, and the spread of biofuels which lead to a closer link between food prices and the more volatile fuel prices. Financing of such programmes through the budget is feasible. A second kind of special programmes will improve skills of workers since industry will need to move up the skill chain to be competitive as wages are higher.

An additional policy might be needed to be considered. The remaining social deprivations may exist in inaccessible pockets. This might require improvement in transport services in order to improve their accessibility, but it might also be necessary to consider facilitating their migration to more developed regions within the country.

---

[14] Also see Esquivel *et al.* (2010). For a more general discussion see Bourguignon (2003), Perry *et al.* (2006) and Ravallion (1997).

(B) Poverty in Asia

Social indicators in EAP have been improving rapidly as these countries have witnessed rapid growth. Two problems need to be tackled if these countries are to achieve the SDGs. These are rising inequality that slows social progress with a given growth (Asian Development Bank, 2012). Also, these countries have not depended on special programmes to reach the disadvantaged as shown by the low elasticities of the improvement of their social indicators with respect to growth of income.

The slow social progress is a special problem in SA. The only target that SA is likely to meet is reducing poverty by half (Desai, 2007). The elasticities with respect to growth of per capita income have been low partly because of limited growth in labor intensive manufacturing and slowing of growth of productivity in small-holder agriculture. Tackling these problems is difficult as these are long standing structural problems. Their solution requires strengthening the physical infrastructure of the countries which would require not only massive investment but changing the working of the public sector. It would also require raising the standards in the countries' educational systems, particularly in the area of research. Raising quality is always more challenging than merely raising enrollments. Also health expenditures as a percent of GDP are much lower in SA than in other regions, as noted above, and so need to be raised, but again there is also the question of the quality of medical services.

(C) Poverty in Africa

Africa has seen the least social progress as its growth rate has been low (Go *et al.*, 2007). However, the high elasticities show that it has been able to very effectively translate what growth has occurred into considerable social progress. What is essential for future progress is a higher rate of growth. SSA is one region that may face a choice in terms of the strategy regarding growth in agriculture.[15] While concentration on growth through development of large scale farms may raise the growth rate and continued sale or leasing of large plots of land may help implementation of such a strategy, its implications for poverty reduction may not be very helpful as small-holder cultivation is significant in SSA. It is necessary to further raise investment rates. This requires both analysis of how to raise domestic savings and a reversal of the decline in international aid. Furthermore, more attention needs to be paid to develop domestic capacity.

We have seen above that the declaration of the MDGs may have energized governments and communities to greater efforts to achieve social progress.

[15] Herbert (2007) stresses the need for higher growth and therefore the need for investment would help achieve this. He believes the MDGs are misconceived as far as SSA is concerned.

However, two questions might be raised about such quantitative indicators. The values are very uncertain. For the same year and the same indicator different agencies and very often the same agency in different years' reports give very different figures. It is very difficult to measure change. The temptation to invent numbers can be very great as happened to casualty figures in the Vietnam war.

Also values for many of these indicators are available at very different time intervals making statistical analysis difficult. For instance, the question has often been raised (Desai, 2007) about whether the constraints to better social indicators are on the demand side. The MDGs are based on the assumption that the constraints are on the supply side, but very often families do not send girls to school even when schools are available so is it a demand constraint (Desai, 2007).

A second issue is that the stress on MDGs risks neglecting aspects of development that cannot be measured and these may be very important (Attaran, 2005). As we move forward to the SDGs it would be necessary for policy makers to keep these aspects in mind.

9 Conclusions

The financial crisis is creating a less favourable external environment. Slower growth in developing countries may have severe adverse effects on their efforts to improve living standards, but some steps can be taken to lessen the impact of the slowdown in the advanced economies of Europe and North America. South–South trade and investment flows have been increasing. In some cases South–South technical cooperation has been increasing, e.g., Brazil's efforts to increase joint research in the area of agriculture. Greater efforts can be made to foster South–South cooperation so that specialization among developing countries can provide the impetus for further growth. Unlike when Prebisch first pushed the idea of greater South–South trade developing countries no longer have very low savings rates. As noted, there are considerable South–South capital flows. Furthermore, initial attempts to foster South–South floundered because of the difficulties of negotiating preferential trade agreements. Today there is a much stronger institutional framework that could be built upon to develop South–South economic cooperation. There is ASEAN along with its agreements with China, India etc. there is MERCOSUR; economic cooperation in Africa is also growing, e.g., SADC, though it remains more limited than in Latin America or Asia.

There is no single answer on how to reduce poverty faster or reduce malnourishment or mortality rates more rapidly. A number of things have to be done and the particular policies to be adopted depend on the particular situation. Access to resources is important. This could be land though it is usually difficult to successfully carry out a land redistribution programme, but in countries where small-holders are important access to ancillary services that would raise land productivity is important. Access to capital for small businesses is also important. For small businesses to succeed in modern conditions often requires that they be part of the supply chain of a large enterprise; they need to develop policies that help in the development of supply chains. As is also well recognized but not always implemented, access to better education and health facilities including cleaner water and better sanitation is critical. In many cases special programmes may be needed to enable the poor to participate in the market.

What is the role of the international community in helping improve living standards? Aid has been declining in importance whether measured as a share of GDP or investment. The only countries, for which it remains important are the least developed countries, but there is another aspect of aid that is important. The share of aid going to support growth has declined. Less of aid is channeled to the production sectors such as agriculture or manufacturing and less goes for infrastructure. The above analysis shows that without growth it will be very difficult to improve living standards, but it is also necessary to make investment in these economies less dependent on foreign resources, whether aid or remittances. So analysis of policies and institutional changes that would raise savings rates is needed, and here the experience of Asia, particularly East Asia, would be very relevant. Also, the past and current efforts to build capacity have not succeeded. It will be imperative to understand the reasons for this failure and to take corrective measures. Again the experience of other developing countries may be more relevant.

Many of the countries in South Asia have already been moved into the middle income category of the World Bank and so would be less eligible for IDA loans, but soft loans are important to reach social goals. While the social returns to these programmes are high the cash returns are not so that governments may be fiscally constrained. It might be necessary to continue to lend to them for the social sectors on IDA terms.

The broad recipes are known, the tricky part is to apply them to specific cases. The international community can help by providing aid, making remittances cheaper and easier, and removing barriers to exports and also perhaps migration. Furthermore, the trend towards less of the aid going for productive purposes, to agriculture, manufacturing and infrastructure, needs to be reversed. Past policies to build capacity have failed. There has to be a proper assessment why this happened and an appropriate shift in approaches. The shift of countries in SA away from loans provided by International Development Association (IDA), the soft loan wing of the World Bank, would not be very helpful for expenditures geared to raising living standards where social returns are high but not financial returns making such expenditures unattractive to fiscally constrained countries. So IDA resources should be made available for social investments.

References

Agarwal, M. (2008), Changing Economic Power. *Discussion Paper No. 143*, New Delhi: Research and Information systems.

Agarwal, M. (2013), Reshaping International Institutions to Achieve MDGs; Paper presented at Conference organized by North South Institute. To be published in Besada, H. and S. Kindornay (Eds.). Future of Multilateral Cooperation in a Changing World Order.

Asian Development Bank (2012), Asian Development: Outlook 2012, Asian Development Bank, Manila.

Attaran, A. (2005), An Immeasurable Crisis? A Criticism of the Millennium. Development Goals and Why they cannot be Measured. *PLos Med 2*. Available from: http://www.plosmedicine.org/article/info:doi/10.1371/journal.pmed.0020318.

Bhagwati, J. (1966), The Economics of Underdeveloped Countries. McGraw-Hill, New York.

Bhagwati, J.N. and J.G. Ruggie (Eds.) (1984) Power, Passions and Purpose: Prospects for North- South Negotiations. M.I.T. Press, Cambridge, MA.

Birdsall, N., N. Lustig, and D. McLeod (2011), Declining Inequality in Latin America: Some Economics, Some Politics, *WP No. 251*. Center for Global Development.

Bourguignon, F. (2003), The Growth Elasticity of Poverty Reduction: Explaining Heterogeneity across countries and Time Periods, in Eicher, T. and S. Turnovsky (Eds.). *Inequality and Growth: Theory and Policy Implications*, MIT Press, Cambridge, MA.

Bradford, C. (2002), Towards 2015: From Consensus Formation to Implementation of the MDGs — The Historical Background, 1990–2002, Brookings Institution. Mimeo, Washington DC.

Cornia, G.A., R. Jolly and F. Stewart (Eds.) (1988), Adjustment with a Human Face, Volume 1, Protecting the Vulnerable and Promoting Growth. Clarendon Press, Oxford.

Desai, M. (2007), Introductory Remarks: Why India Will to Meet the Millennium Development Goals in Agarwal, M. and A. S. Ray (Eds.): *Globalization and the Millennium Development Goals*, Delhi: Social Science Press.

Esquivel, G., N. Lustig and J. Scott (2010), A Decade of falling Inequality in Mexico: Market Forces or State Action? in Lopez Calva, L.F. and N. Lustig (Eds.): *Declining Inequality in Latin America: A Decade of Progress*? Brookings Institutions, Washington, DC.

Fakuda-Parr, S. (2004a), Millennium Development Goals: Why they Matter. *Global Governance*, 10.

Fakuda-Parr, S. (2004b), Millennium Development Goals: The Pledge of World Leaders to End Poverty Will Not Be Met With Business As Usual *Journal of International Development*, 16.

Go, D., D. Nikitin, X. Wang and H. Zou (2007), Poverty and Inequality in Sub-Saharan Africa: Literature Survey and Empirical Assessment, *Annals of Economics and Finance*, 8(2), 251–304.

Government of India (1952), India First Five Year Plan, New Delhi Planning Commission Government of India.

Hulme, D. (2009). The Making of the Millennium Development Goals: Human Development Meets Results-based Management in an Imperfect World. Working Paper 16, Manchester: Brooks World Poverty Institute.

Hulme, D. and S. Fukuda-Parr (2009). International Norm Dynamics and 'the End of Poverty' Understanding the Millennium Development Goals (MDGs). *Working Paper 96*. Manchester: Brooks World Poverty Institute.

Perry, G., O. Arias, H. Lopez, W. Maloney and L. Serven (2006), Poverty Reduction and Growth: Virtuous and Vicious Circlers, World Bank.

Ravallion (1997), Can High Inequality Development Countries Escape Absolute Poverty? *Economic Letters*, 456 (1), 51–57.

Ross, H. (2007), Developing an African Growth Plan in Manmohan, A. and A. S. Ray (Eds.). *Globalization and the Millennium Development Goals*, Delhi: Social Science Press.

Sachs (Ed.) (1989), Developing Country Debt and Economic Performance, Vol. 1, *The International Financial System*, The University of Chicago Press for the NBER, Chicago.

Sen, A. (1980), Equality of What, In McMurrin, M. *The Tanner Lectures on Human Values*.

Salt Lake City: University of Utah Press.

Sen, A. (1985), Commodities and Capabilities. Elsevier Science, Oxford.

Sen, A. (1989), Development as Capability Expansion. *Journal of Development Planning*, 19, 41–58. Reprinted in Fukuda-Parrs, S. and A.K. Shiva Kumar, (Eds.) (2003), *Readings in Human Development*, Oxford University Press, New York, 3–16.

United Nations (2010), *The Least Developed Countries Report 2010: Towards a New International Development Architecture for LDCs*. United Nations Conference on Trade and Development.

United Nations Development Programme (1990), Human Development Report, United Nations, New York.

World Bank (2003), World Development Indicators. World Bank, Washington DC.

World Bank (2008), World Development Indicators. World Bank,Washington DC.

World Bank (2012), World Development Indicators. World Bank, Washington DC.

Williamson, J. (Ed.) (1989), Latin American Adjustment: How Much Has Happened? Institute for International Economics, Washington.

Years of the World Development Report. World Bank. Available from. https://open knowledge.worldbank.org/handle/10986/2586. Last accessed 15 October 2015.

Yusuf, S., A. Deaton, K. Dervis, W. Easterly, T. Ito and J.E. Stiglitz (2009), "*Development Economics through the Decades,*" *World Bank Publications*, The World Bank, number 2586, April.

Chapter 4

Remittances and Development

Manmohan Agarwal*
RBI Chair Professor
Centre for Development Studies
Thiruvananthapuram, Kerala, India
Adjunct Fellow
RIS, New Delhi, India
**manmohan@cds.ac.in*

Abstract: Migration from developing countries has increased considerably in recent years and so are the remittances that the countries of origin get. This migration is in contrast to the 19th century pattern when most emigration was of unskilled labor and there were hardly any remittances. The main effect was on wage rates. Currently, except in some selected segments of the labor market there is no general effect on wage rates. The chapter attempts to analyze the effects of the remittances of growth in the recipient countries. We found no correlation between remittances and investment or growth when we categorized countries according to different criteria or took the entire sample of countries. Similarly, we did not find any effect of remittances on growth in India. However, by easing the current account constraint, it might have enabled the economy to maintain a high rate of growth.

There is a long-standing tradition of research on the effects of migration both in the countries from which migration occurs and the countries to which migration occurs. Migration has been concentrated in two different periods. The first period saw the migration in the 19th century from the countries of Europe to the newly settled area in the Americas and in Australia. The second period the more recent migration from developing countries to the developed countries. In this chapter, we are mainly concerned with the effect of migration from developing countries to the developed countries on the development of the former group of countries but before we analyze this phenomenon, we briefly discuss the research on migration from Europe in the 19th century.

1 Migration from Europe to the Areas of Recent Settlement

Migration from Europe to the New World was about 46 million in the 19th century before 1913 while population increased from 192 million in 1800 to 423 million in 1900. So, annual migration was about 10% of population over the century and even higher after 1880 (Taylor and Williamson, 1994). The extreme case was emigration from Ireland. Around 4 million people migrated and this was partly responsible for the population to decline from 8.2 million in 1841, a level not since exceeded, to 4.4 million in 1911 (O'Rourke, 1995). Almost a quarter of the population emigrated at the rate of about 13 per thousand per annum.

Migration contributed substantially to the increase in Irish living standards between 1850 and 1914 (O'Rourke, 1995). Real agricultural wages doubled between 1860 and 1913, growing at 1.6% a year. They grew even faster, 1.9% a year between 1860 and 1895. Unskilled building wages increased at 2.2% a year (Boyer *et al.*, 1994).[1] This contrasts with the increase in per capita output of 1.6% a year between 1830 and 1913 Kennedy Kieran, Thomas Giblin and Hugh Medeidre (1988) Economic Development of Ireland in the Twentieth Century ,Routledge London. Relative dispersion among Europe and the New Lands declined between 1870 and 1910 by 28% for the real wage, 13% for GDP per capita and 24% for GDP per worker. In the absence of migration, wage, productivity and income, per capita levels would have been higher in the New World and lower in the Old World. For instance, without migration, Irish wages would have been 31% lower, Italian wages 23%, Swedish 10% while Argentine wages would have been 36% higher, Australian by 22%, Canadian by 25% and the US by 12%.[2,3] The simulations suggest that more than all the actual reduced dispersion, 168% was accounted for by migration.[4] The migration particularly helped to raise relative wages in the poorer

[1] They grew even faster if adjusted for lower probability of unemployment.

[2] The relatively poor were more likely to migrate; but not very often as the poorest at least initially, because of the cost of migration (Abramitzky *et al.*, 2010), but later remittances from those who had already migrated helped poorer migrants.

[3] Wages rates grew by 1.3% a year in the UK and so for all these countries wage rates grew faster than 1.3% a year and this was more than the growth of per capita output which was 0.8, 1.2 and 1.3% for Italy Norway and Sweden, respectively.

[4] Analysis shows that the CV is almost cut in half over the three decades, 1870–1900 (Williamson, 1995). Most of this was (60%) due to reduction of gap between the New and Old Worlds. Very little change in CV in the Old World or the New World.

European countries. Real wages in Denmark increased from 52% to 85% of those in Britain, in Ireland from 71% to 88%, Italy from 38% to 40%, Sweden from 41% to 82% and Norway from 41% to 65% (Williamson, 1995).[5,6] The migrants were young male adults, single and unskilled (Hatton and Williamson, 1992). The migrants from Norway were workers with lower productivity and poorer economic prospects (Abramitzky *et al.*, 2010).[7] So there was no brain drain. They were then an immediate addition to the labor market in the host country.

2 Emigration Today

The nature of migration from developing countries today is different. There are basically two different kinds of migration. Migration may be temporary when people go to work for a period and then return to their home country or it may be permanent. Temporary migration is a modern phenomenon as in the 19th century the difficulties of travel usually ensured that migration was permanent.[8] Temporary migration is concentrated among the developing countries themselves and consists of both unskilled and skilled labor. For instance, migration of domestic workers from mainly the Philippines, Indonesia and India to the Middle East is of temporary duration. Such migration is often temporary as workers go on contract employment with the purpose of earning higher wages and so increasing their savings.[9] Migration from developing countries to the developed countries is usually permanent and is mainly of skilled workers as the receiving countries are increasingly allowing only inflow of highly qualified individuals. This skilled migration raises concerns about brain drain since the emigration of well qualified people is believed to harm the growth prospects of the home country.[10] In more recent years, this type of migration is seen to have benefits also. Firstly, there are remittances from the migrants, though it is not clear who are the major remitters,

---

[5] Convergence to real wages in the US must have been even more dramatic as relative real wages fell from being 98% higher than those in Britain in 1855 to only 54% in 1913.

[6] Furthermore, the proportion of the poor fell and of those living in lower quality housing declined from 63% in 1861 to 29% after half a century (Boyer *et al.*, 1994, quoting O'Grada, 1988).

[7] This was likely to be the case for other countries also.

[8] This was not always the case. Even in the 19th century there was temporary migration. This was primarily of Italians to Argentina. They went to save enough to be able to buy a farm in Italy which would enable them to get married.

[9] The contract is usually for two years, but the workers often sign a new contract when their old contract expires. So they may work for an extended period in the host country, but they do not acquire residency rights.

[10] See Sen (1973). Bhagwati (1976) devised various tax schemes to recoup for the home country what had been spent in training these skilled people. Also see Bhagwati and Partington (1976).

Table 1. Emigration.

	Population (in %)	
	1990–1995	**2000–2005**
EAP	0.11	0.14
LAC	0.18	0.20
SA	0.09	0.17
SSA	0.88	1.24

Note: These categories of regions are as defined by the World Bank.
Source: World Development Indicators, 2007.

whether those leaving for temporary migration or the permanent migrants as the latter soon adopt the living style of their new country and also as their links to the home country weaken. But remittances have been important. The second benefit mentioned is that there is a certain amount of return migration and the return migrants bring in new technology.[11]

Emigration from the main developing country regions increased between the early 1990s and the early years of this century. Emigration is particularly high for Sub-Saharan Africa (SSA) (Table 1), though it has also increased substantially for SA. Of course, except in the case of SSA, these levels of emigration are nowhere near what the emigration was from Europe in the pre WWI period. Also, about 75% of migration from SSA is to other countries in SSA and not to the developed economies (International Organization for Migration, 2011).

Remittances as a percentage of GDP are considerable and have been growing rapidly (Table 2). They are particularly high for SSA and SA. Remittances, which were 1.8% and 0.8% of GDP in SA and SSA respectively in the early 1990s, increased to over 4% and 2% respectively by the end of the first decade of the 2000s. They are of considerable importance to the poorer, least developed countries.

3 Remittances and Development

The question arises about the contribution that these remittances are making to sustain growth in the developing world. While it is unclear to what extent the remittances are used for business investment and to what extent for

[11] This was important even in the pre-World War I period, particularly in the case of Italy. While few Irish or Swedes returned, an estimated 49% of Italian migrants to the Americas between 1905 and 1920 returned, many having accumulated the money needed to buy a farm in Italy (Hatton and Williamson, 1998).

Table 2. Remittances.

	GDP (in %)					
	1991–1995	1996–2000	2001–2005	2006–2008	2009–2010	2006–2010
EAP	0.6	0.9	1.4	1.5	1.3	1.4
ECA	1.0	1.3	1.1	1.4	1.2	1.3
LAC	0.7	0.9	1.7	1.7	1.3	1.5
MNA	6.0	3.4	4.0	3.3	3.7	3.5
SA	1.8	2.5	3.4	4.0	4.3	4.1
SSA	0.8	1.4	1.6	2.2	2.4	2.3
Least	3.4	3.8	5.4	5.7	6.3	5.9

Source: World Development Indicators, World Bank Data Bank, World Bank. Washington D.C.

Table 3. Current account balance on goods and services.

	GDP (%)						
Region	1965–1973	1974–1982	1983–1990	1991–2000	2001–2005	2006–2008	2009–2011
World	0.2	0.3	0.4	0.4	0.4	0.8	0.3
High Income	0.4	0.2	0.2	0.6	0.6	0	0.1
EAP	−1.9	−1.2	0.4	1.8	0.2	9.4	4.4
LAC	−0.5	−1.5	3.3	−1.1	3.0	0.5	−1.0
SA	−1.7	−3.8	−4.4	−3.5	−0.8	−2.2	−2.1
SSA	−1.1	−1.5	1.2	−1.3	1.5	0.5	−2.3

Source: World Development Indicators, World Bank Data Bank, World Bank. Washington D.C.

house construction or purely consumption, the remittances have prevented the emergence of a BOP crisis, and balance of payments (BOP) crises had, in the past, resulted in policies that slowed growth.[12]

In the years before the financial crisis, the inflow of remittances were considerably greater than the current account surplus for Latin America and the Caribbean (LAC) and SSA. After the crisis, when the current account position of these regions deteriorated, the deficits would have been twice as large without the very considerable remittances. At least for SSA these deficits may have reached

[12] Stop go policies were a feature of not merely the UK in the 1950s and 1960s. They were also a feature of many countries in Latin America and had sparked a vigorous debate between monetarists and structuralists (Corbo, 1974).

unsustainable levels. Even for SA the current account deficit would have been unmanageable without the very substantial remittances.

Because of the substantial remittances, the current account deficits have been small despite the increasing deficit on trade in goods and services. The deficit on trade in goods and services increased between 1990 and 2007 by 3% of GDP in LAC and by 5% in SSA, but because of higher remittances the current account deficit worsened by only 1% in the case of SSA (World Bank, 2011). The migration from developing countries does not seem to directly contribute to higher wages and living standards in developing countries because of the substantial excess labor in many of these countries. However, the migration may have resulted in higher wage rates in specific areas. The most prominent of these may have been nursing. The effects of the substantial hiring of health workers by developed countries on the delivery of health services in developing countries have resulted in adoption of codes to regulate such hirings Dovlo, 2007.[13]

The remittances have resulted in a relaxation of the foreign exchange constraint and so contributed to higher growth. Remittances have in part played the role that aid was expected to play in the two-gap model of economic growth.[14] While remittances have been increasing, the importance of aid has been declining (Table 4).

Table 4. Net official development assistance.

	GNI (in %)					
	1991–1995	1996–2000	2001–2005	2006–2008	2009–2010	2006–2010
EAP	0.5	0.5	0.4	0.2	0.1	0.2
LAC	0.3	0.3	0.3	0.2	0.2	0.2
MNA	1.2	1.2	1.8	1.9	1.0	1.6
SAS	0.8	0.8	0.9	0.8	0.8	0.8
SSA	4.4	4.4	5.3	4.8	4.6	4.7
Least	7.4	7.4	9.1	7.8	7.4	7.6

Source: World Development Indicators, World Bank Data Bank, World Bank, Washington D.C.

[13]For the Commonwealth declaration, see http://www.aspeninstitute.org/sites/default/files/content/images/%7B7F307830-1FA4-44A3-9EA5-9CC4055D7D4B%7D_CompanionDocument.pdf. See also WHO (2012). Last accessed 15 Sept 2015.

[14]This can be seen most clearly in terms of the two-gap model developed by Chenery and Bruno (1962) and Chenery and Strout (1966). According to traditional aid analysis, e.g., Rosenstein–Rodan (1943), aid was needed to augment domestic savings in order to raise the level of investment. But Chenery and his co-authors argued that apart from this domestic gap there was a foreign gap. Developing countries needed to import more capital goods if they were to raise their investment levels and since earnings from exports of primary products would not keep up, aid would be needed to fill this foreign gap. Aid should fill the larger of the two gaps.

The importance of aid also diminishes when it is measured either as a percent of gross fixed capital formation or of imports.[15] The capital output ratio in Asia, both SA and East Asia and Pacific (EAP) is 4 (Agarwal, 2008), so if remittances are 4% of GDP as they are in SA, they would raise the growth rate of per capita GDP by 1% point if it was all invested and by 0.5% if half was invested.[16] Since the capital output ratio has been higher in SSA, the effect on growth would be lower by about a quarter to half percent. But even with this higher capital output ratio, growth in the least developed countries would have increased by about 0.7% to over 1% a year. The growth effect in LAC and EAP would be negligible because of smaller inflows of remittances coupled in the case of LAC with a higher capital output ratio.

The poorest regions, SA, SSA and the least developed countries, are the most dependent on remittances and these have continued to grow even after the crisis, though for a number of regions the share of remittances in GDP have fallen after the crisis (Table 2).

The importance of remittances can be seen when we can compare their amount with that of aid. Not only has the importance of aid been declining for most regions (Table 3) but it is insignificant for many regions. For regions such as EAP and LAC, remittances are about 7 times as large as aid, and for SA they are 5 or over 4 times as important. Only for SSA and the least developed countries is aid still more important than remittances though even for those areas remittances are becoming more important.

We now discuss in greater detail the effect of remittances in the economies of developing countries.

The growth rate of per capita GDP is the smallest for the LDCs, higher for low income countries, and still higher for the lower middle income countries, but there is not much difference in the share of remittances in GDP for these three groups of countries (Table 5). Nor is there any relation between the share of remittances in GDP and that of foreign direct investment (FDI) in GDP. Presence of workers in the host country does not seem to lead to higher FDI from the host country. Furthermore, there does not seem to be any systematic relation between remittances and fixed capital formation.

We next tried to stratify countries not by income level but by the percent of remittances in GDP. We looked at the spread of this variable and divided the 83 countries for which we had data divided into 4 groups. Those with a percentage greater than 10, those with a percentage between three and ten those with a percentage between one and three and those with a percentage less than 1.

[15] For a more detailed discussion of aid see Agarwal and Ghosh (2016).

[16] It is irrelevant whether this investment was in housing. Research on aid suggests that 1% increase in aid leads to a 0.16% increase in growth Mekasha and Tarp (2011).

Table 5. Some macro indicators by income classes, 2008–2013.

	XGS	FDI	GFCF	Net ODA	Remittances	GDPPC Growth
LDCs	26.5	2.7	25.7	6.6	4.5	2.8
Low income	24.2	4.4	23.1	13.3	4.2	3.2
Lower Middle Income	26.9	2.4	26.6	0.9	4.6	3.9
Upper Middle Income	29.1	3.1	31.0	0.1	0.1	0.7
HIPC	28.5	4.8	22.2	8.9	3.3	2.4

Note: The income categories are as defined by the World Bank. LDCs are least developed countries, HIPCs are the heavily indebted poor countries. XGS are exports of goods and services, FDI is inflow of foreign direct investment, GFCF is gross fixed capital formation, net ODA is net inflow of official development assistance. These variables are all measured as an unweighted average percentage of GDP for the period. GPPC growth is the annual average growth of per capita GDP during the period.

Source: Author's calculations from data in World Bank Development Indicators.

Table 6. Classification by size of remittances.

	Number	XGS	FDI	GFCF	net ODA	Remittances	GDPPC Growth
Less than 1	27	37.7	2.8	24.6	2.9	0.3	2.8
Between 1 and 3	23	36.4	5.1	22.3	7.1	1.7	3.1
Between 3 and 10	21	33.6	4.0	21.9	3.8	6.0	2.2
More than 10	12	35.9	7.9	21.3	11.3	13.8	1.8

The results are somewhat surprising. The group of countries that get the most remittances also, by and large, get the most net ODA and inflow of FDI (Table 6). It may be that getting remittances and aid reduces the probability of running into a BOP crisis and so encourages inflow of FDI. However, for the countries getting the most remittances the total inflow including FDI, ODA and remittances adds to 33% of GDP, and this is more than the GFCF by about 50%. In other words, capital inflows are considerably greater than investment and almost a third of the capital inflows go for consumption.

What is even more puzzling is that the higher the inflows of foreign capital, the lower is the share of GFCF in GDP, and the lower the growth rate. Of course, a major reason behind the lower growth rate would be the lower share of GFCF in GDP. So the main puzzle is why is GFCF so low for countries receiving the most remittances and, in total, the most foreign capital inflow. This would suggest that the remittances are mainly by workers who have neither the technical or entrepreneurial skills to convert their experience and moneys into investments. It is suggested that skilled emigration is mainly a brain drain and does not seem to provide capital or skills to push up the growth rate. Of course, the question remains why the consumption demand by the migrants does not encourage investment. The answer has to lie in the scarcity of technical and entrepreneurial skills.

Table 7. Correlations among the variables.

	FDI	GDPPC Growth	GFCF	net ODA	Remittances
XGS	0.17*	0.02	0.08	–0.11	–0.12
FDI		0.12	0.03	0.68#	0.18*
GDPPC			0.37#	0.01	–0.16
GFCF				–0.12	–0.16
Net ODA					0.17*

*Significant at 10%, #significant.

Most of the remittances flow to countries in SSA and SA. The countries in these regions are lagging behind in the progress towards achieving the MDGs (Agarwal, 2016). Even the increase in consumption is not of the kind that reduces poverty or improves the nutritional status of the people or reduces mortality rates substantially. The impact of remittances needs more detailed analysis.

The aggregate classifications that we have used may hide individual country patterns. We therefore took the values for different variables for our sample of 83 countries and calculated the correlations among variables. [17]Again we find that the share of remittances in GDP has a very low correlation with other variables (Table 7).

We do find, however, that remittances and net ODA have a similar effect on exports of goods and services and GFCF. The former suggests a 'Dutch disease' sort of phenomenon. Inflows of both lead to an appreciation of the exchange rate that hurts export performance. Poor export performance, in turn, inhibits investment so GFCF has a negative correlation with both net ODA and remittances.

The results above about remittances are similar to the results that many analysts have found about other forms of capital flows. Many have found a negative correlation between capital inflows and growth (Aizenman *et al.*, 2007, Obstfeld, 2009, Prasad, Rajan and Subramaniam, 2007). Gourinchas and Jeanne (2009) found a negative relation between capital inflows and productivity growth. On the other hand Barro *et al.* (1995) found no significant effect of capital inflows on growth. Theoretically, capital inflows in the presence of domestic distortions can lead to immiserization (Bhagwati *et al.*, 1998). Undoubtedly, there are distortions in these developing countries; for a beginning many of them have high tariffs on imports. But it is still puzzling that the distortions would outweigh the positive effects across the board.

Furthermore, the two regions with the largest remittances, SA and SSA, are the regions with the worst social indictors and which show the least progress

[17]VAR estimations did not give any significant results.

towards achieving the MDGs (Agarwal, 2016). The lack of an effect on social indicators replicates the effects of European migration in the 19th century.

We then looked at the effect of remittances on the Indian economy. Again we found no effect whether we looked merely at correlations or tried to find a long run relation through time series analysis. But we do know that the trade deficit has been increasing and the remittance inflows have kept the current account deficit in manageable limits (Agarwal and Ghosh, 2016). We know that unmanageable current account deficits lead to a slowdown of growth. In that sense, the large remittances inflows have allowed the economy to experience a prolonged period of rapid growth.

References

Abramitzky, R., L.P. Boustan and K. Eriksson (2010), Europe's Tired, Poor, Huddled Masses, Self-Selection and Economic Outcomes in the of Mass Migration, NBER WP 15684, Jan 2010.

Agarwal, M. (2008), THE BRICSAM Countries and Changing Economic Power: Scenarios to 2050, *CIGI Working paper No. 39*, Canada: Waterloo. Last accessed date Oct. 11, 2008.

Agarwal, M. (2016), India and the MDGs in the Context of Developing Countries Particularly in South Asia, Chapter 3, this volume.

Agarwal, M. and S. Ghosh (2016), Structural Change in the Indian Economy, Chapter 6, this volume.

Aizenman, J., B. Pinto and A. Radziwill (2007), Sources for Financing Domestic Capital — is Foreign Saving a Viable Option for Developing Countries? *Journal of International Money and Finance*, 26(5), 682–702.

Barro, R.J. and X. Sala-i-Martin (1995), Economic Growth. McGraw-Hill, Pennsylvania.

Bhagwati, J. (1976), Taxing the Brain Drain, Challenge, Vol. 19, No. 3 (JULY/AUGUST 1976), pp. 34–38.

Bhagwati, J. and M. Partington (1976), (Ed.), *Taxing the Brain Drain: A Proposal*. North-Holland, Amsterdam.

Bhagwati, J., A. Panagariya and T.N. Srinivasan (1998), *Lectures in International Trade*, MIT Press, Cambridge, MA.

Boyer, H. and O'Rourke (1994), The Impact of Emigration on Real Wages in Ireland, 1850–1914 in Hatton, T.J. and J. Williamson (Eds.). *Migration and The International Labor Market, 1850–1939*, London: Routledge.

Chenery, H. and M. Bruno (1962), Development Alternatives in an Open Economy: The Case of Israel, *Economic Journal*, 72(1).

Chenery H. and A. Strout (1966), Foreign Assistance and Economic Development, *American Economic Review*, 61(4).

Dovlo, D. (2007), Migration of Nurses from Sub-Saharan Africa: A Review of Issues and Challenges, *Health Services Research*, 42(3 Pt 2), 1373–1388.

Gourinchas, P-O and O. Jeanne (2007), Capital Flows to Developing Countries: The Allocation Puzzle, *NBER Working Paper No. 13602*, Cambridge MA: NBER.

Hatton, T.J. and J. Williamson (1992), International Migration and World Development: A Historical Perspective, *NBER Historical Paper No. 41*.

International Organization for Migration (2011), Annual Report, Geneva.

Kieran, K., T. Giblin and D. McHugh (1988), *The Economic Development of Ireland in the Twentieth Century*: Routledge: London.

Mekesha, J.T. and F. Tarp (2011), Aid and Growth: What Meta-Analysis Reveals, *Working Paper No. 2011/22*, Helsinki: UNU World Institute for Development Economics Research (UNU-WIDER).

Obstfeld, M. (2009) International Finance and Growth in Developing Countries: What have we learned? IMF Staff Papers, March 2009.

O'Grada, C. (1988), Ireland Before and After the Famine: Explorations in Economic History, 1800–1925, Manchester University Press, quoted in Boyer G.R. T.J. Hatton and Kevin.

O'Rourke, K. (1995), Emigration and Living Standards in Ireland since the Famine, *Journal of Population Economics*, 8(4), 407–421.

Prasad, E., Raghuram, R. and A. Subramanian (2007), Foreign Capital and Economic Growth, *Brookings Papers on Economic Activity*, 1, 153–230.

Ran, A., L.P. Boustan and K. Eriksson (2012), Europe's Tired, Poor, Huddled Masses: Self-Selection and Economic Outcomes in the age of Mass Migration, *American Economic Review*, 102(5), 1832–1856.

Rosenstein-Rodan (1943), Problems of Industrialization of Eastern and South Eastern Europe, *Economic Journal*, 53(210/211), 202–211.

Sen, A. (1973), Brain Drain: Causes and Effects, in: Williams, B.R. (Ed.): *Science and Technology in Economic Growth*, London: MacMillan.

Taylor, A.M. and J.G. Williamson (1994), *Convergence in the Age of Mass Migration*, NBER Working Paper 4711, Cambridge, MA: NBER.

Williamson, J. (1995), The Evolution of Global Labor Markets since 1830: Background Evidence and Hypotheses, *Explorations in Economic History*, 32, 141–196.

WHO (2010), WHO Global Code of Practice on the International Recruitment of Health Personnel, Geneva. Available from: http://www.who.int/hrh/migration/code/code_en.pdf.

World Bank (2011), World Development Indicators, World Bank, Washington D.C.

Part II

Development of the Indian Economy

Chapter 5

Reflections on India's Emergence in the World Economy

Amit S Ray*,†,‡ and Sunandan Ghosh*,§

**Centre for Development Studies, Thiruvananthapuram, Kerala, India*

†Jawaharlal Nehru University, New Delhi, India

‡asray@cds.edu

§sunandan@cds.edu

Abstract: This paper attempts to capture how India embraced the world economy against the backdrop of the evolving domestic and international economic policy environment. We begin with a brief overview of the evolution of India's development policy framework. Next, we attempt to understand why India failed to join the league of 'Asian Miracle' economies that embarked upon a phenomenal growth path during 1960s, 1970s and 1980s. This is followed by a quantitative presentation of the process of India's integration with the world economy that was effectively set in motion only after a turnaround in its policy regime in the 1990s. Finally, we conclude that India's post-colonial policy thrust on public funded higher education and research in science and technology, creating a strong base of human capital and technological capability, acted as the key drivers of India's economic emergence during the last couple of decades.

1 Introduction

This paper attempts to examine the coordinates of India's emergence as a key player in the world economy. In the history of the world economy, the rise of different nations as economic power hubs at different points in time may be traced back to various factors, going beyond the conventional economic parameters commonly underscored by economic development theories. One could identify distinct (and often unique) social, economic and geo-political explanations for the economic emergence of each nation in the world economy. The prosperity of Britain in its colonial heydays may have a very different genesis and explanation compared to the rise of the USA as an economic superpower in the 20th century. In this paper, our objective is to unfold the mystery of India's economic emergence in the last couple of decades. Our intention is to capture how India embraced the world economy against the backdrop of the evolving domestic and international economic policy environment.

Our paper begins with a brief overview of the evolution of India's development policy framework in the post independent era. Next, we attempt to understand why India failed to seize the opportunity to be a part of the 'Asian Miracle' of the 1960s, 1970s and 1980s, when some of the labor surplus East Asian economies embarked upon a phenomenal growth path unprecedented in human history. This section will posit India against its East Asian neighbors to give us a comparative Asian perspective. This will be followed by a quantitative presentation of the process of India's integration with the world economy that was effectively set in motion much later, only after a turnaround in its policy regime in the 1990s. Finally, we discuss the key drivers of India's economic emergence into the world economy. We show that India's success may be attributed largely to its post-colonial policy thrust on public funded higher education and research in science and technology, creating a strong base of human capital and technological capability that proved to be the cornerstone of India's economic emergence during the last couple of decades.

2 Evolution of India's Development Policy Framework[1]

The conventional discourse on India's development policy has invariably confined itself to the paradigm of inward vs. outward looking strategies, dividing it into two distinct regimes — import substituting industrialization extending till the 1980s, followed by a paradigm shift in 1991 towards a liberalized trade and industrial policy regime. We refrain from such a broad brush depiction of India's development policy evolution. We demarcate four distinct phases of India's development policy distinguished by their guiding philosophies and compulsions.

2.1 Policy planning driven by ideology: 1950s and 1960s

India followed an inward looking development strategy and remained a virtually closed economy for almost four decades after its independence in 1947. The key

[1] This section draws largely upon a recent paper by one of the authors Ray (2015).

goal was to achieve *self-reliance* in all possible dimensions of economic activities of the nation.

According to Ray (2006), the immediate aspiration of independent India was perhaps to mimic the development trajectories of the 'advanced' industrialized nations, although very much within the framework of import substitution and self-reliance. It was perhaps important for Indian policy makers to signal to the rest of the world that India could do whatever the advanced nations can. Accordingly, diversification of industrial production base was given a high priority in India's planning with a view to achieving self-reliance in the entire array of industrial production from simple consumer items to sophisticated capital goods and heavy machinery. Indian planners paid little attention to the notion of comparative advantage and did not even hesitate to focus on highly complex and resource intensive activities like space research and nuclear technology.

This policy approach was perhaps a result of the hangover of prolonged colonial rule that fostered a process of "drain of wealth" through tripartite and unequal trading relations dictated by the British rulers. This hangover was reinforced by the contemporary scholarship on *dependency theories*[2] pioneered by the Latin American school of thought, highlighting notions of elasticity pessimism and inequalizing trade. All this led to deep cynicism about trade and openness among the founding fathers of India's development policy. The goal was, therefore, to achieve 'self-reliance' by doing away with all elements of dependence on the western world. However, the idea of *self-reliance* itself has gone through a metamorphosis in India's development policy that we shall discuss in due course.

The architecture of India's post-colonial development policy framework was inspired by the soviet model of development. Indeed, India's Second Five Year Plan model closely resembled the one that Feldman developed for the Soviet Union in the 1920s.[3] India's first Prime Minister Jawaharlal Nehru, with his Cambridge exposure, had a strong faith in socialist ideals, which left a significant imprint on India's post-colonial development model. If we consider the Nehruvian era that extends probably till the mid-1960s, we note that socialist sentiments went a long way in defining India's own understanding of development, both in terms of its means as well as its ends. There are several pointers to substantiate this claim.

Soviet style Central Economic Planning was the cornerstone of India's initial development strategy that aimed at a "socialistic pattern of development". There was lack of faith in the market and the role of the state was emphatically highlighted. Although a mixed economy was envisaged, there was a clearly

[2] See, for instance, Prebisch (1950).

[3] See Bhagwati and Desai (1970).

assigned role earmarked for the private sector, primarily restricted to the consumer goods segment, and even that was subjected to pervasive regulatory control by the state. On the other hand, a progressively expanding list of priority sector industries was reserved for the public sector that was supposed to reach the "commanding heights" of the economy.

India's post-colonial development strategy paid very little attention to trade. India's trade policy was characterized by pervasive import and exchange control, relying primarily on quantitative restrictions (QRs). From 1962 onwards, QRs were supplemented by increasing use of import duties. There was a pessimistic neglect of exports to begin with, but from the Third Plan (1961–1962), there were some piecemeal and *ad -hoc* attempts towards export promotion through various export incentives (subsidies, fiscal incentives and import entitlements). There was, of course, a temporary and short-lived trade-liberalization attempt during the devaluation of 1966 with an announced goal of eliminating/rationalizing export subsidies and liberalizing import licensing and reduction in import duties, but only to be followed by a reversal to the protectionist policy framework.[4]

Socialist ideals were also reflected in the deliberate policy attempts on several other fronts — (1) reduction of monopoly and concentration of economic power, (2) promotion of the small scale sector that generates income and livelihood for the common man through a policy of industrial reservation, (3) balanced regional development through freight equalization policy to eliminate regional disparities in growth and development and (4) price controls, aimed at ensuring availability of certain "essential" ("crucial") products at "reasonable" prices — fertilizer, cement, iron and steel, pharmaceuticals.

Another area that deserves special attention in India's development policy during the Nehruvian era is its concerted focus on social sector policies, driven by the ideals of the so-called *Nehruvian Socialism*. The need for a proactive role of the government in the provision of merit goods such as health and education was clearly highlighted. An elaborate public health care system and infrastructure was envisaged and created during this period. Likewise, government funded higher education and research, especially in the fields of science and technology, was emphasized with the creation of an elaborate network of public funded colleges and universities as well as other institutions of higher learning in science, technology and management.

2.2 Deeper penetration of self-reliance: 1970–1985

The decade of the 1960s witnessed several changes in the global political economy scenario. Two neighborhood conflicts (1962 China and 1965 Pakistan) exposed

[4] Wolf (1982).

the ground realities of India's limited military capabilities and the consequent vulnerabilities against global forces and alliances. Moreover, the acute food crisis of 1966 revealed India's economic vulnerability vis-à-vis the USA, when it withdrew its food aid to India under PL480. This was followed by an acute currency crisis and a major devaluation of the rupee.

Despite being one of original founders of the non-aligned movement in a bipolar world, India slowly started aligning with the Soviet Union, both on strategic and economic fronts. There was urgency to rapidly march towards the goal of self-reliance, both economic as well as strategic. India's achievement of nuclear capability in 1974 was a clear step in this direction. This was also a period when private capitalists were emerging as a powerful class in India as an outcome of the original vision of a mixed economy. This class had a vested interest in protecting their business from international competition and a policy of self-reliance and import substitution was in perfect harmony with their narrow self-interest. The policy of license-raj had already created a rent-seeking vested interest among the bureaucracy. Against this backdrop, India's development policy framework tilted towards deeper penetration of self-reliance in every sense of the term. However, with the private capitalist class now being allowed to operate more pervasively, the initial policy goal for the public sector reaching the "commanding heights" of the economy was substantially diluted. Nevertheless, industrial licensing continued in full steam. With a change in the political regime in 1977, there was an announced intention to relax licensing policies, but it never quite materialized and was promptly reversed in 1980.

This period also witnessed a passage of several legislative acts that have a direct bearing on India's development model. These include the Foreign Exchange Regulation Act (FERA) 1973 intended to restrict and regulate the operations of foreign (multinational) companies in India, the Monopolies and Restrictive Trade Practices (MRTP) Act of 1970 to prevent the concentration of economic power in hands of a few rich, the Patent Act of 1970 granting only process patents *for chemical substances including pharmaceuticals* with a reduced duration of seven years from the date of filing or five years from the date of sealing whichever is lower and placing the burden of proof on the plaintiff in case of infringement.

All these acts introduced in the 1970s, in conjunction with several other policy initiatives towards active promotion of indigenous technology creation and adoption, resulted in a policy framework that took the goal of *self-reliance* beyond mere manufacturing capabilities to technological *self-reliance*. Given the protectionist environment, considerations of costs and quality as per global standards were not considered to be of much relevance during this phase of India's development model.

Another important dimension of this deepening of *self-reliance* during this era was evident in India's strive towards attaining self-sufficiency in food grain production. India's *green revolution* was made possible through the Government's concerted effort and investment in agricultural research and extension services.

2.3 Policy ambivalence and sporadic reforms: 1985–1990

The flip side of this protectionist policy regime soon revealed itself in the form of inefficiencies of various kinds. For example, the Indian industry, protected from foreign competition, was reluctant to adapt itself to the fast changing global technology frontier and hence, in the process, became inefficient with regard to global standards of cost and quality. India's industrial sector was characterized by very high effective rates of protection and associated domestic resource costs. The country settled at a "Hindu" rate of growth (2–3% p.a.) and was branded by development scholars as a growth laggard in the world.[5]

From the mid-1980s, with a young leader taking over as Prime Minister with a dynamic appeal, along with his team of technocrat advisors, a technological view of development was getting imprinted in India's development policy framework. It was realized that the ability to produce a wide range of objects is of little value if it is not matched by the ability to produce them efficiently. This may require opening up the doors to latest global technologies, even if it entails a deviation from the original policy framework of inward looking industrialization. At the same time, global scholarship on development strategy was also going through a metamorphosis, fueled by the trumpeting of the success stories of East Asian economies that had adopted an outward oriented industrialization strategies. There was some serious rethinking about India's development path among Indian scholars and policy makers, albeit with a lot of scepticism and hesitation.

Although this period marked the beginning of India's liberalization policy, the policy response was at best feeble and sporadic. There was an attempt to liberalize particular aspects of the control system without affecting the system itself in any fundamental way. These attempts have, arguably, been piecemeal and ad hoc and lacked a comprehensive program of reforms that some of the other inward looking economies had already adopted (including China from 1978).

2.4 Paradigm shift: 1991 onwards

The year 1991 marked a radical departure in India's development policy from inward looking industrialization to an outward oriented trade regime. This was

[5] Lal (1988).

precipitated by an exceptionally severe balance of payment crisis compelling India to borrow from the IMF. The massive economic reforms package adopted in 1991, consisting of short-term stabilization measures along with a longer-term program of comprehensive structural reforms, was much wider and deeper than earlier piecemeal attempts. There was a complete paradigm shift in India's development policy that now emphasized not only relaxation of government controls and greater integration with the world economy, but also a larger role for the private sector as the engine of growth in a free market framework nurturing competitive forces in order to boost efficiency. Interestingly, this paradigm shift in India's policy framework coincided with the Uruguay Round of negotiations culminating in the establishment of the World Trade Organization (WTO). This ushered in a new era of WTO driven world order of globalization, against which we should try to understand India's economic reforms.

In terms of outcomes, the reforms process, over a period of time, puts in place a trade regime compatible with the diktats of the WTO, with the removal of all QRs on trade, reduction of tariff rates, market aligned foreign exchange rates with full current account and limited capital account convertibility and a liberal, transparent, investor friendly foreign direct investment (FDI) policy in place. On the industrial front, the reforms led to virtual elimination of industrial licensing and de-reservation. The number of sectors reserved for small-scale enterprises was drastically reduced. Most significantly, the role of the public sector was redefined with the stated objective of disinvesting public sector units. Finally, the establishment of bodies like the Investment Commission and the National Manufacturing Competitiveness Council clearly highlights a major shift in the role of the government from 'control' to 'regulation' insofar as the industrial sector is concerned.

On the fiscal front, to achieve fiscal consolidation and stabilization, the *Fiscal Responsibility and Budget Management Act* was passed. This act enjoined the central government to eliminate its fiscal and revenue deficits in a phased manner in the medium term. In another significant move aiming to create a common market for goods and services in the country, a uniform system of VAT has been adopted and services sector (contributing to more than 50% of GDP) has been brought under the tax net in a comprehensive manner. Finally, subsidies on petroleum products are being progressively dismantled by linking domestic retail prices to international prices. This has considerably reduced government expenditure on the petroleum account.

3 The Asian Miracle: A Lost Opportunity for India?

India had to wait for five long decades after its independence before it could make its presence felt in the world economy. Despite its illustrious history of an ancient civilization dating back to 5000 BC and a rich cultural heritage, intellectual and scientific capacities and enlightened leadership at the time of independence,[6] India remained a poor under-developed nation for more than half a century. It is rather intriguing to note that much of the labor surplus Asia (East and Southeast, in particular) forged ahead with economic prosperity from the 1960s and 1970s, even though they started from a much lower base of economic and scientific capacities compared to India. Some of the economies in the East and Southeast Asia grew at rates, unprecedented in human history. By contrast, India remained stuck at low levels of growth rates of per capita income.

The extraordinary growth performance of East Asia, popularly known as the Asian Miracle, cannot be understood as an isolated regional phenomenon. Rather, it depicts an unfolding pattern of international specialization, where labor surpluses of Asia get integrated into the mainstream of world trade. Within labor surplus East Asia, the development of different national economies followed an orderly sequence — the so-called 'flying geese' pattern.[7]

> *"The initial leader Japan was followed by the Four Tigers (Korea, Taiwan, Hong Kong and Singapore), then by the three Cubs (Indonesia, Malaysia and Thailand) and finally by China and Vietnam. At each stage, rapid economic growth driven by labor-intensive manufactured exports produced a Stolper-Samuelson effect in the current leaders setting off a wage-explosion there. This drove labor-intensive industries out to the next tier of low-wage economies while the current leaders graduated to more sophisticated activities that were not however at the cutting edge of technology. The final destination of this migration of labor-intensive manufacturing was, of course, China. In part, this was due to its vast surplus of low-wage labor (generating a Lewis effect)."*[8]

The pattern of emergence of the Asian Miracle economies is captured in Table 1 which presents the GDP growth trajectories and the degree of openness in selected Asian countries.

Japan, the leader of the Asian Miracle, experienced an average GDP growth rate of 10.4% during the 1960s. This abruptly turned negative at the beginning of the 1970s and never regained its past levels. During the next two decades, the

---

[6] By 1947, India had already produced two Nobel laureates (CV Raman in Physics and Sir Rabindranath Tagore in Literature who also happened to be the first one to receive a Nobel prize in Literature outside the English speaking world), several civil servants, barristers, professors and scientists of global repute.

[7] Akamatsu (1962).

[8] Guha and Ray (2004).

Table 1. Growth and openness of Asian economies.

Countries	Period	Average GDP Growth Rate	Openness (Trade/GDP ratio)
Japan	1961–1969	10.4	Steadily increased:
	1970–1991	4.3	5% in 1960
	1992–2013	0.8	30% now
Singapore	1961–1981	9.3	Fully open throughout
	1982–1997	7.9	150–450%
	1998–2013	5.3	
Hong Kong	1969–1981	9.3	Fully open throughout
	1982–1997	5.9	150–450%
	1998–2013	3.4	
Korea, Rep. of	1961–1991	9.5	Steadily increased:
	1992–2013	5.0	5% in 1960
			90% now
Indonesia	1961–1967	2.0	Open throughout:
	1968–1996	7.5	Hovering around 50% rising to 65% now
	1997–2013	4.0	
Malaysia	1961–1996	7.7	Open to highly open:
	1997–2013	4.5	100–170%
Thailand	1966–1996	7.8	Open to highly open:
	1997–2013	3.0	50–160%
China	1961–1978	4.7	Opened up in 1979: steadily increased
	1979–2013	9.9	30–70%
India	1961–1984	3.8	Opened up in 1991:
	1985–1994	5.3	Below 15% till then, and thereafter
	1995–2002	5.8	steadily rising to above 50%.
	2003–2010	8.3	
	1995–2010	7.1	
	2010–2013	5.5	

Source: Authors' calculations from World Development Indicators.

average rate of growth was only 4.3%. Since 1990, Japan's growth rates further tapered off to less than 1% on an average.

Among the tigers, the growth spurt in Singapore and Hong Kong continued till 1981 while South Korea's growth spurt lasted till 1991. The average growth rates achieved by these tigers were 9.3–9.5%, respectively, very close to the rates achieved by Japan.[9] The three cubs also experienced growth spurts beginning in the 1960s continuing till 1996 before being hit by the East Asian currency crisis.

[9] Data for the fourth tiger Taiwan was not available.

The levels achieved by the cubs were much below that of the leader and the tigers, the average varying between 7.5 and 7.8%.

With regard to openness, with the exception of Japan and South Korea, all others were fully open economies and remained so throughout their period of growth explosion that began in the 1960s. Japan and South Korea started as virtually closed economies with trade-GDP ratios as low as 5% in 1960. However, both progressively opened up their economies over time, with their trade/GDP ratios steadily rising to the present levels of 30% and 90% respectively. Trade and openness were, therefore, at the core of the Asian Miracle which integrated labor surplus Asia into the mainstream of world trade.

After East Asia, it was the sleeping dragon China that took off in the 1980s, again propelled by rapid expansion of labor-intensive manufactured exports. China opened up its economy in 1979 and its trade GDP ratio steadily rose from 30% to 70%. China's growth explosion was imminent as soon as it opened up. The average growth rate of GDP during 1961–1978 stood at 4.7% and it doubled during the period 1979–2013 at 9.9%. This spectacular growth performance of China, spanning over more than three decades, surpasses the miraculous achievements of all East Asian star performers, including Japan. As we noted above, the Stolper–Samuelson process[10] that was setting in for other Asian Miracle economies and eventually eroded, at least in part, their low labor cost advantage, was delayed in the case of China which enjoys almost a Lewisian "unlimited supply of labor". No wonder, China continues to dominate the global market for labor-intensive mass manufactures!

Despite its bulging population, where was labor surplus *India* in this Asian Miracle? When the rest of Asia, including the late riser China was bubbling with export driven growth, India continued with its autarkic trade policy regime that created strong anti-export bias in the relative incentive structures (Wolf, 1982; Bhagwati and Srinivasan, 1975). As a result, India could never experience the Asian Miracle driven by rapid expansion of labor- intensive manufactured exports. India settled at a low rate of GDP growth averaging 3.8% till the mid-1980s. With its sporadic attempts to liberalize trade restrictions from 1985, there was some improvement in its growth performance with an average rate of 5.3% during 1985–1994, but nothing compared to the phenomenal growth rates experienced by its East Asian neighbors during the Asian Miracle.

Comparing GDP trajectories of India and China (Figure 1), we note that the paths nearly overlap till the early 1980s, when China begins to forge ahead after opening up its economy in 1979, leaving India hovering at the same level for

[10]According to the Stolper and Samuelson (1941) theorem, a rise in the price of a commodity leads to a rise in the price of the factor used more intensively in the production of that commodity.

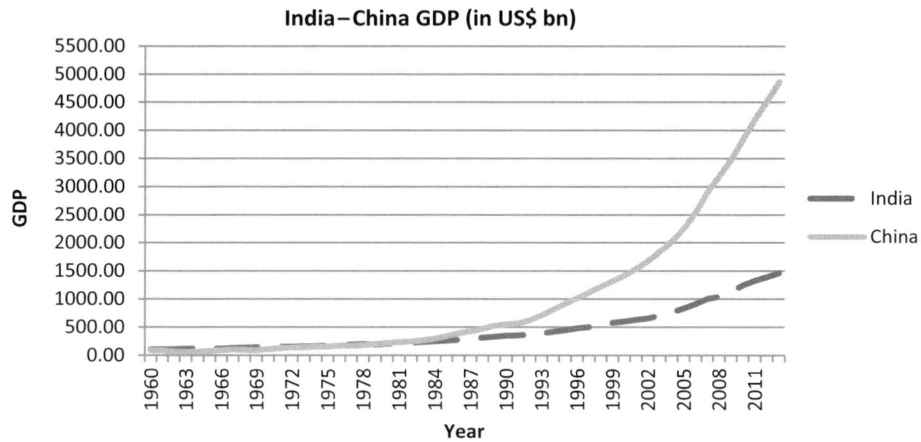

Figure 1. GDP paths of China and India.

Source: World Development Indicators.

another decade or two. India opened up only in 1991 and took off much later than China. Even after taking off, India has never been able to match up with Chinese growth rates. As indicated in Table 1, during 1995–2010, India achieved an average growth rate of 7.1%, somewhat comparable to the growth spurt experienced by the three cubs. It was only in some of the years between 2005 and 2010 that India achieved growth rates exceeding 9% matching that of the Asian tigers. But even during this period (2003–2010), the average growth rate was barely 8.3%, much below China's average of 9.9% sustained over 35 long years after its opening up. In other words, India's growth performance clearly indicates that it could not come on board the spectacular Asian Miracle.[11]

In common discourse, India's inability to join the miraculous growth experience of the Asian Miracle economies has been solely attributed to its inward looking trade regime. However, if this was indeed the case, one would naturally expect India, with low labor cost advantages, to surge ahead and flood the global markets for labor-intensive mass manufactures after it opened up its trade in 1991. But this never happened. By the time India's policy shift took place, competition in the global mass market in labor-intensive manufactures had intensified and India had already lost out in the race against East and Southeast Asia. It was the conquest of this market that propelled China's boom of the 1990s.[12]

---

[11] One could, of course, argue that the Asian Miracle was not an unmixed blessing. Many of these countries following an outward oriented policy got severely hit by the East Asian Currency Crisis of 1997 and suffered a major setback in their growth process (with the exception of China), whereas India remained by and large insulated from such external shocks.

[12] Guha and Ray (2004).

The Asian Miracle was indeed a lost opportunity for India! But this did not prevent India from charting out its own trajectory of emergence in the world economy that transgressed simple labor cost advantage. In the following section, we explore how India could capitalize on these new vistas and opportunities to emerge as a major player in the world economy.

4 The Story of India's Emergence Post-1991

Before getting down to the nitty-gritty of India's economic emergence, we examine the trajectories of GDP and openness for India over the entire period of 1960–2013. Estimating an exponential growth function, we find that India's GDP grew at an average rate of 4.9% during the entire period. Using the methodology proposed by Bai and Perron (1998, 2003) for estimating multiple structural breaks in linear models, we find that there are two structural breaks in India's GDP path — the first one in 1989 and the second one in 2000.[13] In other words, it was from the late 1980s that India could eventually escape the "Hindu" equilibrium stagnation. While the average growth rate in the period 1961–1988 was only 3.7%, it shot up to 6.4% during 1989–2013. In fact, the period 2000–2013 experienced an average growth rate of 7.2% — a growth rate almost similar to those of the Asian Cubs in their heydays.

Alongside this growth trajectory, if we analyze the composition of India's GDP (agriculture, manufacturing and services) in Figure 2, we fail to observe the

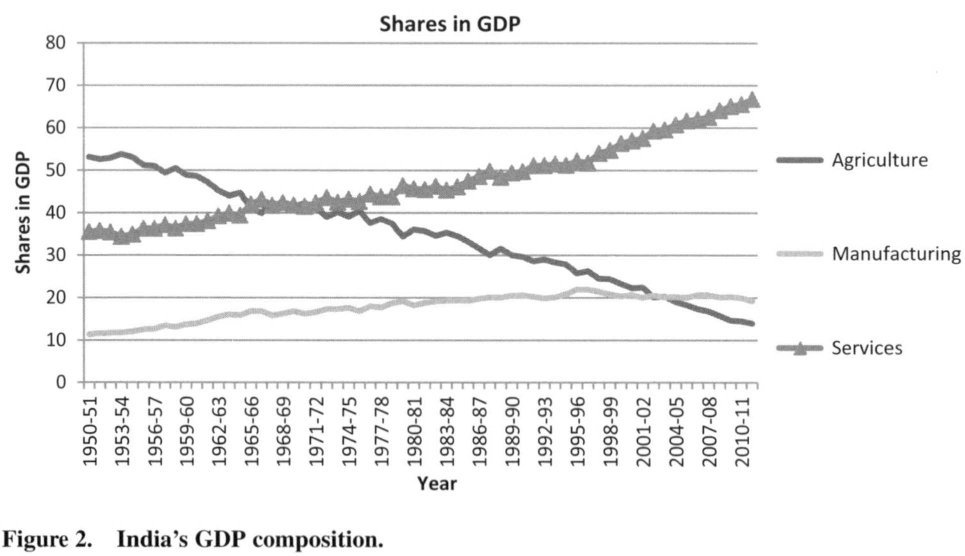

Figure 2. India's GDP composition.

Source: Authors' calculations based on data from Reserve Bank of India.

[13] See Table A1 in the appendix.

associated structural transformation in the framework of the conventional paradigm of phases of development a la Chenery and Syrquin (1975). The Indian model seems to have skipped the middle phase of an expanding manufacturing sector as the share of manufacturing remained low and almost stagnant throughout India's development transition. From an agriculture dominated economy to begin with, India straightaway jumped to an economic structure, with a transition period of two decades or so, where services assumed the lead role right from the mid-1970s. Its share in GDP rose to above 50% in the 1990s. Presently, services account for a whopping 67% of India's GDP.

It was from the mid-1980s that India started experimenting with policy reforms and trade liberalization during its brief period of policy ambivalence (1985–1990) as described earlier. However, in the trajectory of India's openness as reflected in its trade/GDP ratio, we identified endogenous structural breaks in 1992 and 2003 using the same Bai–Perron methodology. In fact, the real shift in India's path of openness can be traced back to India's opening up in 1991 when India's trade/GDP ratio jumped from 0.14 in 1991 to 0.23 in 1995. Figure 3 clearly demonstrates that India openness index started moving steadily upwards only from the early 1990s.

Therefore, in India's case, contrary to the Asian Miracle experiences, improvement in growth seems to precede the turnaround in openness. Does this really mean India's economic transformation had little to do its integration with the world economy resulting from its comprehensive policy reform initiated in 1991? This may be a hasty conclusion. India posted average growth rates of 6.1% during the period 1992–2000 and 7.4% during 2003–2013 as compared to 4.1% during 1989–1991. Hence, for India, the two trajectories of growth and openness exhibited similar patterns and went hand-in-hand to mark the beginning of India's

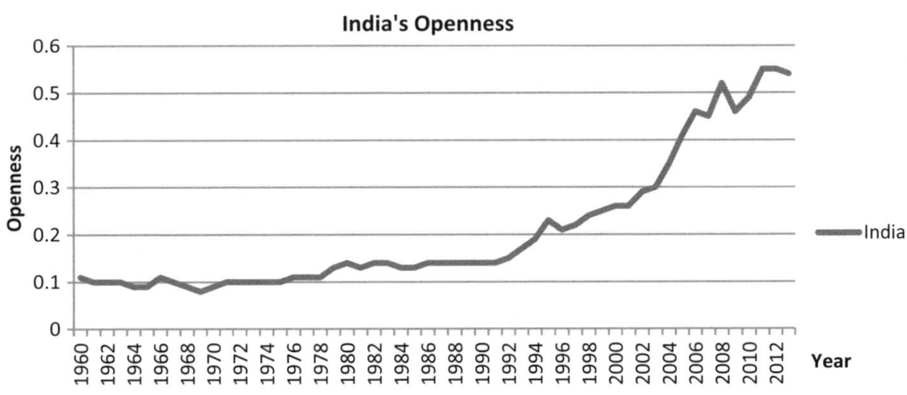

Figure 3. India's openness.

Source: Authors' calculations based on data from World Development Indicators.

economic emergence in the beginning of this new millennium. Like the Asian Miracle economies, trade and openness therefore proved to be the cornerstone of India's economic emergence. However, unlike the Asian Miracle, export of labor-intensive mass manufactures was not the driver of growth in this case.

4.1 Evolving trade structure

To unfold the story of India's economic emergence, we now examine India's trade structure, as it evolved over the past 50 years.

India's trade structure reflects highly diversified export (and import) bundles, consisting of 160–180 items (at the SITC three digit level of disaggregation) during the entire period of 1962–2013. However, over these 52 years, one can identify a clear shift in India's export pattern. Initially, India's export basket was dominated by low value added primary goods and natural resources like tea, coffee, spices, cotton, leather, hides and skins, tobacco, iron-ore and concentrates, crude vegetable materials, other crude minerals, woven textile fabrics, etc. However, new items began to emerge in India's export basket from the 1980s and the 1990s, leading to a shift towards high value added and skill intensive manufactures like petroleum products, medicinal and pharmaceutical products, organic chemicals, road motor vehicles, etc. In order to capture this structural change in India's export pattern in a quick and simple manner, we focused on those export items whose share in India's total exports exceeds 1% in any particular year and clubbed them in five categories as presented in Table 2.

The two major items that dominated India's exports during the 1960s and 1970s are tea and mate and woven textile fabrics. The former contributed to more than 10% of total exports (as high as 18.7% in 1962) but eventually disappeared from the list, in spite of its natural comparative advantage coupled with Geographical Indication in Darjeeling Tea. Woven textile fabrics contributed more than 13% of India's total export on an average till mid-1970s, but subsequently the share has been consistently declining falling below 1% since 2005. Apart from these, other traditional items that had moderate shares in total exports in the initial decades, like coffee, spices, fruits, tobacco, crude vegetable materials, leather, cotton fabrics, iron ore, other crude minerals, floor coverings, made-up articles, etc., have either disappeared or are almost on the verge of disappearing from the export basket.

Fish, rice and feed stuff for animals are the only traditional items which still contribute to around 1.5–2.5% of the total exports throughout the period. Cotton is another item that needs to be highlighted. Its share has never been more than 2% and it has been disappearing from the list periodically. However, it may be of interest to note that its share is displaying a rising trend from 2001 and has

Table 2. Changing pattern of India's exports.

1 Items that no longer feature in the 1% list	2 Items that remain in the list but with a declining share	3 Items that remain in the list with a low but steady share	4 Items that remain in the list with rising share	5 Items that are new
Fruits (051)	Iron Ore (281)	Fish (031)	Petroleum Products (332)	Organic Chemicals (512)[#]
Spices (075)	Textile Fabric Woven (653)	Rice (042)	Med & Pharma (541)[##]	Plastic Materials (581)[*]
Coffee (071)	Made-up Articles (656)	Feed Stuff for Animals (081)	Textile Yarn and Threads (651)	Chemical Materials (599)[**]
Tea and Mate (074)	Clothing ex fur (841)		Pearls etc. (667)	Universals (674)
Tobacco (121)			Machinery Non-electrical (719)	Copper (682)
Crude Vegetable Materials (292)			Electric Power and Switch (722)	Telecom Equipments (724)
Leather (611)			Road Motor Vehicles (732)	Aircraft (734)
Leather Manufactured (612)			Jewellery (897)	Ships and Boats (735)
Cotton Fabrics (652)				
Floor Coverings (657)				
Work of Art (896)				

*Plastic Materials (581) was there throughout, but its contribution was insignificant before 1993.
**Chemical Materials (599) was there throughout, but its contribution was insignificant before 1991.
#Organic Chemicals (512) was there throughout, but its contribution was insignificant before 1987.
##Med & Pharma (541) was there throughout, but its contribution was insignificant before 1977.

reentered the list (of those items constituting of more than 1% of total exports) from 2010. The only item that not only retained but also improved its position in this low value-added category is textile yarn and threads. The share of textile yarn and threads grew at a rate of 1.4% on an average over the 52-year period.

The shift in India's export pattern becomes evident when we focus on the last two columns of Table 2. Presently, India's export basket is dominated by petroleum products which contribute to more than 15% of total exports on an average over the last 10 years (with an export share as high as 20.2% in 2013).[14] The other prominent item in India's exports is pearls and precious and semi-precious stones. This item has been contributing to 12.5% on an average since late 1970s.

Items like organic chemicals, plastic materials, chemical materials and universals, plates and sheets of iron have made their entry into this group of prominent contributors since late 1980s. In particular, the share of organic chemicals in India's total export has been 3.5% on an average since the mid-1990s. Medicinal and pharmaceutical products emerged as a prominent item in the late 1970s and its share has been consistently rising since then reaching 4% at present.

India has been exporting non-electric machinery, electric power machinery and switch and road motor vehicles right from the beginning. However, the shares of these three items have been increasing consistently. In particular, road motor vehicles have registered an average growth rate of 5.3% over this period of 52 years and its present share is about 4% of total exports.

Table 2 also captures India's evolving comparative advantage in technology intensive items like telecom equipment, aircrafts and ships and boats. The shares of these items are increasing consistently since their entry in India's export basket from the mid-1990s, although the shares are still rather low (currently at just above 1%).

A couple of other items require special mention at this point. Jewellery became a prominent export item since early 1990s. The export share of this item has increased at an average rate of 8.2% and it has contributed to 4.6% of the total exports on an average over the last 10 years making it a major export item at present. Clothing materials became a prominent export item in the late 1960s and then turned out to be a major one in the following years. Particularly during the period 1985–2003, clothing material contributed to a whopping 13% of total exports on an average. Subsequently, however, the share started declining rapidly reaching nearly 5% at present.

Works of art entered the export basket as a prominent item in the early 1970s. It remained so till 1986 after which it abruptly vanished from India's exports.

[14] It may be pertinent to note that crude and partly refined petroleum has been India's major import item accounting for 35% of total imports at present. This not only serves India's energy requirements but also acts as an intermediate input into India's major export item, petroleum products.

Copper presents an interesting story of reversal of trade pattern for India. India used to import Copper till 1997 but has started exporting it from 2005.

Finally, we would like to note that there are several items like organic chemicals, plastic materials, non-electrical machinery, electric power machinery and switch, telecom equipments and ships and boats that are prominently featuring in both the export and import baskets of India in recent years, perhaps reflecting intra-industry trade, although at the three digit level of disaggregation one cannot conclusively arrive at this conclusion.[15]

By and large, the metamorphosis of India's manufactured exports basket is evident from Table 2. Standard labor-intensive and resource based manufactures, some of which featured in India's export basket in the initial periods, have been losing out in recent years, while high-end knowledge and skill intensive items are emerging as the new flag bearers of India's emergence in the world economy. One must, however, note that India is yet to become a major player in global merchandise exports with its share in total world merchandise exports remaining as low as 1.66% in 2014 (WTO, 2014). It is in the export of commercial services that India has made some kind of a mark, contributing to 3.25% of global exports. The appearance and subsequent domination of services exports, therefore, must be highlighted as a key feature of India's evolving trade structure.

As we have already noted above, service sector has been the largest and fastest growing sector in the Indian economy, contributing to 67% of its total GDP. Naturally, this lead sector is also emerging as the driver of its integration with the world economy through exports. Unfortunately, data on service trade for India are not available too far back in time.

Figure 4 shows how services exports from India grew exponentially from 1991 at a rate of 18% per annum.[16] Figure 5 depicts that in 1991 exports of services already started accounting for a significant share (one fifth) of India's total exports. This share rose to one-third in recent years. According to the World Development Indicators, services exports accounts for a significant 7.8% of India's GDP. Looking at the composition of services exports from India (Figure 6), IT and ITES have the lion's share (70%). Travel, transport, financial and insurance services together account for another 25%.

4.2 Drivers of India's take-off

Unlike the rest of labor surplus Asia, India could not capitalize on its low labor cost advantage to embark on a growth path driven by labor-intensive mass

[15] Agarwal and Ghosh (2016) have analyzed India's intra-industry trade in greater detail.

[16] RBI reports services exports data only from 1991.

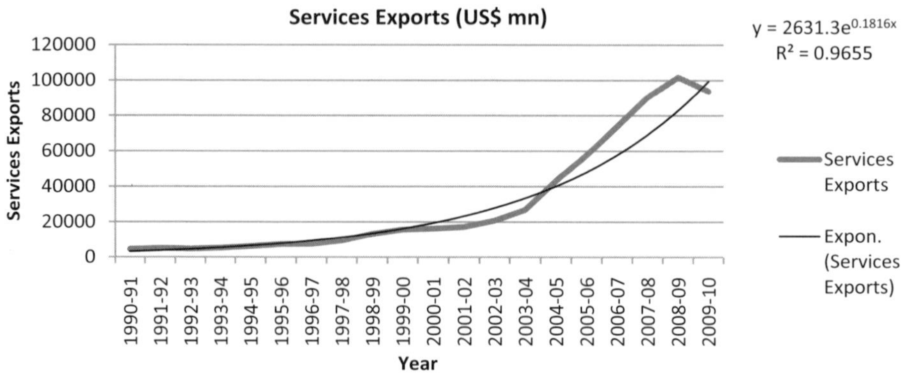

Figure 4. Services exports from India.

Source: Reserve Bank of India.

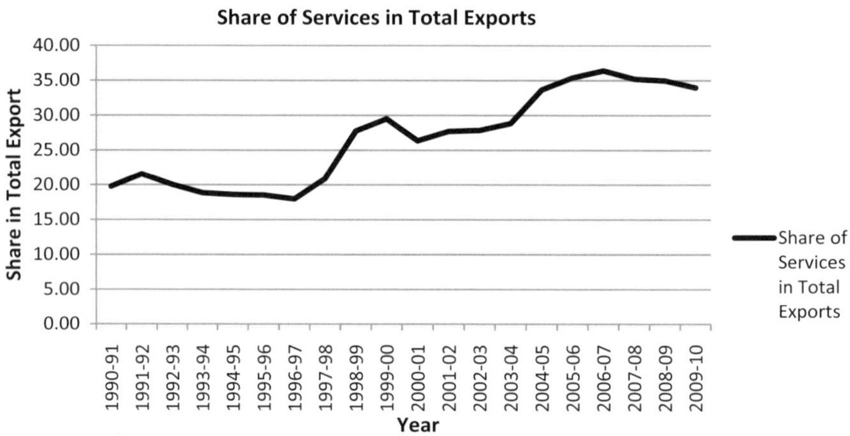

Figure 5. Share of services in India's total exports.

Source: Reserve Bank of India.

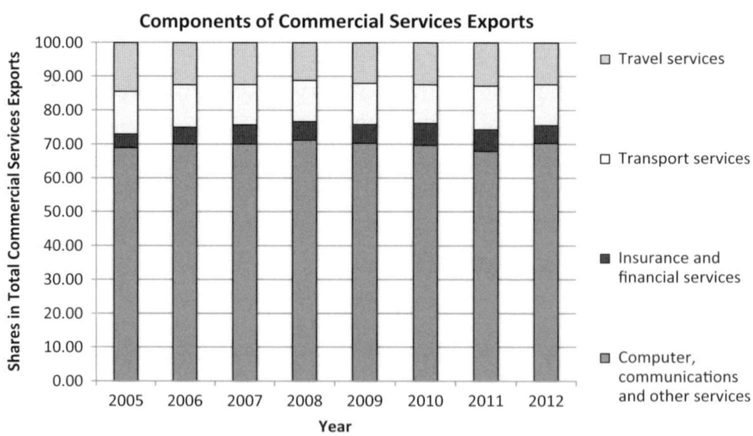

Figure 6. Compositions of services exports from India.

Source: World Bank.

manufactures. Fortunately, the advantage conferred by low labor costs is pervasive, transgressing the narrow realm of traditional labor-intensive mass manufactures into new industries and services like software, information technology (IT) and IT enabled services (ITES), biotechnology (BT) and pharmaceuticals, where knowledge inputs prove to be the key source of comparative advantage.

India's opening up in the 1990s coincided with a new era where these knowledge-intensive sectors began to dominate the world economy. India's could successfully exploit these opportunities on account of several distinct advantages.

First, India's post-colonial policy emphasis on expanding public funded higher education resulted in creation of an extensive network of publicly funded colleges and universities throughout the length and breadth of the country. Such indiscriminate expansion of higher education naturally resulted in enormous quality variations and heterogeneity in the levels of higher education in the country. Nevertheless, through this India could create a large base of university-educated middle class, translating its labor abundance into skill abundance that eventually proved to be a key pillar of India's economic emergence where skill intensive manufacturing and services played a dominant role.

Secondly, India's commitment to creating a foundation in science and technology also proved crucially important. India has pursued a well-articulated technology policy providing the broad guidelines for technological development within the country. Thanks to this policy effort, India has been able to create and nurture technological capability, broadly defined as the capacity to select, absorb, assimilate, adapt, imitate and perhaps improve upon given (imported) technologies.[17] Although India is yet to arrive at the frontiers of global technological advances, it has been able to create a niche for itself in inventing around process technologies to achieve a distinct competitive edge in some of the high tech and knowledge intensive areas, like IT and pharmaceuticals.

Finally, as noted by Guha and Ray (2004), apart from skills, knowledge, and S&T capacity, a key source of India's strength has been its "knowledge of English language which we had inherited from our colonial past." This has proved to be "an asset of incalculable value in an age of instant world-wide communication, basically in the English language." Thus, while China continues to dominate the vast world market for traditional labor-intensive manufactures, new vistas have opened up for India, where knowledge resources, as opposed to simple labor abundance, prove to the key source of comparative advantage.

Given that India's emergence has centered on a limited number of specific sectors, one obvious question that arises is whether (and to what extent) it has been ignited by sector specific policies. We find quite a divergence among sectors in

---

[17] Lall (1987).

this regard. According to Ray (2015), India's success in IT and ITES has largely been self driven that took off on its own, in response to the new global economic opportunities created by an IT driven global production structure in a globalized world. Of course, India's advantages in terms of skilled (university educated) manpower and English language naturally led to the flourishing of IT and ITES in India, even without any specific government policies towards IT in the initial phases. It is interesting to note that the National Policy on IT was announced only in 2011, long after the successful emergence of India's IT sector.

In case of the pharmaceutical sector, however, the story is somewhat different. Here, India could create a unique policy space for itself that fostered technological capability in the domestic pharmaceutical industry.[18] The carefully designed targeted policy framework adopted in the 1970s helped this industry to become self-reliant, initially only in manufacturing capabilities but eventually also in technological capability that helped this sector (the generic segment) compete successfully in global markets. From the 1970s, the pharmaceutical industry in India embarked on a new trajectory of technological learning in terms of process development through reverse engineering and reached new heights of process capabilities to "knock off" any new drug with a non-infringing process and market them at low prices. This phenomenon has often been referred to as the *process revolution* in the Indian pharmaceutical sector and India is now poised to make a major dent in the global generics market.[19]

5 Concluding Remarks

India's emergence in the world economy, as it has unfolded in the last couple of decades, is based on a foundation of knowledge resources. But India is yet to make a successful transition towards a fully knowledge-driven economy — creating, disseminating and using knowledge to enhance growth and development.[20]

Indeed, these assets and advantages (namely, educated workforce, technological capability and knowledge of English) that have fueled India's economic emergence are by no means permanent in character. With some effort, they can be replicated in other countries. As a matter of fact, some of the other emerging economies, like China and Brazil are catching up with India very fast on these assets. More seriously, these assets created by our colonial history and post-colonial policy effort, can be damaged or destroyed by insipid policy.

[18] Ray and Bhaduri (2014).

[19] Ray (2008).

[20] World Bank (2005).

Another key point to reflect on is the tragic neglect of *low-end* labor-intensive mass manufactures in India's economic progress that has been principally driven by rapid expansion of *high-end* knowledge intensive sectors. This raises two imminent questions: (1) *how high is India's high end?* and (2) is this a sustainable model in a democratic structure?

On the first issue, ironically India's high end is not quite so "high". Ray (2009) shows that although India has demonstrated significant competitive strength in routine, though skill intensive, tasks like coding (in software) or process development (in pharmaceuticals), it has been lacking creativity and innovativeness to reach the global frontiers of technological advancement. India is yet to make a mark in cutting edge global technologies. For instance, it is noteworthy that despite India's global presence in the generic market and its declared effort to reach newer heights in pharmaceutical R&D, we are yet to see a *new chemical entity* (drug) from India hitting the global market. Effectively then, India cannot compete with advanced nations in the truly high tech segments in terms of creating new technologies and ideas. India has created a niche for itself in the so-called lower-end activities of the high end sectors (like customized IT and ITES and generic medicines) that do require skills and technological capability that India has acquired, but it is yet to reach the levels of the league of technologically advanced nations. As we have shown above, in the framework of the conventional structural transformation paradigm, the Indian model of development seems to have skipped the middle phase of an expanding manufacturing sector. In the process, however, India completely lost out to other emerging economies (mainly China) in the low-end segment of mass manufactures. At the same time, it has not been able to compete with the technologically advanced nations in the truly high tech segment.

It is in the *lower end activities* of the *high-end sectors* that India has carved out a niche for itself in the global economy. India's success in this niche segment has created unprecedented opportunities for a limited section (creamy layer) of the society, mainly for the upwardly mobile English speaking, university educated urban elite — what has in popular parlance come to be known as the *Great Indian Middle Class*. However, this can never be a truly inclusive strategy of economic development as it relies on an educated middle class as the key driver of growth in the midst of vast illiteracy and poverty. This creates extreme inequality and becomes a prescription for political volatility. This is surely not a sustainable development model, especially in a democracy.

To employ the billion strong population productively, it is essential to tap the potentials for labor-intensive "low end" sectors (mass products) that create job opportunities for the masses. This may require a proactive policy framework that resolves infrastructure deficits and improves labor productivity through investments in health, education and technology. Ironically, the neo-liberal world order often dictates the retreat of the state from active engagement in many of these activities. Social sector allocations, in particular education, health and poverty reduction, often become the soft targets for public expenditure compression for fiscal discipline. This not only directly affects the poor in a material sense but also raises questions about the political viability and sustainability of India's economic progress.

Acknowledgment

We are grateful to participants at the seminars at Centre for Development Studies, Trivandrum, India and at Sheffield Political Economy Research Institute, UK for comments. We thank Dr. M Parameswaran and Dr. S Kundu for valuable inputs into an earlier working paper version. The usual disclaimer applies.

References

Agarwal, M. and S. Ghosh (2016), The Effect of RTAs on India's Trade, Forthcoming in M. Agarwal and J. Whalley (Eds): *China and India: The International Context and Economic Growth, Manufacturing Performance and Rural Development*, Singapore: World Scientific Press.

Akamatsu, K. (1962), A Historical Pattern of Economic Growth in Developing Countries, *The Developing Economies*, Vol. 1, No. S1, 3–25.

Bai, J. and P. Perron (1998), Estimating and Testing Linear Models with Multiple Structural Changes, *Econometrica*, 66, 47–78.

Bai, J. and P. Perron (2003), Computation and Analysis of Multiple Structural Change Models, *Journal of Applied Econometrics*, Vol. 18, 1–22.

Bhagwati, J. and P. Desai (1970), *India: Planning for Industrialization*. Oxford University Press, London.

Bhagwati, J. and T.N. Srinivasan (1975), *Foreign Trade Regimes and Economic Development: India*. National Bureau of Economic Research, New York.

Chenery, H. and M. Syrquin (1975), *Patterns of Development 1950–70*. Oxford University Press, Oxford.

Guha, A. and A.S. Ray (2004), India and Asia in the World Economy: The Role of Human Capital and Technology, *International Studies*, 41, 299–311.

Lal, D. (1988), *Hindu Equilibrium: Cultural Stability and Economic Stagnation, India, 1500 BC–AD 1980*. Clarendon Press, Oxford.

Lall, S. (1987), *Learning to Industrialize: The Acquisition of Technological Capability by India*. Macmillan, London.

Prebisch, R. (1950), *The Economic Development of Latin America and its Principal Problems*. United Nations, New York.

Ray, A.S. (2006), India's Economic Reforms: Opportunities, Challenges and Political Economy Perspectives, in L. White (ed): *Is there an Economic Orthodoxy? Growth and Reform in Africa, Asia and Latin America*, Johannesburg: South African Institute of International Affairs.

Ray, A.S. (2008), Learning and Innovation in the Indian Pharmaceutical Industry: The Role of IPR and other Policy Interventions. RECIIS Electronic *Journal of Communication, Information and Innovation in Health* (Brazil), 2, 71–77.

Ray, A.S. (2009), Emerging through Technological Capability: An Overview of India's Technological Trajectory, in M. Agarwal (ed): *India's Economic Future: Education, Technology, Energy and Environment*, New Delhi: Social Science Press.

Ray, A.S. (2015), The Enigma of the 'Indian Model' of Development, *Discussion Papers in Economics (No. 15-01), Centre for International Trade and Development, JNU, New Delhi.*

Ray, A.S. and S. Bhaduri (2014), Competing through Technological Capability; the Indian Pharmaceutical Industry in a Changing Global Landscape, in D. Drache and L. Jacobs (eds): *Linking Global Trade and Human Rights: New Policy Spaces in Hard Economic Times*, New York: Cambridge University Press.

Stolper, W.F. and P.A. Samuelson (1941), Protection and Real Wages, *The Review of Economic Studies*, 9, 58–73.

Wolf, M. (1982), *India's Exports*. Oxford University Press, New York.

World Bank (2005), India and the Knowledge Economy: Leveraging Strengths and Opportunities. Report No. 31267-IN, World Bank Finance and Private Sector Development Unit South Asia Region and the World Bank Institute.

World Trade Organization (2014), Available from: http://stat.wto.org/CountryProfile/WSDBCountryPFView.aspx?Country=IN&Language=F. Last accessed on 13th February, 2015.

Appendix

Table A1. Structural breaks.

Series	GDP	Openness
UDmax	23.4054	625.4882
(critical value)	(14.8500)	(12.5900)
WDmax	26.6551	625.4882
(critical value)	(16.0700)	(13.6600)
supF(l+1|l)	16.8150	39.1761
(critical values for l =1, 2)	(14.60, 16.53)	(12.25, 13.83)
Break Dates	1989, 2000	1992, 2003

Critical values given are at 5% level of significance.

Chapter 6

Structural Change in the Indian Economy

Manmohan Agarwal* and Sunandan Ghosh†

Centre for Development Studies,
Thiruvananthapuram, Kerala, India
**manmohan@cds.ac.in*
†sunandan@cds.edu

Abstract: We analyze the evolution of the Indian economy over the past six decades, particularly identifying structural breaks. We find that usually there has been a gradual change in the indicators of the economy. The growth rate of per capita GDP after falling in the decade mid 1960s to mid 1970s has been accelerating gradually since then. Since 1991 exports have played an important role in this growth. The various crises and the measures taken to tackle them have not disturbed this evolution, except the policy changes ushered from 1991. The structural breaks we identify do not usually coincide with these crises. The structural breaks suggest certain patterns which are investigated using the Vector Autoregression (VAR) estimations.

1 Introduction

Indian policy makers embarked on their journey to raise living standards and reduce poverty and inequality soon after independence, and they employed the mechanism of Five Year Plans to bring coherence to their attempts. The process of designing explicit five year plans went on for nearly 60 years. But the process of growth and planning did not proceed smoothly. It was interrupted by a number of crises and sometimes these crises led to the suspension of plan implementation for a few years while new policies were adopted to tackle the problems identified or caused by the crisis. This paper seeks to analyze whether the different crises were caused by exogenous factors or because of faulty domestic policies. Exogenous factors themselves could be of two kinds one those emanating from the world economy and those emanating in the domestic sphere. We next analyze what the effect of these crises reveal about the interrelationships between different aspects of the Indian economy.

Our analysis proceeds in Section 2 by first noting the various crises that have struck the Indian economy over the past six decades and their effects on growth and investment. We find that the effect on GDP is ephemeral while that on investment is longer lasting. We then examine in Section 3 the evolution of the Indian economy over the past six decades. We do this planwise as the plans governed the government's policies. We find that GDP growth gradually accelerates over the plan periods except for a slowdown in the 1960s and early 1970s. The gradual growth acceleration is accompanied by increases in investment and saving rates. A significant change over this period is that the share of exports of goods and services (XGS) in GDP declines till the Fourth Plan, 1969–1973, and shows rapid growth after the Eighth Plan, 1992–1996, reflecting the significant change in India's trade and industrial policies initiated in 1991. While the improved export performance can be ascribed to the policy changes initiated in 1991, the gradual acceleration in growth of GDP cannot be similarly ascribed to any particular policy changes. In Section 4, we more formally identify structural breaks in the Indian economy using the Bai–Perron technique. In Section 5, we compare the impacts of the manufacturing and service sectors on the Indian economy. The findings suggest certain patterns which are further analyzed in Section 6 to reveal interrelationships in the Indian economy using Vector Autoregression (VAR) estimations. Section 7 concludes the paper.

2 Crises in the Indian Economy

The Indian economy has experienced a number of crises in the past six decades as shown in Table 1. There was a balance of payments (BOP) crisis in 1957–1958 as the policy makers were implementing the Second Five Year Plan, 1956–1960, that called for much higher rates of investment and needed much greater imports of capital goods. Another crisis struck in the mid 1960s because of a severe drought that resulted in very poor harvests in 1965–1966 and 1966–1967. This necessitated large imports of food from the US under the food aid programme and resulted in very high rates of inflation. The drought was followed by cutoff of aid from the US and the World Bank forcing adoption of severe adjustment

Table 1. Crises for the Indian economy.

Date of crisis	Cause				What
	Endogenous	Exogenous	Domestic	External	
1957–1958	✓		✓		Excess Investment
1965 on		✓	✓	✓	Drought and Aid Cut
1973–1974		✓		✓	Oil Price Rise
1979–1980		✓		✓	Oil Price (Iran–Iraq War)
1990–1991	✓	✓	✓	✓	Oil Price (Gulf War)

policies. Subsequently, a BOP crisis was precipitated by the large increases in prices of oil and many commodities in 1973–1974. The price increases followed on the heels of the large influx of refugees from the present Bangladesh and the subsequent war that resulted in the independence of Bangladesh. The effects of the oil price rise in 1979 following the revolution in Iran and the subsequent Iran–Iraq war generated another BOP crisis. The invasion of Kuwait by Iraq and the First Gulf War resulted in a severe BOP crisis as the larger trade deficit because of higher oil prices was aggravated by the fall in remittances as many Indian workers in the Gulf returned home.

Though the immediate factor behind the 1991 crisis was the Gulf war with the rise in oil prices and fall in remittances because of return of workers from the Middle East, the domestic situation was fragile both economically, high short-term borrowings, and politically, weak governments unable to take decisions.

2.1 Impact of crises on GDP and investment

The effect of the crises on growth of GDP was usually short lived. In 1957–1958, GDP declined by 1.2%, but rebounded in the next year as it grew by 7.6%. Similarly, the GDP after growing at merely 1.2% in 1974–1975 grew by 9% the following year and after falling by 5.2% in 1979–1980 grew by 7.2% in 1980–1981. However, while GDP rebounded rapidly, that was not the case with investment.

The drop in the investment ratio after a crisis recovered only after a considerable lag. For instance, after gross fixed capital formation (GFCF) as a percentage of gross domestic product (GDP) reached a peak of 15.9% in 1957–1958, it fell after the 1957–1958 BOP crisis and did not recover to the earlier ratio till 1963–1964 (RBI 2012). The fall in the GFCF ratio after the 1965–1967 crisis was particularly severe — from 20.4%–16.7% — and it did not recover till 1977–1978.

2.2 Response to the crises

The government responded by a mixture of financing and adjustment. For instance, following the 1957–1958 crisis, the Indian Government approached the World Bank for financial assistance. The World Bank responded favorably and organized the Aid India Consortium. Under the leadership of the US, the Aid India Consortium provided considerable help during the Second and Third Five Year Plans.[1] This aid financed a quarter to a third of public investment in these plans. Following the 1973–1974 crisis, India borrowed from the trust fund that had been set up at the International Monetary Fund (IMF) to provide BOP financing for countries severely affected by the oil price rise. India also started tapping non-resident Indians. It provided various incentives, including a higher interest rate than they could earn in the country of residence. In the crisis following the oil price rises of 1979 and the Gulf War, India borrowed from the IMF. The only crisis when India did not tap external financing was the 1965–1967 crisis. This crisis was partly caused by the cutoff of aid and at that time the availability of private financing was very limited.

At the time of the first crisis in 1957–1958, there was a vigorous debate about the size of the Plan. Many analysts and policy makers believed that the Plan was too large and beyond the capacity of the economy. As a result of this debate, the Plan was divided into two, a core plan and the rest which would be implemented if resources permitted. Subsequent crises also saw similar adjustments on the expenditure side. For instance, the fiscal and monetary policy became so contractionary after the 1973–1974 oil price rise that wholesale prices which had risen by 25.2% in 1974–1975 fell by 1.1% in 1975–1976. The reduction in domestic absorption also resulted in the country running current account surpluses for a few years in the mid-1970s. As we saw above investments declined following a crisis and recovered only after a time lag. Also in subsequent crisis, a somewhat greater emphasis was given to raising the rate of savings as we shall see below.

3 Progress of the Indian Economy

We first look at the evolution of the Indian economy to identify major interruptions to the growth process. Since the intended overall macro and development policy changes were made in the plans we analyze the performance planwise.

The growth rate of the economy plummeted to a relatively low level for almost a decade from the mid-1960s to the mid-1970s as the economy struggled to cope

[1] The US promised to match aid given by the other countries of the Consortium.

with the cutback in aid during 1966–1968.[2] The savings rate had to be raised before investment and growth could recover. In the short run, the higher rate of savings had a deflationary effect on the economy.[3] Furthermore, as noted below, lack of demand for capital goods created by the aid cutback created substantial excess capacity. Since this was a period when the world economy was growing rapidly as were also other developing countries, India missed the opportunity to take advantage of favorable international conditions.[4]

Since the mid-1970s there has been a steady acceleration of the growth rate, except for a slight deceleration during the Ninth Plan, which is difficult to prima facie ascribe to any policy measures (Table 2). The effects of poor harvests in the mid-1960s can be seen in the negative average rate of growth of value added in agriculture during the Third Plan.

The effect of the subsequent cutback in aid can be seen in the sharp drop in the growth of the manufacturing sector during the periods of the annual plans and the Fourth Plan. The cutback in aid, the investment needs accompanying the green

Table 2. Growth rate of GDP and major sectors in India.

	GDP	Agriculture	Manufacturing	Services
First Plan (1951–1955)	3.9	3.2	5.8	5.2
Second Plan (1956–1960)	4.1	3.3	6.3	4.9
Third Plan (1961–1965)	3.5	–0.3	6.6	5.4
Annual Plans (1966–1968)	3.7	4.4	2.2	4.3
Fourth Plan (1969–1973)	3.2	2.8	4.9	3.2
Fifth Plan (74–78)	5.0	3.6	6.5	5.4
Sixth Plan (80–84)	5.5	6.3	5.2	5.5
Seventh Plan (85–89)	5.7	3.1	6.3	7.2
Eighth Plan (92–96)	6.5	4.9	9.5	6.8
Ninth Plan (97–01)	5.7	2.5	3.6	8.0
Tenth Plan (02–06)	7.6	2.5	9.0	9.2
Eleventh Plan (07–11)	8.0	3.8	7.7	9.9
2012–2013	4.5	1.7	1.1	6.8

Source: Reserve Bank of India (2012).

[2] The slowdown in the economy was similar to that experienced by many Latin American countries in the 1980s as they struggled to cope with their debt crisis.

[3] There was considerable analysis at that time about the demand constraint to investment and growth (Chakravarty, 1979).

[4] The period till 1973 is called the "Golden Age of Capitalism" (Marglin and Schor, 1990). The growth rates of the different regions are analyzed in Agarwal (2008).

revolution in agriculture and priority accorded petroleum exploration and refining following the oil price rises in 1973–1974 forced a changed allocation of the government's investments and a smaller allocation for manufacturing (Lele and Agarwal, 1991). The poor performance of the manufacturing sector was because the Government's industrialization strategy stressed investment in heavy industries in the public sector. The output of these basic industries would be used for further investment in heavy industries in the public sector. Such a strategy was growth maximizing and a higher rate of growth would lead to a greater reduction of poverty in the long run (Mahalanobis 1953 and 1955; Bhagwati and Chakravarty, 1969; Chakravarty, 1969). A large part of this public sector investment was financed by aid and the aid cutoff had very serious consequences. Without the aid, investment fell. So there was no demand for the output of the public sector units that had been set up resulting in considerable excess capacity and very high capital output ratios. Also, as noted above, other sectors claimed a larger share of the government's investment budget.

It has been contended that the rapid growth of the economy since the 1990s has been based on service growth rather than growth of manufacturing.[5] This is not borne out by the data. The average growth rate for services during the period 1980–1996 is 6.4%, not statistically different from the 6.3% growth rate for manufacturing during that period. Again, the average growth rates for the two sectors are not statistically significantly different for the period 2002–2010. The significant difference is during the Ninth Plan (Table 2). The large reduction in tariff rates for imports of manufactures could have resulted in shrinking of the sector as happened in many Latin American countries where the share of manufactures in GDP has fallen considerably since the debt crisis (Agarwal and Chakravarty, 2016).

The behavior of investment mirrors that of the growth rate of the economy. The investment to GDP ratio was stable during the Third to Fourth Plan periods and then there was a sharp increase from the Fifth Plan to the Sixth Plan with further increase in the Tenth and Eleventh Plans (Table 3). The increase in the investment ratio is usually preceded by increase in the share of gross domestic savings in GDP so that the financing of the higher investment would not depend on foreign aid (Table 3). We see a very sharp increase in the savings rate after the cutoff in aid in the mid-1960s to the Fifth Plan. The increase in the savings ratio predates the increase in the investment ratio. Again, the savings ratio starts to increase in the Ninth Plan before the investment ratio shot up in the Tenth Plan.

---

[5] For a discussion of this aspect of Indian growth see Kotwal *et al.* (2011).

Table 3. Economic performance some indicators (% of GDP).

Plans	GFCF	Gross domestic savings	Current account balance	XGS
First Plan (1951–1955)	9.5	9.8	0.2	—
Second Plan (1956–1960)	13.0	11.0	–2.8	—
Third Plan (1961–1965)	14.3	12.7	–1.8	3.9
Annual Plans (1966–1968)	14.3	12.7	–0.2	4.0
Fourth Plan (1969–1973)	14.3	14.9	–0.7	3.8
Fifth Plan (74–78)	16.3	18.6	0.5	5.9
Sixth Plan (80–84)	20.5	17.6	–1.5	6.6
Seventh Plan (85–89)	21.4	19.6	–2.2	6.0
Eighth Plan (92–96)	22.4	22.5	–1.2	8.8
Ninth Plan (97–01)	24.3	24.3	–0.6	11.2
Tenth Plan (02–06)	28.1	31.0	0.2	17.9
Eleventh Plan (07–11)	33.7	33.5	–2.6	22.6
2012–2013	33.2	30.1	–4.7	24.4

We now discuss the state of India's external sector by examining both export performance and the balance between exports and imports. It has been contended that India's growth has been driven by domestic demand and not exports unlike China's growth.

The importance of exports both of goods and non-factor services (NFS) declined through the first three plans (Table 4).[6] They then stabilized before experiencing a sharp increase in the Fifth Plan.[7] Exports of goods, NFS and transfers, mainly remittances started growing very rapidly from the Eighth Plan onwards, namely since the liberalization process started. A number of policies were changed following the BOP crisis of 1991 all of which contributed to this rapid expansion of exports. The rupee was devalued and later was made market determined so it tended to devalue and imports were liberalized.

[6] Indian exports at the time of independence consisted mainly of agricultural products such as tea, jute and cotton in all of which India had a large market share. Improved export performance had to wait for development of the manufacturing sector (Government of India, 1952). Actually, the export target for the Third Plan had been achieved by the third year. The droughts of 1965–1967 and the subsequent aid cutback required an entirely different strategy.

[7] This increase reflected the analysis of the effects of a permanent increase in the price of imported oil and the subsequent terms of trade loss (Persson and Svensson, 1985).

Table 4. India's export performance (% of GDP).

Plans	Goods	Non-factor services	Income	Transfers
First Plan (1951–1955)	5.5	1.0	0.2	0.6
Second Plan (1956–1960)	4.1	0.9	0.1	0.6
Third Plan (1961–1965)	3.2	0.7	0.0	0.6
Annual Plans (1966–1968)	3.3	0.7	0.1	0.5
Fourth Plan (1969–1973)	3.2	0.5	0.1	0.9
Fifth Plan (74–78)	4.9	0.9	0.2	1.1
Sixth Plan (80–84)	4.5	1.5	0.3	1.5
Seventh Plan (85–89)	4.6	1.3	0.2	1.1
Eighth Plan (92–96)	8.1	1.9	0.2	2.4
Ninth Plan (97–01)	8.6	3.1	0.5	2.8
Tenth Plan (02–06)	11.8	5.8	0.7	3.3
Eleventh Plan (07–11)	14.7	7.6	0.9	3.7

This helped exports in two ways. One, if fewer import competing goods are produced following the trade liberalization then resources would be freed to move to export production and the devaluation of the exchange rate would provide an incentive for such a shift.[8] Two, better quality imports could be acquired to improve the competitiveness of exports. The import content of Indian exports increased following the liberalization. The elimination of industrial licensing also allowed entry of more firms and some of them would export.[9] So removal of entry restrictions resulted in a large increase in exports.

We now examine whether China's growth was more export driven and India's growth more dependent on domestic demand.

The share of XGS is much higher in China than in India (Figure 1). However, the behavior of the share shows a very striking similarity. This is borne out if we compare the evolution since the respective reforms. So we form an index number of the share with the value of 100 for China's share in 1979, the beginning of

[8] This analysis reflects the absorption approach to the BOP (Johnson, 1962).

[9] For the effect of entry on exports see Agarwal and Barua (2004). They show that if a monopolist in the domestic market is a perfect competitor in the export market and exports say 5% of his output, then entry of a second firm leads to a 14 fold increase in exports. While the extent of the increase depends on the elasticity of domestic demand because that determines the extent of price decline after entry and so the incentive to export, the increase is quite robust to variations in the parameters.

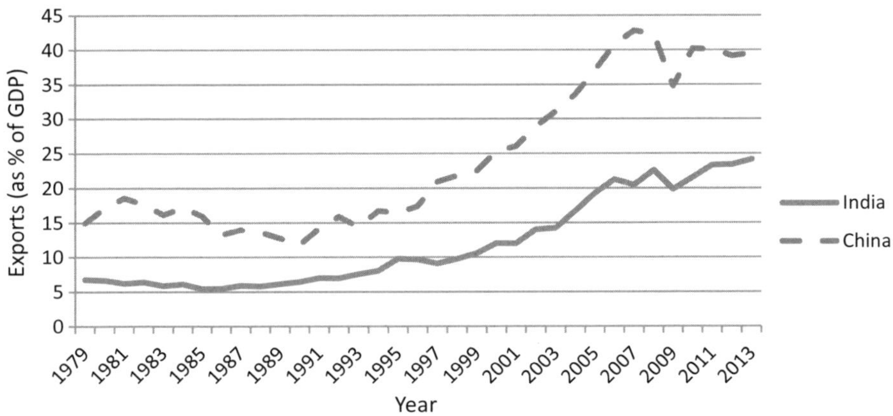

Figure 1. Exports (% of GDP), 1979–2013.

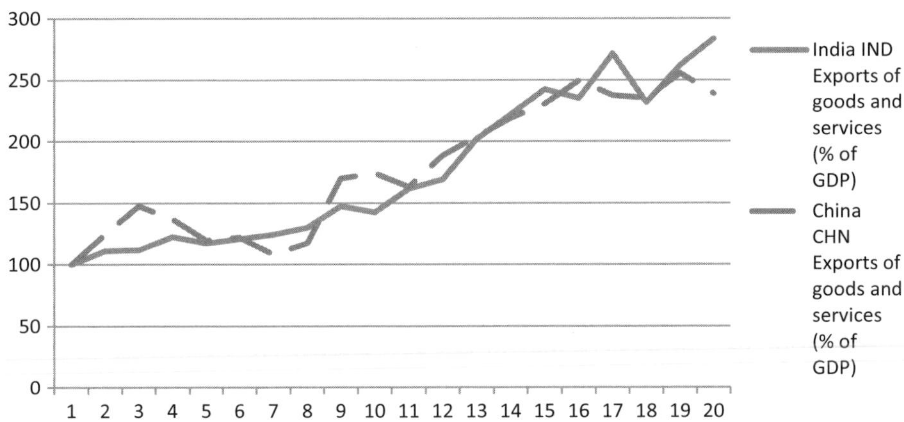

Figure 2. Index of share of goods and services in GDP since the reforms.
(Index = 100 for China's share in 1979 and for India's share in 1992).

China's reform and for India's share in 1992, the beginning of India's reform. So the year 10 represents 10 years after the reform and so corresponds to 1989 for China and 2001 for India.

The increase in share of XGS was 239% for China, but 283% for India and this is not merely because of the spurt in the last three or four years. The shares track well throughout the 20 year period since the respective reforms (Figure 2).[10]

[10] There is considerable similarity between the Chinese and Indian performances when seen from the perspective of change since their respective reforms (Agarwal and Whalley, 2015a).

Table 5. The current account balance and its components (% of GDP).

Plans	Current account	Goods	NFS	Income	Transfers
First Plan (1951–1955)	–0.3	–1.4	0.4	0.0	0.6
Second Plan (1956–1960)	–2.2	–2.8	0.4	–0.2	0.5
Third Plan (1961–1965)	–2.1	–2.5	0.3	–0.5	0.6
Annual Plans (1966–1968)	–1.4	–1.3	0.2	–0.6	0.4
Fourth Plan (1969–1973)	–0.4	–1.0	0.1	–0.5	1.0
Fifth Plan (1974–1978)	0.3	–1.5	0.4	–0.2	1.5
Sixth Plan (1980–1984)	–1.8	–3.7	0.6	–0.2	1.5
Seventh Plan (1985–1989)	–2.5	–3.2	0.3	–0.9	1.1
Eighth Plan (1992–1996)	–1.3	–3.4	0.2	–1.1	3.0
Ninth Plan (1997–2001)	–0.1	–3.1	0.7	–0.9	3.2
Tenth Plan (2002–2006)	–0.4	–6.2	2.9	–0.8	3.7
Eleventh Plan (2007–2011)	–3.9	–10.7	3.8	–1.0	4.0

There is no evidence that India has depended more on domestic demand for growth while China has depended more on exports for growth.

Exports can provide a fillip to the economy because of the backward linkages, though of course in strict national accounting terms it is net exports which contribute to GDP. But export performance has another effect on economic growth. Export performance influences the current account deficit and its sustainability. A large current account deficit can usually not be sustained and it is usually corrected by a period of slower growth. So we now examine the state of India's current account over the years.

The current account has usually been negative except in the Fifth Plan when for a few years in the mid-1970s it was positive and again for some years during the Ninth Plan (Table 5). The 1991 reforms led to an improvement in the current account balance as the deficit fell from 2.5% of GDP in the Seventh Plan to 1.3% in the Eighth Plan and only 0.1% in the Ninth Plan, before ballooning again in the Eleventh Plan.

Within the current account, the balance on goods and on income has been negative. However, that on non-factor services (NFS) and on transfers has been positive (Table 5). A second feature is that the imbalances have been generally growing especially since the Fourth Plan. The reforms initiated in 1991 temporarily halted the trend of increasing deficits in merchandise trade. However, the reforms did not reduce the deficit on merchandise trade to any significant extent as it jumped again almost to 4% in the Eleventh Plan. But there was a surge in exports of NFS and of incoming remittances.

4 Structural Breaks

The above analysis has pointed to significant structural changes in the Indian economy over the past six decades.[11] We now examine more formally whether there were structural breaks in the Indian economy during this period by using Bai and Perron (1998, 2003) method for estimating multiple structural breaks in linear models. We used two sets of data to test for structural breaks. We used data from the World Bank from 1960 to 2013 to test for breaks not only in the series for India but also the series for low income countries (LIC), the group to which India belonged for most of this period and also for the entire world. This was done to isolate factors emanating from the world economy that may account for the structural breaks in the Indian economy. We also used data from the Reserve Bank of India from 1951–1952 to 2012–2013. This longer time series allowed us to see whether there was a structural break in the mid-1960s. Since the data from the World Bank was only from 1960, it would not identify a break in the mid-1960s.

From the World Bank data, we find no breaks in the growth rate for per capita GDP in India (Table 6).[12] For the world, there is only one break in 1972 whereas the LIC experienced two breaks in 1993 and 2002.

In general, while there are breaks in growth rates for the world and for low LIC, there are hardly any for India. The technique compares growth rates before a possible break with the growth rate after the possible break. Only if the two growth rates are significantly different does the technique denote the point as a break point. While the growth rate has fluctuated considerably in India, there is no point at which there is a sharp break in the later growth rate compared to the earlier growth rate. But that does not mean that there is no point of time at which there is

Table 6. Breaks in growth rates.

	India	LIC	World
GDP per capita	None	1993, 2002	1972
Agriculture	None	2003	None
Manufacturing	None	1986, 1991	No Data
Services	2003	1985, 1989	No Data

[11] An earlier analysis had concentrated on the behavior of 12 significant economic indicators and had found improvement in these indicators in the 1990s as compared to the 1980s and in the 2000s as compared to the 1990s (Agarwal *et al.*, 2015).

[12] However, several authors have identified structural break in India's GDP growth rate during mid-1970s or early 1980s [see Agarwal *et al.* (2015) for a detailed discussion]. Using the Bai and Perron (1998, 2003) method, we do find multiple structural breaks in India's GDP or GDP per capita series, however, as already discussed, we find no statistically significant structural break in the GDP growth rate for India over the period 1951–2013.

a sharp interruption in the rate of growth. But what the lack of a structural break implies is that any interruptions in the growth process are temporary. The existence of breaks in the rate of growth of per capita GDP for the world and LICs implies that the rate of growth varied for a substantial period of time.

For the world, there is a break in 1972. During this period, there were increasing global imbalances and rising inflation that culminated in the collapse of the fixed exchange rate regime in 1971. This break in the growth rate of the world per capita GDP is not reflected in either the growth rate in developing countries whether low income or middle income or in India. There are two breaks in the growth rate of per capita GDP in LICs. These occur in 1993 when the growth rate increased from an average of –0.7% in the period 1975–1993 to an average of 1.2% in the period 1994–2002 and in 2002 when the average growth rate of per capita GDP increased further to 3.6 for the period 2003–2013.

We analyze temporary interruptions in the growth process in India by seeking breaks in the series. We take the log of the series as shifts in slopes then represent changes in the growth rate. We find three break points for the economy, namely the performance of the economy can be divided into four periods (Table 7). In the

Table 7. Breaks in the Indian economy (taking natural log series).

Variables	Break years	Average growth rates
GDP at Factor Cost	1977–1978	3.74 (1950–1951–1977–1978)
	1986–1987	4.03 (1978–1979–1986–1987)
	2003–2004	5.86 (1987–1988–2003–2004)
		7.55 (2004–2005–2013–2014)
GDPPC at Factor cost	1963–1964	1.79 (1950–1951–1963–1964)
	1977–1978	1.38 (1964–1965–1977–1978)
	1988–1989	2.30 (1978–1979–1988–1989)
	2003–2004	3.73 (1989–1990–2003–2004)
		6.05 (2003–2004–2012–2013)
Manufacturing	1964–1965	6.63 (1950–1951–1964–1965)
	1978–1979	4.62 (1965–1966–1978–1979)
	1989–1990	4.95 (1979–1980–1989–1990)
	1999–2000	5.84 (1990–1991–1999–2000)
		7.53 (2000–2001–2012–2013)
Services	1960–1961	3.65 (1950–1951–1960–1961)
	1971–1972	5.22 (1961–1962–1971–1972)
	1984–1985	4.37 (1972–1973–1984–1985)
	1994–1995	5.41 (1985–1986–1994–1995)
		6.97 (1995–1996–2012–2013)
Agriculture	1986–1987	2.52 (1950–1951–1986–1987)
	2000–2001	3.40 (1987–1988–2000–2001)
		3.31 (2001–2002–2012–2013)

first period from 1950–1951 to 1977–1978, the growth rate averaged 3.7%. Then there are increases in the growth rate first to 4% during the period of the Sixth Plan and later to almost 6% from the middle of the Seventh Plan to the beginning of the Tenth Plan and subsequently it further accelerated.[13] Again the picture is one of almost steady acceleration in the growth rate.

The breaks in manufacturing growth coincide partly with the breaks in the GDP growth rate. For instance, the growth of manufacturing accelerates in 1978–1979 to almost 5% and in 1989–1990 to 5.8% and these breaks roughly correspond to the accelerations in the growth rate of GDP in 1977–1978 and 1986–1987. We get an additional break for per capita GDP because of variations in the rate of growth of population.

It is interesting to note that the break in the GDP series occurs before that in manufacturing suggesting that manufacturing responded to the higher growth of GDP which would in turn imply that the manufacturing sector faced a demand constraint; overall exports were a small part of GDP and exports of manufactures of manufacturing output. But later the manufacturing sector's growth accelerated in 1999–2000 before that of GDP and we note that exports of goods accelerated in 1996–1967 suggesting that the last growth acceleration in value added in manufactures was export driven. We explore the relation between the manufacturing sector and GDP further in Section 5.

The breaks in the growth rate of services are usually independent of that in GDP except the acceleration in services growth rate in 1984–1985 pre-dates that in GDP in 1986–1987. However, there is a break in the growth rate of value added for services in 2003.

What is surprising are the breaks in the growth rate of agriculture. There are only two — acceleration after 1986–1987, which is well after the onset of the green revolution, and a marginal decline after 2000–2001. This behavior of the agricultural growth rate we believe is because the value added in agriculture fluctuates very extensively with growth rates varying from –12.77 to 15.63. Consequently, the application of the technique of structural breaks to the agricultural series may be problematic.

We now consider the performance of the external sector, trying to see to what extent it can explain the performance of GDP. As evident from Table 8, a number of variables show structural breaks in the late 1990s or in the early 2000s. In particular, it is worth noting that the merchandise trade deficit went up to 8.5% of the GDP in the last decade from 3.2% of GDP during 1977–2002.

---

[13] The deceleration in 2012–2013 and 2013–2014 is too short a period for it to qualify as a separate period.

Table 8. Breaks in Indian exports and balances.

Variables	Break dates	Average values
Export of goods (% of GDP)	1964–1965	4.51 (till 1964–1965)
	1973–1974	3.21
	1985–1986	4.66
	1996–1997	6.52
		12.30 (till 2013–2014)
CAB (% of GDP)	1965–1966	–1.53 (till 1965–1966)
	1977–1978	–0.36
	1988–1989	–1.85
	1998–1999	–1.43
		–1.54 (till 2012–2013)
Merchandise Trade Balance (% of GDP)	1976–1977	–1.74 (till 1976–1977)
	2001–2002	–3.21
		–8.48 (till 2013–2014)
Imports (% of GDP)	1972–1973	5.61 (till 1972–1973)
	1984–1985	6.16
	1996–1997	7.38
		16.79 (till 2013–2014)
Non-oil Imports (% of GDP)*	1992–1993	4.53 (till 1992–1993)
	2002–2003	7.34
		13.88 (till 2013–2014)
Exchange Rate (Re/US$)	1978–1979	7.03 (till 1978–1979)
	1989–1990	10.51
	2002–2003	32.68
		46.27 (till 2013–2014)

* For non-oil imports, the data period is 1970–1971 to 2013–2014. For the rest, data period is 1950–1951 to 2013–2014.

Now, one point is worth mentioning at this stage. The relationship between India's exports and India's exchange rate with the US is non-unique. As elaborated in Agarwal and Essid (2015), an expansionary monetary policy of the US may both increase (real effect) and decrease (monetary effect) India's exports to the US. An expansionary monetary policy in the US increases US import demand and hence, exports of partner country will increase. This is the real effect. On the other hand, an expansionary monetary policy of the US will reduce US interest rates. This will lead to a depreciation of the US dollar. Hence, the currency of the partner country will appreciate and in turn will lower the exports of the partner country. This is the monetary effect. The total effect, hence, will depend on the relative strengths of the real and monetary effects.

5 Impact of Manufacturing and Services Sectors on the Indian Economy

In this section, we compare the effects of the manufacturing and services sectors on the economy by examining the sectors' backward and forward linkages. We used national input–output tables for India from the World Input Output Database (2013) to aggregate the sectors into five sectors — primary, manufacturing, utilities, construction and services. We did these for the years 1995 and 2011. The input–output tables for India are given below (Table 9).

Table 9. Input–output table (India).

	Primary	Manufacturing	Utilities	Construction	Services
			1995		
Primary	0.117	0.116	0.072	0.030	0.105
Manufacturing	0.050	0.328	0.085	0.317	0.017
Utilities	0.007	0.039	0.241	0.015	0.000
Construction	0.005	0.002	0.019	0.005	0.000
Services	0.054	0.181	0.169	0.144	0.015
			2011		
Primary	0.080	0.085	0.056	0.017	0.014
Manufacturing	0.088	0.261	0.388	0.391	0.079
Utilities	0.010	0.026	0.030	0.015	0.006
Construction	0.012	0.013	0.090	0.045	0.022
Services	0.014	0.223	0.196	0.056	0.114

Now, we invert these matrices to analyze the contribution of each of these sectors on the final demand of all the sectors.

Table 10. The inverse of the input–output table [$(I — A)^{-1}$], 1995.

	Primary	Manufacturing	Utilities	Construction	Services
Primary	1.156	0.244	0.169	0.134	0.127
Manufacturing	0.093	1.527	0.200	0.498	0.036
Utilities	0.016	0.081	1.330	0.047	0.003
Construction	0.006	0.006	0.027	1.008	0.001
Services	0.084	0.309	0.278	0.254	1.030

The above table shows that the primary sector supplies 0.244 units for the production of one unit of final demand for manufactures and supplies 0.127 units for the production of one unit of final demand for services (Table 10). So per unit the manufacturing sector provided a larger market for primary goods than did the services sector. This is true for the other sectors also except for the services sector that provides 1.03 units for production of one unit of final demand for the services sector but only 0.309 for one unit of the manufacturing sector.

We can also examine what each sector provides to the other sectors for their production. The manufacturing sector provides 0.093 for the agriculture sector whereas the services sector provides 0.084. Again, we find that the manufacturing sector usually provides more inputs for production in the other sectors than does the services sector. So, by and large, the manufacturing sector has larger backward and forward linkages.

Table 11. The inverse of the input–output Table [(I — A)$^{-1}$], 2011.

	Primary	Manufacturing	Utilities	Construction	Services
Primary	1.104	0.143	0.135	0.082	0.033
Manufacturing	0.157	1.452	0.678	0.617	0.152
Utilities	0.016	0.043	1.055	0.035	0.012
Construction	0.019	0.034	0.120	1.065	0.031
Services	0.062	0.379	0.414	0.232	1.172

The above table shows that the manufacturing sector continues to have stronger backward and forward linkages in 2011 (Table 11).

We know that exports of both goods including manufactures and NFS have increased considerably, that of services increasing faster. We use the input–output table to calculate the contribution of the exports to output. In 1995, service exports were 2.0%[14] of GDP and this contributed 2.4% of GDP as greater amounts of goods of the other sectors were produced to get the output of services. Exports of manufactures were 8.8% of GDP and this resulted in a contribution to GDP of 19.2%. For 2011, exports of services were 7.6% of GDP and this contributed 10.6% of GDP; exports of manufactures were 16.45% of GDP and this contributes 33.7% of GDP. Despite exports of services increasing faster than exports of manufactures, the latter continued to contribute more to GDP because of stronger linkages.

In the next section, we try to analyze the interrelationships between the performance of India's manufacturing sector and India's external sector and, hence, in turn, try to identify the dynamics of India's growth. We do the analysis using VAR estimations.

[14] The source of data on exports of manufacturing and non-factor services as a percentage of GDP is Reserve Bank of India.

6 VAR Estimations

As discussed in the last section, the relationship between India's exports and India's exchange rate with the US is non-unique and a more formal analysis is warranted to have a better understanding of this relationship. We do this with the help of VAR estimation using three variables — exports, CAB and exchange rate. We used data on India's exports, CAB (as a percent of GDP) and INR exchange rate (vis-à-vis US$) for the period 1962–1963 to 2012–2013. However, while testing for stationarity, we applied (natural) log transformation of each of the three series. In doing so, we further modified the CAB series by adding 10 to all the values on an ad hoc basis, that is, we just performed a shift of origin for the CAB series in order to make this transformed series free of negative values and ready for log transformation. Phillips–Perron test (see Phillips and Perron, 1988) for unit roots exhibited that each of the three series are integrated of order one I(1), and hence, are stationary after first difference. The results of unit root test are given in Table 12.[15]

Before testing for cointegration, we tested for the optimal lag structure of the system. Table 13 summarizes the VAR lag order selection results. As evident from the results, the optimal lag structure turns out be 3 from maximum number of criteria.

Table 12. Summary of unit root tests.

Series	*t*-values at level	*t*-values at first difference
lnexp	−1.259891 (0.8863)	−7.615512 (0.0000)
lnexrt	−1.572066 (0.7900)	−4.747715 (0.0019)
lnmodcab	−3.233962 (0.0896)	−8.208772 (0.0000)

* Probability values are given in parentheses.

Table 13. VAR lag order selection criteria.

Lag	LogL	LR	FPE	AIC	SC	HQ
0	−61.54419	NA	0.003129	2.746561	2.864656	2.791001
1	142.9427	374.1675	7.64e–07	−5.572029	−5.099651*	−5.394270
2	155.4935	21.36317	6.61e–07	−5.723130	−4.896468	−5.412051*
3	167.3015	18.59131*	5.94e–07*	−5.842619*	−4.661673	−5.398221
4	172.9976	8.241120	7.01e–07	−5.702026	−4.166797	−5.124309

* Significant

[15] As in Section 4, we have already identified multiple structural breaks in almost all the variables, we incorporated the structural breaks while testing for unit roots for all the variables using Perron (1994) technique. We found that all the variables have unit roots.

Table 14. Unrestricted cointegration rank test (maximum Eigenvalue).

Hypothesized no. of CE(s)	Eigenvalue	Max-Eigen statistic	0.05 critical value	Prob.**
None*	0.369415	22.13315	21.13162	0.0361
At most 1	0.230777	12.59400	14.26460	0.0903
At most 2*	0.086529	4.344178	3.841466	0.0371

Max-eigenvalue test indicates 1 cointegrating eqn(s) at the 0.05 level.
* Denotes rejection of the hypothesis at the 0.05 level.
** MacKinnon-Haug-Michelis (1999) *p*-values.

Table 15. VEC estimation results.

Cointegrating Eq:	CointEq1		
LNEXP(–1)	1.000000		
LNEXRT(–1)	–0.519837		
	(0.28239)		
	[–1.84083]		
LNMODCAB(–1)	6.712904		
	(1.47127)		
	[4.56267]		
C	–24.54734		
Error Correction:	D(LNEXP)	D(LNEXRT)	D(LNMODCAB)
CointEq1	0.033208	–0.022445	–0.069297
	(0.01457)	(0.01150)	(0.02122)
	[2.27946]	[–1.95226]	[–3.26547]

Using the optimal lag structure thus obtained, we test for cointegration using Johansen cointegration test (see Johansen, 1991). The results, given in Table 14, indicate that there exists one cointegrating equation using the Maximum Eigenvalue criterion for unrestricted VAR.

Given the original series are non-stationary, we perform Vector Error Correction (VEC) estimation to establish the significance of the relationship between these three variables as captured by the cointegrating equation. Finally, we run Granger causality test (see Granger, 1969) to understand the dynamics of the system.

As evident from the results, changes in exchange rate and exports significantly influence CAB (Table 15). The other causalities, were however, statistically insignificant (Table 16).

Table 16. VEC granger causality tests results.

Dependent variable: D(LNMODCAB)			
Excluded	**Chi-sq**	**df**	**Prob.**
D(LNEXP)	10.14594	2	0.0063
D(LNEXRT)	3.233140	2	0.1986
All	14.55783	4	0.0057

Before proceeding further, we return our focus to one more interesting observation made in the last section. As evident from Table 7, the structural breaks in India's GDP and manufacturing output do not reveal any unique pattern. To have a better understanding of this causality between GDP and manufacturing output, we estimated a VAR model using data for 1950–1951 to 2012–2013. We find that there exists one cointegrating equation implying a long-run positive relationship between GDP and manufacturing output growth rates. The rationale is pretty straightforward — manufacturing is a component of GDP itself and hence, there will exist a positive relation between the two. Interestingly, Granger causality test results reveal that there does not exist any statistically significant causality among the two growth rates.[16]

Even though we do not find any causal relationship between the performance of India's manufacturing sector and overall GDP, we know that the percent of value manufacturing exports of manufacturing value added has increased from 16.4% in the sixth Plan (1980–1984) to almost 60% in the period 2007–2010 (Agarwal and Whalley, 2015b). The manufacturing sector's growth accelerated in 1999–2000 before that of GDP and we note that exports of goods accelerated in 1996–1967 suggesting that thc last growth acceleration in value added in manufactures was export driven. To delve deeper into the matter, we resort to VAR estimation to analyze the relation between growth of the Indian manufacturing sector with India's exports and imports. In doing so, we can identify whether it is the growth in the manufacturing that led to the growth in exports or the other way round. In fact, it might be the growth in exports which might finance growth in the import of intermediate goods needed for the manufacturing sector.

First, we consider three variables — exports, imports and manufacturing (all as percentage of GDP) data for India for the period 1950–1951 to 2012–2013 to

[16] The estimation results, as given in Tables A5 and A6 the appendix, show that though there exists a long-run positive relation between ***lngdp*** and ***lnman***, there is no significant short-run causality either way. In other words, both GDP and Manufacturing growth rates move in the same direction (as manufacturing is just a part of GDP), but there is no significant causal relation among them.

Table 17. VAR estimation results summary.

	DEXP	DIMP	DMAN
DEXP(−1)	−0.045614	−0.047413	−0.114349
	(0.15574)	(0.18642)	(0.05674)
	[−0.29288]	[−0.25433]	[−2.01539]*
DIMP(−1)	0.048164	−0.003699	−0.063578
	(0.12424)	(0.14872)	(0.04526)
	[0.38766]	[−0.02487]	[−1.40467]
DMAN(−1)	−0.105117	0.392407	0.180624
	(0.34755)	(0.41601)	(0.12661)
	[−0.30245]	[0.94326]	[1.42658]
C	0.015131	0.018139	0.006353
	(0.01393)	(0.01668)	(0.00508)
	[1.08606]	[1.08772]	[1.25166]

construct a structural VAR model. To achieve stationarity[17] in all the series, we performed a (natural) log transformation of these three series and found that all of them are integrated of order one, that is, they are stationary after first differencing. Next, we tested for the optimal lag structure of the VAR[18] and found the optimal lag structure, to be one. Using the optimal lag structure, we test for cointegration using Johansen cointegration test. However, the results, as given in Table A3 in the appendix, show that there exists no cointegrating equation, that is, there is no long-run equilibrium relation between the three growth rates in this sample. Therefore, we performed an unrestricted VAR to find out the short-run relations among these variables. Table 17 gives the results of the VAR estimation results.

As evident from the above table, it is only the last period's growth in exports which has a significant impact on the present period's growth rate in manufacturing. To complete the analysis, we test for pairwise Granger causality. The results are given in Table 18.

The Granger causality results not only reinforce the results of the unrestricted VAR model but also show that growth rate of imports has significant impact on growth rate of manufacturing. These results imply that it is the growth of exports which influence growth of manufacturing via growth in imports rather than the growth in manufacturing influencing growth of exports.

---

[17] See Table A1 in the appendix for the results of the Augmented Dickey–Fuller test for unit roots (see Fuller, 1976; Dickey and Fuller, 1979).

[18] See Table A2 for the results of VAR lag order selection.

Table 18. Pairwise granger causality test results.

Null hypothesis:	F-statistic	Prob.
DIMP does not Granger Cause DEXP	0.11994	0.7304
DEXP does not Granger Cause DIMP	0.01579	0.9004
DMAN does not Granger Cause DEXP	0.06014	0.8071
DEXP does not Granger Cause DMAN	9.32847	0.0034*
DMAN does not Granger Cause DIMP	0.85461	0.3591
DIMP does not Granger Cause DMAN	7.02541	0.0103*

Table 19. Unrestricted cointegration rank test (Trace).

Hypothesized no. of CE(s)	Eigenvalue	Trace statistic	0.05 critical value	Prob.**
None *	0.344017	30.94459	29.79707	0.0367
At most 1	0.219514	13.65819	15.49471	0.0928
At most 2	0.081752	3.496814	3.841466	0.0615

Trace test indicates 1 cointegrating eqn(s) at the 0.05 level.
* Denotes rejection of the hypothesis at the 0.05 level.
** MacKinnon-Haug-Michelis (1999) *p*-values.

However, till now we have used total import data for the Indian economy. Hence, we repeat the above exercise using non-oil imports instead of total imports. Now, such a decision is not an arbitrary one. If we look into the trends of exports, imports and non-oil imports for India (though we have data only from 1970–1971 for non-oil imports), it becomes evident that the exports and non-oil imports series almost coincide with each other and they grow almost smoothly during the period 1970–1971 to 2012–2013. On the other hand, oil imports show an increase till 1980–1981 followed by a sharp fall till 1986–1987 after which it increased gradually till 2004–2005 and after 2004–2005, there is again a sharp increase.[19]

Now, the Johansen test for cointegration reveals (Table 19) that there exists one cointegrating equation when we consider the non-oil imports (natural log transformed).

Given there is one cointegrating equation, we opted for a VEC model this time to have a closer look into the exact relationship between these three variables in the long-run equilibrium.

This time, the results (as given in Table A4 in the Appendix) clearly exhibit significant influence of last period's growth rate of imports on present period's

[19] See Figure 3 in the appendix.

Table 20. VEC granger causality tests results.

Excluded	Chi-sq	df	Prob.
Dependent variable: D(LNNOIMP)			
Excluded	Chi-sq	df	Prob.
D(LNEXP)	0.561869	1	0.4535
D(LNMAN)	0.807996	1	0.3687
All	1.017143	2	0.6014
Dependent variable: D(LNEXP)			
D(LNNOIMP)	1.582940	1	0.2083
D(LNMAN)	0.360388	1	0.5483
All	2.169366	2	0.3380
Dependent variable: D(LNMAN)			
D(LNNOIMP)	5.337462	1	0.0209
D(LNEXP)	2.475464	1	0.1156
All	7.556824	2	0.0229

growth rate of manufacturing. Further, VEC Granger causality tests (Table 20) reveal that growth rates of exports and non-oil imports have significant impacts on growth rate of manufacturing while the reverse does not hold.

Hence, the results from the analyses done in this section clearly reveal that the growth in the manufacturing does not have a statistically significant impact on the growth rate of exports. On the contrary, growth of exports financing growth of imports, in particular, non-oil imports has a significant impact on growth of manufacturing. There is lag of one period in such causality, that is, last period's export and non-oil import influence present period's manufacturing.

7 Conclusion

Since the 1970s, there has been a continuous growth of the Indian GDP. However, a priori, it is not easy to identify any structural break in the GDP series. On the other hand, there seems to be an increase in exports and investment as evident from Tables 2 and 7. Manufacturing sector experienced a sharp fall after aid was cut off in the mid-1960s following a reversal in the pattern in the late 1980s and a continuous increase after that.

In this paper, we performed structural break analyses of several macroeconomic variables for the Indian economy to have a clear picture about the evolution of the economy from various dimensions. Interestingly, though GDP and GDP per capita series exhibit multiple structural breaks, we do not find any statistically significant structural break in India's GDP growth rate. Hence, unlike many analysts[20] who claim that the policy changes began in 1991 had resulted in a significant acceleration of the growth rate, we find that no such significant acceleration has occurred.

Our analysis casts doubt on two perception about India's growth. First, India's growth is domestic demand-led as compared to the export-led growth story of China. We show that India's export performance is very similar to that of China's. Hence, one cannot claim that China's growth is export-led and that India's growth is domestic demand-led.

Second, India's development is service sector led rather than manufacturing sector led. We found no significant difference between the growth rates of the value added in manufacturing and services. Furthermore, we found that the backward and forward linkages are stronger for the manufacturing sector vis-à-vis the services sector. Hence, we do not find evidence in support of this perception that India's growth can be largely attributed to the growth of the services sector.

While analyzing the components of GDP, we found multiple breaks in the manufacturing and service sectors. However, agriculture exhibited only two structural breaks. So far as the external sector is concerned, almost all the indicators like exports, imports, non-oil imports, CAB and exchange rate (vis-à-vis US dollar) exhibit multiple structural breaks.

Interestingly, the structural breaks in all the major series of the Indian economy exhibit a similar pattern — there is one break in almost in every decade from the 1960s to the 1990s. To have further insight to the long-run dynamics of these variables, we performed multiple VAR estimation models. In the external sector, we found that changes in exports and exchange rates have a significant impact on the changes in current account balance. Reverse causalities were not statistically significant.

While analyzing the long-and short-run relations among the external sectors and manufacturing growth, we found that the growth in the manufacturing does not have a statistically significant impact on the growth rate of exports. On the contrary, growth of exports and imports (particularly, non-oil imports) of the

[20] Kotwal *et al.* (2011).

previous period have a significant impact on the current period growth of manufacturing.

Our analysis provides an alternative narrative for India's development process. A correct appraisal is important for appropriate policy design. Further analyses of exact sectoral and dynamic interlinkages are required to improve our understanding of the operation of the Indian economy.

Acknowledgment

The authors deeply acknowledge the suggestions by Dr. Srikanta Kundu of the Centre for Development Studies. Comments by Dr. M. Parameswaran, Prof. Sunil Mani, Dr. PL Beena and other participants of seminar in the Centre for Development Studies and an anonymous referee on an earlier draft of the paper are also acknowledged. The usual disclaimer, however, is applied.

References

Agarwal, M. (2008), The BRICSAM Countries and Changing Economic Power: Scenarios to 2050. *CIGI Working Paper, No. 39*, Waterloo, Canada. Oct. 11 2008.

Agarwal, M. and A. Barua (2004), Entry Liberalisation and Export Performance: A Theoretical Analysis in a Multi-Market Oligopoly Model, *Journal of International Trade and Development*, 13(3), 287–303.

Agarwal, M. and A. Chakravarty (2016), *The Manufacturing Sector in BRICS*, mimeo, CDS, Thiruvananthapuram.

Agarwal, M. and B. Essid (2015), The Effect of US Monetary Policy on G20 Emerging Countries, In Agarwal, M. and J. Whalley (Eds): *India and China: Comparative Experience and Prospects*, Singapore: World Scientific.

Agarwal, M. and J. Whalley (2015a), China and India: Reforms and the Response — How Differently have the Economies Behaved? in M. Agarwal and J. Whalley (Eds): *India and China: Comparative Experience and Prospects*, Singapore: World Scientific.

Agarwal, M. and J. Whalley (2015b), The 1991 Reforms, Indian Economic Growth and Social Progress, in M. Agarwal and J. Whalley (Eds): *India and China: Comparative Experience and Prospects*, Singapore: World Scientific.

Agarwal, M., S. Mitra and J. Whalley (2015), Indian Economic Growth: Its Ups and Downs, in M. Agarwal and J. Whalley (Eds): *Sustainability of Growth: The Role of Economic, Technological and Environmental Factors*, Singapore: World Scientific.

Bai, J. and P. Perron (1998), Estimating and Testing Linear Models with Multiple Structural Changes, *Econometrica*, 66(1), 47–78.

Bai, J. and P. Perron (2003), Computation and Analysis of Multiple Structural Change Models, *Journal of Applied Econometrics*, 18, 1–22.

Bhagwati, J. and S. Chakravarty (1969), Contributions to Indian Economic Analysis: A Survey, *American Economic Review*, 59(4), 1–73.

Chakravarty, S. (1969), *Capital and Development Planning*. MIT Press, Cambridge, Mass.

Chakravarty, S. (1979), On the Question of Home Market and Prospects for Indian Growth, *Economic and Political Weekly*, 14(30/32), 1229–1242.

Dickey, D.A. and W.A. Fuller (1979), Distribution of the Estimators for Autoregressive Time Series with a Unit Root, *Journal of the American Statistical Association*, 74(366a), 427–431.

Fuller, W.A. (1976), *Introduction to Statistical Time Series*. John Wiley and Sons, New York.

Government of India (1952), The First Five Year Plan. Planning Commission, Government of India, New Delhi.

Granger, C.W.J. (1969), Investigating Causal Relations by Econometric Models and Cross-Spectral Methods, *Econometrica*, 37(3), 424–438.

Johansen, S. (1991), Estimation and Hypothesis Testing of Cointegration Vectors in Gaussian Vector Autoregressive Models, *Econometrica*, 59(6), 1551–1580.

Johnson, H. (1962), *Money, Trade and Economic Growth (Collected Works of Harry Johnson): Survey Lectures in Economic Theory*. Routledge, London.

Kotwal, A., B. Ramaswami and W. Wadhwa (2011), Economic Liberalization and Indian Economic Growth: What's the Evidence? *Journal of Economic Literature*, 49(4), 1152–1199.

Lele, U. and M. Agarwal (1990), Aid in India's Development: Experience of Four Decades, in U. Lele and I. Nabi (Eds): *Transitions in Development: The Role of Aid and Commercial Flows*, San Francisco: International Center for Economic Growth, Institute for Contemporary Studies Press.

MacKinnon, J.G., A. Haug, and L. Michelis (1999), Numerical Distribution Functions of Likelihood Ratio Tests for Cointegration, *Journal of Applied Econometrics*, 14(5), 563–577.

Mahalanobis, P.C. (1953), Some Observations on the Process of Growth of National Income, *Sankhya: The Indian Journal of Statistic*s, 12(4), 307–312.

Mahalanobis, P.C. (1955), The Approach of Operational Research Planning in India, *Sankhya: The Indian Journal of Statistics*, 16(1/2), 3–130.

Marglin, S. and J. Schor (Eds.) (1990), *The Golden Age of Capitalism*. Clarendon Press, Oxford.

Persson, T. and Lars E.O. Svensson (1985), Current Account Dynamics and the Terms of Trade: Harberger-Laursen-Metzler Two Generations Later, *Journal of Political Economy*, 93(1), 43–65.

Phillips, P.C.B. and P. Perron (1988), Testing for a Unit Root in Time Series Regression, *Biometrika*, 75(2), 335–346.

Svensson, Lars E.O (1984), Oil Prices, Welfare and the Trade Balance, *Quarterly Journal of Economics*, 99(4), 649–672.

World Input Output Database (2013), Available from: http://www.wiod.org/protected3/data/update_sep12/niot/IND_NIOT_row_sep12.xlsx. Last accessed date 18 June 2015.

Appendix

Table A1. Summary of unit root tests.

Series	*t*-values at first difference*
lnexp	–8.865972 (0.0000)
lnimp	–8.576165 (0.0000)
lnman	–7.547305 (0.0000)

* Probability values are given in parentheses.

Table A2. VAR lag order selection criteria.

Lag	LogL	LR	FPE	AIC	SC	HQ
0	38.88952	NA	5.82e–05	–1.237570	–1.130995	–1.196057
1	220.8142	338.7562*	1.50e–07*	–7.200488*	–6.774190*	–7.034437*
2	226.4820	9.967525	1.69e–07	–7.085585	–6.339563	–6.794994
3	231.8369	8.863327	1.93e–07	–6.959893	–5.894147	–6.544763
4	236.8810	7.827093	2.23e–07	–6.823484	–5.438013	–6.283815
5	242.1003	7.558913	2.60e–07	–6.693113	–4.987919	–6.028905

* Indicates lag order selected by the criterion.

Table A3. Test for cointegration.

Unrestricted cointegration rank test (trace)

Hypothesized no. of CE(s)	Eigenvalue	Trace statistic	0.05 critical value	Prob.**
None	0.226952	27.74282	29.79707	0.0847
At most 1	0.173799	12.04058	15.49471	0.1550
At most 2	0.006448	0.394629	3.841466	0.5299

Trace test indicates no cointegration at the 0.05 level.
* denotes rejection of the hypothesis at the 0.05 level.
** MacKinnon-Haug-Michelis (1999) *p*-values.

Unrestricted cointegration rank test (Maximum Eigenvalue)

Hypothesized no. of CE(s)	Eigenvalue	Max-Eigen statistic	0.05 critical value	Prob.**
None	0.226952	15.70224	21.13162	0.2427
At most 1	0.173799	11.64595	14.26460	0.1247
At most 2	0.006448	0.394629	3.841466	0.5299

Max-eigenvalue test indicates no cointegration at the 0.05 level.
* Denotes rejection of the hypothesis at the 0.05 level.
** MacKinnon-Haug-Michelis (1999) *p*-values.

Table A4. Results of VEC estimates.

Cointegrating Eq:	**CointEq1**		
LNNOIMP(–1)	1.000000		
LNEXP(–1)	–0.732755		
	(0.17168)		
	[–4.26806]		
LNMAN(–1)	6.667456		
	(1.78057)		
	[3.74455]		
C	–18.78447		
Error Correction:	D(LNNOIMP)	D(LNEXP)	D(LNMAN)
CointEq1	–0.079501	–0.086788	–0.055877
	(0.04360)	(0.03960)	(0.01505)
	[–1.82360]	[–2.19184]*	[–3.71280]*
D(LNNOIMP(–1))	–0.102506	0.184389	0.128691
	(0.16136)	(0.14656)	(0.05570)
	[–0.63527]	[1.25815]	[2.31029]*
D(LNEXP(–1))	–0.140160	–0.211625	–0.101560
	(0.18698)	(0.16983)	(0.06455)
	[–0.74958]	[–1.24609]	[–1.57336]
D(LNMAN(–1))	0.391674	0.237583	0.113697
	(0.43573)	(0.39576)	(0.15042)
	[0.89889]	[0.60032]	[0.75586]
C	0.051060	0.041379	–0.001784
	(0.01762)	(0.01600)	(0.00608)
	[2.89772]	[2.58550]	[–0.29329]
R-squared	0.103022	0.149013	0.331760
Adj. R-squared	0.003357	0.054459	0.257511
Sum sq. resids	0.313078	0.258270	0.037310
S.E. equation	0.093256	0.084700	0.032193
F-statistic	1.033687	1.575952	4.468216
Log likelihood	41.75844	45.70361	85.36566
Akaike AIC	–1.793095	–1.985542	–3.920276
Schwarz SC	–1.584122	–1.776570	–3.711304
Mean dependent	0.041572	0.040764	–0.000381
S.D. dependent	0.093413	0.087105	0.037361
Determinant resid covariance (dof adj.)		6.26E–08	
Determinant resid covariance		4.24E–08	
Log likelihood		173.4783	
Akaike information criterion		–7.584306	
Schwarz criterion		–6.832006	

* Statistically significant at 5% level of significance.

Table A5. VEC estimation results (GDP and manufacturing growth rates).

Cointegrating Eq:	**CointEq1**	
LNGDP(−1)	1.000000	
LNMAN(−1)	−1.004999	
	(0.00921)	
	[−109.063]	
C	−1.870911	
Error Correction:	D(LNGDP)	D(LNMAN)
CointEq1	−0.280878	−0.122863
	(0.05162)	(0.06427)
	[−5.44075]	[−1.91175]
D(LNGDP(−1))	0.119223	0.187798
	(0.14314)	(0.17820)
	[0.83290]	[1.05387]
D(LNMAN(−1))	−0.224999	−0.076101
	(0.13898)	(0.17301)
	[−1.61894]	[−0.43985]
C	0.124172	0.103331
	(0.01586)	(0.01974)
	[7.83092]	[5.23463]
R-squared	0.411763	0.137222
Adj. R-squared	0.380803	0.091813
Sum sq. resids	0.090331	0.139991
S.E. equation	0.039809	0.049558
F-statistic	13.29992	3.021885
Log likelihood	112.1568	98.79472
Akaike AIC	−3.546125	−3.108024
Schwarz SC	−3.407707	−2.969606
Mean dependent	0.111259	0.115231
S.D. dependent	0.050590	0.052003
Determinant resid covariance (dof adj.)		2.33E−06
Determinant resid covariance		2.04E−06
Log likelihood		226.5760
Akaike information criterion		−7.100851
Schwarz criterion		−6.754806

Table A6. Granger causality results (GDP and manufacturing growth rates).

Excluded	Chi-sq	df	Prob.
Dependent variable: D(LNGDP)			
D(LNMAN)	2.620971	1	0.1055
Dependent variable: D(LNMAN)			
D(LNGDP)	1.110650	1	0.2919

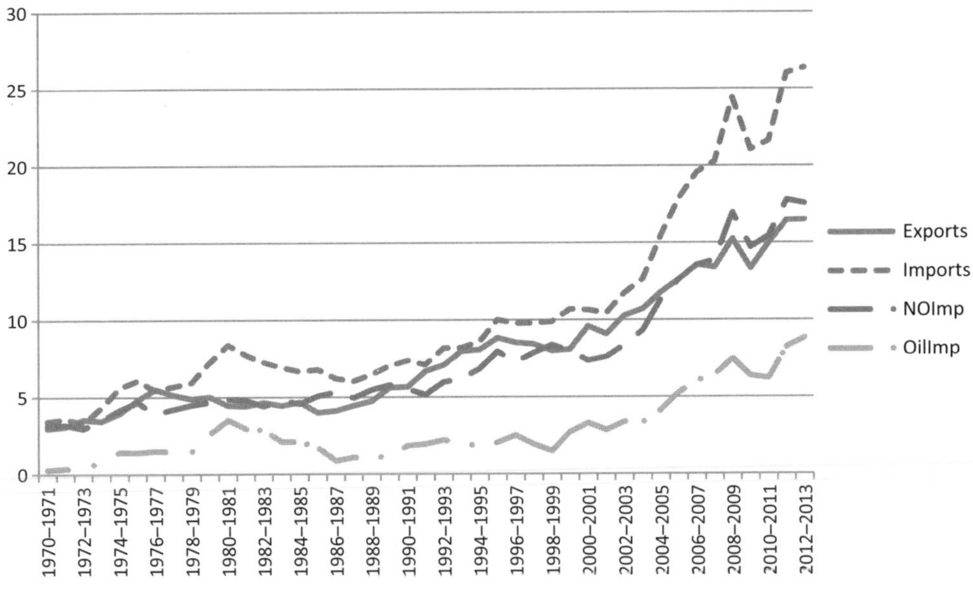

Figure 3. Trends of Indian exports, imports and non-oil imports.

Chapter 7

Inclusiveness of Information Access in Agriculture: Evidence from India

Aritri Chakravarty and Upasak Das*
Centre for Development Studies, Thiruvananthapuram, Kerala, India
**upasak.das@gmail.com*

Abstract: Information plays a crucial role in important and effective decision-making in any economic activity. This becomes especially relevant for agriculture, where the vagaries of climate change and price fluctuations can make information necessary for the marginal and vulnerable farmers. Using representative data in 2012–2013 this chapter examines the inclusiveness of access to information by the marginal famers. It also studies if poor and deprived farmers in terms of social group, household headship and consumption expenditure are likely to get the agricultural information. Further, the chapter explores if government information agencies are more inclusive than the private agencies, both when compared to the external agencies passed on by television/media/internet/newspaper and progressive farmers. Our findings show access to agricultural information is less likely to reach the marginal, poor and deprived farmers. We also find government agencies are more inclusive to the marginal farmers than the private ones.

1 Introduction

Information plays a crucial role in effective decision-making in any economy. Any economic activity can be improved with the correct use of relevant and timely information. For instance, if information is available on the internal environment of a production unit such as the correct proportion of input mix or on the external environment like weather, market conditions, etc.), then both losses and uncertainties can be mitigated (Citroen, 2011). Traditionally, the most popular sources of information were newspapers, radio and television. However, with advancement in information and communication technology, the internet has revolutionized access to information (Chapman and Slaymaker, 2002). Information creates awareness, dissipates knowledge on technical know-how and external factors and gives relevant insights to the appropriateness of any production technique (Hussain *et al.*, 2004). These are extremely important for any economic activity and particularly for activities prone to high risks (Kahan, 2008). Internet can have the advantage of ease of access.

These risky activities include agriculture, where several factors can hamper the production process in agriculture. Apart from natural calamities, most of these other factors can be taken care of with the access to timely information. For instance, information on the accurate and timely use of fertilizers and pesticides can prevent the crop from failing. Also prior information about extreme weather such as droughts or floods can give farmers time to prepare for it. Soil tests and use of efficient input bundles can be availed because of availability of appropriate information. Thus, risks of crop failure can be avoided or at least mitigated and also productivity can be increased through proper access and utilization of information. Information on prices would allow farmers to choose the proper output mix. Furthermore, price information can prevent the farmers from being cheated by sellers while procuring inputs and also by middlemen while selling their output. Many studies have shown that information enables farmers to decide on the cropping pattern, use of high-yielding seeds, fertilizer application, pest management and marketing (Segrave, 2004; Lio and Liu, 2006; Nazari and Hasbullah, 2008; Gandhi, 2011).

Access to adequate knowledge and information regarding farming practices is a major constraint to farmers in India thus reducing constraining and efficiency of agriculture. It is hence crucial to provide farmers with the knowledge and information in a timely and proper manner. Several studies have found a significant linkage between access to information through institutions and/or agents and agricultural efficiency (Helfand and Levine, 2004; Ali, 2011). The government has come up with several policy initiatives to ensure that farmers have access to proper information through agricultural extension services and universities. Also several non-government entities have started providing information. For example, the organization PRADAN (Professional Assistance for Development Action) has been assisting in disseminating information on agricultural practices to enhance productivity and diversification among others in parts of Madhya Pradesh, West Bengal, Rajasthan and other states (www.pradan.net). However, accessing, processing and executing the information not only depend on its availability but also on a variety of socio-economic traits of the farmer.

Though there is ample research evaluating the impact of access and adoption of information on agricultural productivity, farming practice and farmer income, there is a dearth of literature studying the inclusiveness of information access. This is important as the marginal farmers with small land holdings are more vulnerable to the vagaries of monsoon clubbed with the inherent risks of farming and rising input costs rendering farming quite unviable as a profitable source of income. Under such circumstances, information can play a key role in improving agriculture and hence help the sector to grow.

In this backdrop, this paper attempts to examine the inclusiveness of access to information by the marginal famers having small land holdings. It also explores if poor and deprived farmers in terms of social group, household headship and consumption expenditure are likely to get the required agricultural information. Further, the chapter studies if government information agencies are more inclusive than private agencies, both when compared to the external agencies such as television/media/internet/newspaper and progressive farmers. Our results, derived from both an econometric exercise and non-parametric analysis show access to agricultural information is less likely to reach the marginal, poor and deprived farmers. We also find government agencies are more inclusive to the marginal farmers than the private ones.

The structure of the chapter is as follows. Section 2 explains the data used in the analysis and Section 3 gives out details of the variables used. Section 4 presents the estimation strategy used. Section 5 discusses the results from the regression and non-parametric analysis. The chapter ends with a conclusion in Section 6.

2 Data

To conduct this analysis, we have used data from the Situation Assessment Survey of Agricultural Households schedule of the 70th Round of National Sample Survey (NSS). It captures several aspects of farming such as farming practices and preferences, availability of resources, awareness of technological developments and access to modern technology and level of living measured in terms of consumer expenditure, income and indebtedness of the agricultural households in rural India. The survey was divided into two visits each of six months, July–December 2012 and January–June 2013, to make a comprehensive assessment of the situation of the agricultural households for the agricultural year July 2012 to June 2013. The survey was conducted only for rural households. Each household was visited twice. About 35,200 households were surveyed across all the states and Union Territories in first visit, which diminished to 34,907 in the second.

This round differs from the 59th Round of the Situation Assessment Survey of Farmers on the ground as it does not consider possession of land as the prerequisite to qualify as a farmer household since agricultural activity can be performed without the possession of land. In this round, any household that has earned at least Rs. 3000 from agriculture and has at least one member self-employed in agriculture, either in principal or subsidiary status in the last 365 days qualifies to be an agricultural household. The survey canvasses information on (i) characteristics of agricultural households, (ii) some aspects of farming and (iii) income, expenditure, productive assets and indebtedness of agricultural households.

3 Variables

3.1 Dependent variable

Our research objectives in this chapter are two-fold. Firstly, we examine if access to information on agriculture and farming practice is inclusive or covers mainly the better-off farmers. For this purpose, we create a dichotomous variable which takes the value "1" if the household has accessed information on agriculture from at least any of the following sources:

(i) Krishi Vigyan Kendra, which is a center formed by the State Agricultural Universities, Indian Council of Agricultural Research and Agricultural Research Institutes of the State Governments. They act both as information and service centers to dissipate new farming technology to farmers through training and demonstration. They also supply certain inputs to facilitate the adoption of new technology.
(ii) Extension agent is a government employee in the Department of Agriculture/Horticulture/Animal Husbandry/Forestry/Soil conservation or Agricultural Universities or Indian Council of Agricultural Research Institutes who provide necessary information and guidance to farmers. Para-technicians/para-veterinarians visiting from government departments are also classified as extension workers.
(iii) Agricultural university/college.
(iv) Veterinary department.
(v) Private commercial agents.
(vi) Non-Government Organization (NGO).
(vii) Radio/Television/Newspaper/Internet.
(viii) Progressive farmers.

The variable takes the value "0" if the household has not accessed any of these sources for information.

The second objective of the paper is to find if government agencies are more inclusive of the worse-off farmers in terms of information dissemination than the private agencies when compared to the external agencies. For this purpose, we create a dependent variable with three unordered categories:

(i) Public/Government Source if information has been accessed from Krishi Vigyan Kendra, extension agent, agricultural university/college and/or veterinary department.
(ii) Private Source if information has been accessed from private commercial agents and/or NGOs.
(iii) External source if information has been accessed from progressive farmers and Information and Communication Technology comprising of radio/television/newspaper/internet. This has been taken as the base category.

3.2 Explanatory variables

Taking into account the context of India, we use several explanatory variables in our model as indicators of socio-economic characteristics and well-being. We use dummies for caste and religion to characterize the households by social group and religion. The variable for caste is coded into four categories: "Scheduled Tribe (ST)", "Scheduled Castes (SC)", "Other Backward Castes" (OBC) and "General" (taken as reference).[7] The religion dummy has been coded into Hindus (taken as reference), Muslims, Christians and other religions.

To capture the economic condition of the household, a number of variables are incorporated. We use a dummy to indicate if the house of the household is hired or not. We also use dummies for types of houses: Pucca, which indicates cemented houses (taken as reference); kaccha, which indicates if the house is non-cemented and semi-pucca. Amount of land possessed is included because it is accepted as indicator of wealth status especially in rural areas for farmers. Since consumption expenditure is considered to be the prime indicator for well-being, household Monthly Per Capita Consumption Expenditure (MPCE) is used by dividing it into quintiles (Q1, Q2, Q3, Q4 and Q5). Households in Q1 are the poorest and those in Q5 are the richest. Apart from these controls, demographic variables like the gender of the household head and his/her education are used.

4 Estimation Strategy

4.1 Probability to estimate access to information

To examine the probability of households accessing agricultural information, we use the widely recognized logistic regression model, which fits a logit model for a binary response by maximum likelihood. Since the dependent variable is dichotomous in nature, it is considered to be the most appropriate regression strategy.

4.2 Government agencies vs. the private agencies

In this case, we categorize the dependent variable (source of information) in three components: Government agencies, private agencies and external agencies, comprising of information through Information and Communication Technology (ICT) (TV/Radio/Newspaper/Internet) and progressive farmers. Since these categories are not ordered in nature, we use multinomial logistic regression, which fits maximum likelihood models with discrete dependent variables when the dependent variable takes on more than two outcomes and the outcomes have no natural ordering (Greene, 2012).

5 Results

5.1 Descriptive statistics

Table 1 gives a list of the variables used in the regression. It also presents the mean/proportion of these characteristics (variables) for (i) all households; (ii) households with no information access and (iii) households which have accessed information. Among all the households in the sample, about 44% had accessed information on agricultural issues.

In terms of social group, the sample of households which have accessed information is dominated by the General caste category in comparison to those who have not accessed information. However the representation of the lower groups (SC and ST) is significantly lower among households, who have accessed information. More than 67% of the households that have accessed information are found to possess pucca houses, whereas for households who have not accessed information, it is only 59%.

The households accessing information for agriculture are found to be better-off in terms of land possession and MPCE too. The average land possessed by the farmers, who have accessed information is about 1.9 ha and that for those, who did not access information is 1.4a. The difference is found to be statistically significant at the 5% level (two group mean comparison test). Further, the households which have accessed information on agriculture are found to be significantly poorer than those which have not. For example, among the households that accessed information, 34% belong to the poorest two quintiles of MPCE. For households with no information access, this figure is about 45%.

In terms of headship too, we get similar results. Expectedly, households with female heads are the ones which have accessed information, relatively lesser than households with male heads. Similarly, proportion of households with illiterate heads form a significantly larger proportion of those who have not accessed

Table 1. Descriptive statistics (mean/proportion) and variables used in the regressions.

	Total sample	Did not access information	Accessed information	Difference
All households		0.562	0.437	
Caste				
General	0.286	0.258	0.321	0.062*
ST	0.204	0.244	0.152	–0.092*
SC	0.114	0.123	0.102	–0.021*
OBC	0.396	0.374	0.425	0.051*
Religion				
Hindu	0.791	0.786	0.797	0.011*
Muslim	0.094	0.084	0.108	0.024*
Christian	0.074	0.086	0.058	–0.028*
Others	0.041	0.044	0.037	–0.007*
House not hired	0.017	0.017	0.016	–0.002
Hired house	0.983	0.983	0.984	0.002
Type of house				
Pucca	0.625	0.588	0.672	0.084*
Kaccha	0.084	0.102	0.061	–0.041*
Semi-pucca	0.291	0.310	0.267	–0.043*
Total land possessed (mean)	1.635	1.432	1.895	0.463*
MPCE quantiles				
Q1 (poorest)	0.204	0.236	0.164	–0.072*
Q2	0.198	0.213	0.178	–0.035*
Q3	0.198	0.200	0.196	–0.004
Q4	0.200	0.187	0.215	0.028*
Q5 (richest)	0.200	0.164	0.247	0.083*
Received training in agriculture	0.038	0.020	0.060	0.039*
Gender of household head				
Male head	0.921	0.912	0.932	0.02*
Female head	0.079	0.088	0.068	–0.02*
Education of the household head				
Illiterate head	0.339	0.377	0.290	–0.087*
Below primary	0.129	0.130	0.127	–0.003
Primary and middle	0.294	0.286	0.303	0.017*
Secondary and higher secondary	0.177	0.156	0.204	0.048*
Above higher secondary	0.062	0.051	0.076	0.025*

Note: Unless otherwise mentioned, the figures give the column proportion, that is they represent the proportion of a particular characteristic in the respective groups — accessed and did not access information. For some characteristics as mentioned, the mean is given for that group. *Significant at 5% level.

Source: Author's calculation based on NSSO 70th round Situation Assessment Survey of Agricultural Households.

information as compared to those who have accessed some information. These findings very clearly suggest that household with access to agricultural information are better-off in terms of consumption expenditure, land possession, education and social group, when compared to those who have not accessed information.

5.2 Regression results

(i) *Probability to estimate access to information*

Table 2 gives the logit estimation of the probability of households to access information on various independent variables as discussed. We used three different specifications for the logit estimations for robustness checks. In the first specification, we kept all the variables as listed out in Table 1 except the dummy for whether the house is a hired one or not. In the second specification, we dropped the dummies indicating the types of house (pucca, kuccha or semi-pucca) along with the dummy indicating whether the house is hired or not. In the third specification we retained all the variables in the model. It should be noted that we tried out other specifications too but the results remain largely invariant.

In all the three specifications, we find that most of the variables behave similarly, signifying that our estimates are robust and invariant to specification changes.

Table 2. Logistic regression to estimate the probability of households accessing agricultural information.

	(1)	(2)	(3)
Caste (Ref. General)			
ST	–0.368***	–0.394***	–0.369***
	(0.102)	(0.105)	(0.102)
SC	–0.131	–0.144*	–0.131
	(0.072)	(0.072)	(0.072)
OBC	0.017	0.017	0.017
	(0.066)	(0.066)	(0.066)
Religion (Ref. Hindu)			
Muslim	0.231*	0.225	0.230*
	(0.116)	(0.117)	(0.116)
Christian	–0.277	–0.284	–0.276
	(0.175)	(0.177)	(0.175)
Others	–0.336	–0.348	–0.337
	(0.195)	(0.196)	(0.196)
Hired			0.082
			(0.118)

(*Continued*)

Table 2. *(Continued)*

	(1)	(2)	(3)
Ref (Pucca household)			
Kaccha	–0.318***		–0.317***
	(0.084)		(0.084)
Semi-pucca	–0.030		–0.030
	(0.083)		(0.083)
Total land possessed	0.124***	0.127***	0.124***
	(0.018)	(0.018)	(0.018)
Ref. MPCE Q5	0.000	0.000	0.000
Q1	–0.538***	–0.560***	–0.538***
	(0.112)	(0.107)	(0.112)
Q2	–0.422***	–0.434***	–0.422***
	(0.098)	(0.096)	(0.098)
Q3	–0.268**	–0.275**	–0.268**
	(0.092)	(0.090)	(0.093)
Q4	–0.170*	–0.174*	–0.170*
	(0.078)	(0.077)	(0.078)
Formal training in agriculture	0.983***	0.988***	0.984***
	(0.116)	(0.117)	(0.116)
Gender of household head (Ref. Male)			
Female head	–0.183***	–0.176**	–0.182***
	(0.054)	(0.054)	(0.054)
Ref. Education of head (illiterate)			
Below primary	0.182**	0.186**	0.182**
	(0.059)	(0.059)	(0.059)
Primary and middle	0.192***	0.203***	0.192***
	(0.055)	(0.054)	(0.055)
Secondary and higher secondary	0.303***	0.319***	0.303***
	(0.058)	(0.057)	(0.058)
Above higher secondary	0.311***	0.332***	0.312***
	(0.075)	(0.076)	(0.075)
Constant	–0.227*	–0.258*	–0.307*
	(0.109)	(0.113)	(0.154)
N	30517	30521	30517
R^2	0.04	0.04	0.04

Note: Figures not in parentheses show coefficient values. Figures in parentheses represent standard error. *, ** and *** represent significance at 1, 5 and 10% respectively.

Source: Author's calculation based on NSSO 70th round Situation Assessment Survey of Agricultural Households.

In all the models, ST households are found to have significantly lower chances of accessing information compared to the households belonging to the General Social group. As inferred form Table 1, we find households with kaccha households are less likely to access information on agriculture in comparison to those with pucca houses and this relationship is significant at the 1% level. We also find households which have at least one of its members receiving formal training in agriculture are more likely to access information probably because these are the households that know about different issues of agriculture and would be more open to access any new information. Controlling for other factors, we also find female headed households to be less likely to access information. One reason of this might be the fact that female headed households are less likely to be socially connected and hence would not get opportunity to access information.

In terms of land possession, we find that farmers with more land have higher probability of accessing information. This indicates that information might not be used by marginal farmers and may be kept closed within the circle of the big farmers. This is accentuated by the fact that poor farmers in terms of consumption expenditure are significantly less likely to access agricultural information.[1] For example, households in the first three quintiles of MPCE, Q1, Q2 and Q3 are found to have significantly less chances of accessing any information on agriculture in comparison to the richest households (at 1%, 5% and 10% level, respectively). Further, we also find education to be an important determinant of households accessing information. Compared to households with an illiterate head, those with literate heads (at primary, secondary and higher secondary level) have higher probability of accessing information for agricultural purpose.

All these findings reveal that access to information on agriculture has not been inclusive.[2] Clearly, it is found that small and marginal farmers with low income and education lag behind in accessing the much needed information for improving agricultural yield and productivity. This opens up another question as to whether government-run information agencies perform better than the private agencies in terms of dissemination of information to the poor and vulnerable farmers. We attempt to examine this in the following sub-section.

(ii) *Government agencies vs. private agencies*

As discussed, for this part we apply a multinomial logit model to compare Government information agencies and the private information agencies with the

---

[1] The variables used in the regression may be correlated. Hence, the regressions are carried out checking the multicollinearity.

[2] It is true that different forms of information may need different cost. At this stage, we are focusing only on information access. At a later stage, cost, both monetary and non-monetary can be invoked to study the association between information and cost.

external sources (ICT and progressive farmers) to examine who among the two is more inclusive in dissemination of information.

Table 3 presents the estimates from the regressions. The first two columns give the coefficient values along with the standard errors for the regression for estimating the probability of farmers accessing the information from Government sources as compared to the external sources like ICT and progressive farmers. We find that

Table 3. Multinomial logistic regression to estimate the probability of households accessing government information agencies and private agencies.

	Probability of government information		Probability of private information	
	Coefficient	Standard error	Coefficient	Standard error
Base: external (media + progressive farmers)				
Caste (Ref. General)				
ST	0.056	0.070	–0.007	0.075
SC	0.039	0.076	–0.010	0.081
OBC	–0.011	0.049	–0.027	0.052
Religion (Ref. Hindu)				
Muslim	0.05	0.069	0.095	0.072
Christian	0.012	0.094	–0.038	0.102
Others	–0.103	0.113	0.040	0.114
Hired house	0.036	0.165	0.018	0.174
House (Ref. Pucca)				
Kaccha	0.194**	0.088	0.098	0.096
Semi-pucca	0.074	0.049	0.031	0.053
Land holdings	–0.044*	0.011	–0.011	0.009
MPCE (Ref. Q5)				
Q1	0.324*	0.071	0.211*	0.076
Q2	0.158**	0.067	0.121***	0.071
Q3	0.129**	0.065	0.090	0.069
Q4	–0.058	0.062	0.038	0.065
Training in agriculture	–0.357*	0.091	0.005	0.088
Gender of household head (Ref. Male)				
Female head	–0.014	0.083	–0.035	0.089
Education of head (Ref. Illiterate)				
Below primary	–0.081	0.069	–0.114	0.074
Primary and middle	–0.013	0.055	–0.068	0.058
Secondary and higher secondary	–0.043	0.063	–0.040	0.066
Constant	–0.155	0.178	0.379**	0.188

Note: *, ** and *** represents significance at 1, 5 and 10%, respectively.
Source: Author's calculation based on NSSO 70th round Situation Assessment Survey of Agricultural Households.

farmers residing in kaccha houses are significantly more likely to access information from Government sources when compared to those residing in pucca houses (at 5% level of significance). Land possession is negatively correlated with the probability of households to access information from Government sources. Of note is the fact that the Government information agencies have been able to target the worse-off groups in terms of MPCE as we find households in the second quintile and the third quintile of MPCE most likely to access information from these sources. However, it should be acknowledged that the association of the poorest households in the Q1 quintile, though positive, is weaker with the probability of them accessing information from Government agencies. This indicates that there is a kind of bias in the inclusivity of access of information from these sources with the ultra-poor farmers left out, but the relatively better-off ones among the poor mostly getting information from Government agencies.

The last two columns of the table give the coefficient values and the standard errors respectively for the regression to estimate the probability of households seeking information from private sources as compared to the external sources. The findings suggest that private sources are less inclusive in terms of reaching out to the poorest and vulnerable farmers. Indicators of deprivation like belonging to scheduled groups (SC/ST), residence in kaccha households and education of the household head do not have a significant association with the probability of accessing agricultural information from the private agencies. In fact land possession also does not bear a strong correlation with access to information. However, middle income households from the 40th percentile to 60th percentile of MPCE are significantly more likely to access information pertaining to agriculture from private sources in comparison to the richest households. Nevertheless, if we compare the estimates of the first regression, it is clear that Government sources have been more proactive in disseminating information to the poor and deprived farmers, who would need the agricultural information more than anyone else.

(iii) *Non-parametric approach*

One of the main advantages of multi-variable regression method of analysis is the control for variables, other than the ones of interest that might affect a decision. However, the regression approach forces us to assume a function form to the model. This approach also requires assumptions on the underlying distribution of the data. To avoid these problems, we also use non-parametric kernel weighted local polynomial regressions to examine the relationship between the logarithmic value of the land possessed by a household and their probability of accessing information on farming practices (Fan and Gijbels, 1996). Further, we use these plots to observe the probability of households accessing information from Government and private agencies with respect to the external sources. Figures 1–3 plot these three graphs, respectively.

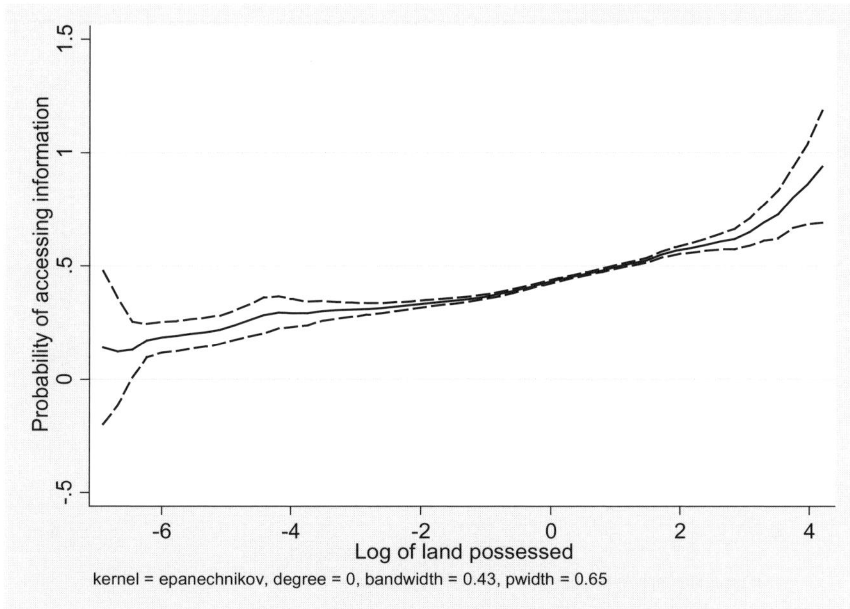

Figure 1. Local polynomial smoothing regression plot for probability of households accessing information on log of land possessed by the household.

Source: Author's calculation based on NSSO 70th round Situation Assessment Survey of Agricultural Households.

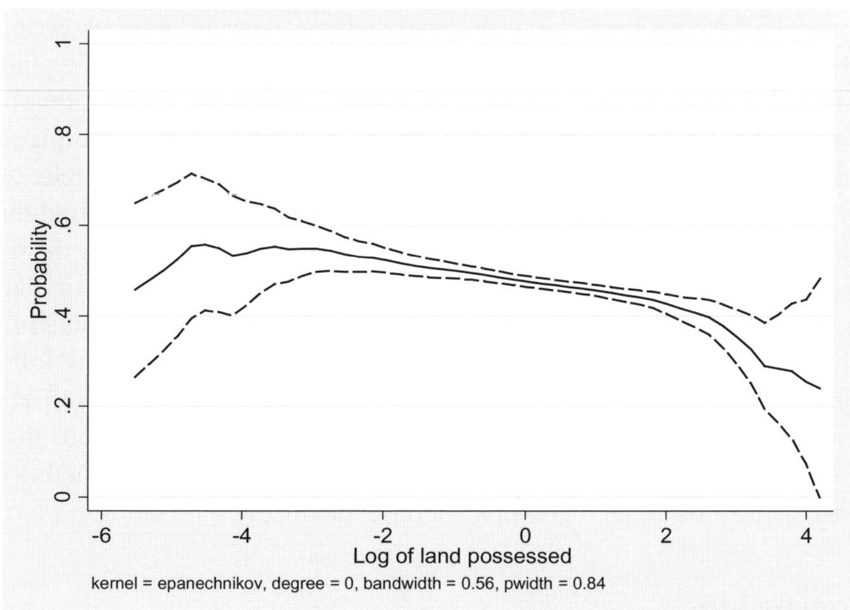

Figure 2. Local polynomial smoothing regression plots to estimate the probability of households accessing information from government sources with respect to external sources.

Source: Author's calculation based on NSSO 70th round Situation Assessment Survey of Agricultural Households.

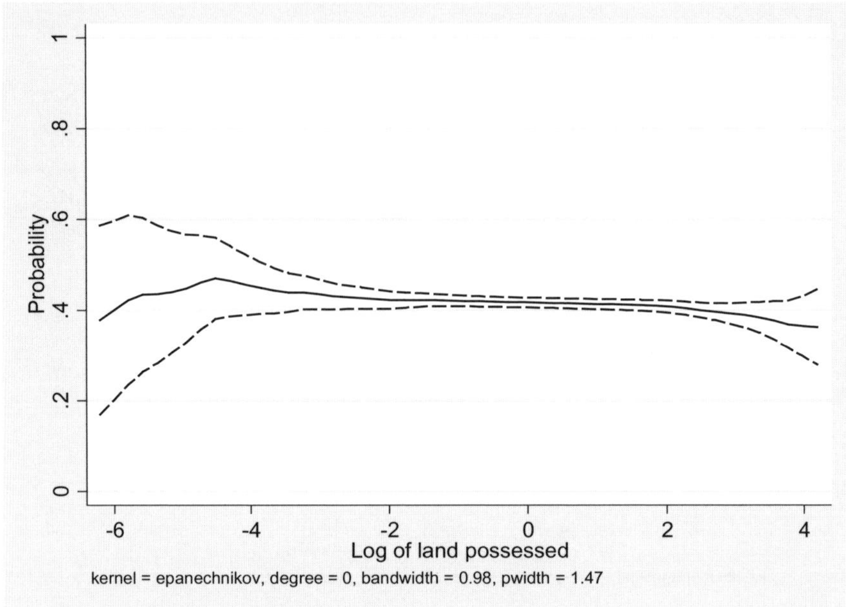

Figure 3. Local polynomial smoothing regression plots to estimate the probability of households accessing information from private sources with respect to external sources.

Source: Author's calculation based on NSSO 70th round Situation Assessment Survey of Agricultural Households.

It is found from Figure 1 that the association between land possession and probability of the households accessing agricultural information is an upward sloping curve. This reiterates the fact noted in the regression analysis that better-off farmers in terms of land possession are more likely to access information on agriculture and farming practices. Findings from Figures 2 and 3 also reiterate the results obtained from the regression estimates shown in Table 3. We find that the probability of households accessing Government agencies follows a decreasing path with the land possession showing that worse-off farmers are more likely to access information from Government sources. However, the plot obtained for the probability of households accessing information from private sources follows a near straight line parallel to the X-axis. This indicates that the worse-off farmers are not substantially more likely to access information on agriculture than the better-off ones. This non-parametric exercise lends support to the findings and inferences drawn from the regression exercise and makes our claims more robust.

6 Conclusion

Information plays a crucial role in important and effective decision-making in any economy. Any economic activity can be improved with the correct usage of relevant and timely information. The importance of information becomes especially relevant for agriculture, which is the mainstay for almost 60% of the population in India. Also attached with agriculture are the vagaries of climate change and price fluctuations, which make information necessary for the marginal and vulnerable farmers.

In this backdrop, this chapter examines the inclusiveness of access to information by the marginal famers. It also finds if poor and deprived farmers in terms of social group, household headship and consumption expenditure are likely to get the agricultural information. Further, the chapter explores if government information agencies are more inclusive than the private agencies, both when compared to the external agencies passed on by television/media/internet/newspaper and progressive farmers. Our findings show access to agricultural information is less likely to reach the marginal, poor and deprived farmers. We also find government agencies are more inclusive to the marginal farmers than the private ones.

The results lay stress on the fact that though marginal farmers may be the ones, who require information on farming practice so as to reduce vulnerability and enhance yield, their penetration in terms of information access is low. This is also true for farmers belonging to lower caste and income. However, we find government agencies performing better in terms of inclusiveness to these households compared to the private agencies. Hence, it is important for the government to identify areas dominated by agricultural risks and marginal farmers and increase the outreach of the information agencies. Establishment of an agricultural extension service or Krishi Vighyan Kendra in poor tribal areas with agriculture as the main occupation can go a long way to improve it and reduce vulnerability.

References

Ali, J. (2011), Adoption of mass media Information for Decision-making Among Vegetable Growers in Uttar Pradesh. *Indian Journal of Agricultural Economics*, *66*(2), 241.

Chapman, R. and T. Slaymaker (2002), ICTs and Rural Development: Review of the Literature, Current Interventions and Opportunities for Action. *Working Paper 1929* London. Overseas Development Institute.

Citroen, C.L. (2011), The Role of Information in Strategic Decision-making. *International Journal of Information Management*, 31, 493–501.

Gandhi, V.P. (2011), ICT Based Knowledge and Information System for Brand-variety Selection by Farmers: Study and Design Using the Crop-cutting Survey System in Cotton. *Indian Journal of Agricultural Economics*, 66(3), 498.

Greene, W. (2012), *Econometric Analysis*, 7th Edition. Boston, Columbus, Indianapolis, Pearson.

Helfand, S.M. and E.S. Levine (2004), Farm Size and the Determinants of Productive Efficiency in the Brazilian Center-West. *Agricultural Economics*, 31(2–3), 241–249.

Hussain, A., C. Lucas and M. A. Ali (2004), Managing Knowledge Effectively. *Journal of Knowledge Management Practice.*

Kahan, D. (2008), Managing Risk in Farming, Farm Management Extension Guide. *Food And Agriculture Organization Of The United Nations.*

Lio, M. and M. C. Liu (2006), ICT and Agricultural Productivity: Evidence from Cross-country Data. *Agricultural Economics*, 34(3), 221–228.

Nazari, M.R. and A.H. Hasbullah (2005), Farmers' Approach and Access to Information and Communication Technology in the Efficient Use of Modern Irrigation Methods. *Editorial Advisory Board e*, 21(1), 37–44.

NSSO (2005), Situation Assessment Survey of Farmers: Some aspects of farming.

NSSO (2014), Situation Assessment Survey of Agricultural Households.

Segrave, R. (2004), Communication Technologies and Knowledge Building in Agriculture. *Australian Journal of Adult Learning*, 44(1), 27–43.

Chapter 8

Choice and Design of Policy Instruments Towards Promoting Renewable Energy Technologies: Conceptual Framework and Guiding Principles

Rita Pandey
National Institute of Public Finance and Policy, New Delhi, India
rita.pandey@nipfp.org.in

Meeta Keswani Mehra
Jawaharlal Nehru University, New Delhi, India
meetakm@mail.jnu.ac.in

Abstract: There exists a consensus in the international community that clean energy technologies will significantly contribute toward mitigation of climate change as well as adapting to the impacts of climatic variations. The emissions control policies (e.g., market-based — getting prices right approach) have been argued to be efficient (cost minimizing) instruments to achieve greenhouse gas emissions reduction. These policies could also potentially work as an incentive for technological innovation in low-carbon energy and bring about changes in consumer behaviour as compared to the command and control or regulatory methods. However, government intervention towards the innovation process through additional complimentary policies to promote low-carbon energy technology might be necessary because both market and policy failures pose a barrier to their market penetration. This chapter reviews the best practices associated with the choice and design of such instruments toward promoting research, development and deployment of renewable energy technologies, and identifies the main lessons learned from their implementation (e.g., how to identify and design a policy to ease specific barriers for a given technology and other background variables; and how to identify a slowing down and an exit strategy). It is concluded that the issue of design and implementation of support measures for renewable energy technologies is complex and require a nuanced, case-by-case approach. Foremost, the design of the support instrument needs to be placed in a specific policy context (e.g., energy and climate policies), with clear identification of drivers for and barriers to its design and deployment. In this regard, the role of the regulatory, institutional, and political environment needs to be emphasized. It is also found that price-based instruments have worked better as compared to quantity-based instruments, and amongst various technologies, wind technology has had the maximum potential for cost reduction and dissemination. Finally, the costs of renewable energy technologies tend to fall as there is learning-by-doing and market maturation. Thus, the instrument design needs to have in-built flexibility in the price or quantity domain so as to adapt to the changing market situation and allow for a smooth phasing out/exit policy for the renewable energy technology.

1 Background

There exists a fair consensus amongst the international community that clean energy technologies will play a crucial role in the mitigation of climate change as well as adapting to the impacts of climatic variations. The Center for Climate and Energy Solutions estimates that carbon capture and storage (CCS) technologies can absorb around 90% of carbon emissions from coal-fired power plants and industries, and store them underground. Besides, some other potential opportunities that clean energy technologies offer include energy security, development benefits in the form of poverty reduction, improved health, opportunities for growth and employment generation, and gains from trade on account of an enlarged international market for energy. Needless to say, some sectors of the economy would have to contract, thus causing offsetting loss in output and employment. Gainful exploitation of clean energy opportunities would depend, on the one hand, on policies, capacities, local situations and the drive of individual countries, and on the other, entail technological breakthroughs that have not been witnessed before, thus warranting research, development and deployment (RD&D) in clean energy to be put on center stage. The magnitude and pace of technological transformation required in this context is highly challenging and unprecedented. However, so far the progress in this regard has been rather inadequate. For instance, the International Energy Agency (IEA) estimates a shortfall between the current $10 billion in annual public RD&D spending and the $40–$90 billion of investment needed for low-carbon energy technologies (IEA, 2010).

The emission control policies [(e.g., market-based approaches to get prices right — emissions pricing, emissions trading, environmental fiscal reforms)] have been argued to be efficient (cost minimizing) instruments to achieve reduction of greenhouse gas (GHG) emissions. These could also potentially work as an incentive for technological innovation in low-carbon energy and bring about changes in consumer behavior as compared to the command and control methods (Popp *et al.*, 2010; Downing and White, 1986; Millimen and Prince, 1989). However, the theoretical and empirical literature suggests that government intervention towards the innovation process through additional complementary policies to promote low-carbon energy technology might be necessary because environmental externalities are not the only market failure posing a barrier to penetration of low-carbon energy technologies. For instance, there exist problems associated with policy failures (Brown, 2001; Henriques and Sardorsky, 2008; van den Bergh and Bruinsma 2008; IPCC, 2011) economies of scale and market power (Neuhoff, 2005; Jamasb and Pollitt, 2008) and information distortions (Jaffe and Stavins, 1994; Levine *et al.*, 1995).

Consequently, countries across the world have implemented a wide range of public policy instruments to promote RD&D of low-carbon energy technologies, including renewable energy technologies (RETs) (Azuella and Luiz, 2011). This, however, has been achieved with varying levels of success and with both direct and indirect costs. Public policy instruments by their very nature put pressure on governments' budgets and thus, in turn, have implications for their ability to sustain funding support to investment flows in low-carbon energy sector (Gillingham and Sweeney, 2012; UNEP, 2011). This is a serious concern and requires that public policy instruments towards fostering the necessary investment in RD&D of low-carbon energy technologies be efficiently designed and implemented.

Against this backdrop, this chapter reviews the best practices associated with the choice and design of such instruments toward promoting RD&D of RETs, and identifies the main lessons learned of their implementation (e.g., how to identify and design a policy to ease specific barriers for a given technology and other background variables; and how to identify a slowing down and an exit strategy).[1] This chapter also presents a conceptual discussion which identifies the characteristics of drivers and barriers in innovation of RETs, sequencing of various steps involved in promoting innovation, and various policy tools in the context of each barrier that will help accelerate the process and enhance the outcomes; as well as outlines a set of guiding principles — based on a review of literature on the subject — in identifying and designing appropriate instruments.

[1] An assessment of Indian policies in this framework is undertaken in Mehra and Pandey (2016).

2 Policy Framework and Drivers for and Barriers to Complementary Instruments for Technology D&D

A number of domestic and international considerations inform and influence the choice and design of policy instruments towards D&D of RETs in a country. The entire process from planning to development of complementary policy instruments can be broadly divided into two stages: (i) setting the stage (that is, articulating an energy R&D framework and clearly identifying the barriers faced by different technologies), and (ii) basic guiding principles in actual design and implementation stage. Although the focus of this study is on the latter, some discussion on the former is necessary in order to put things in perspective and set the context.

3 Need for an Energy RD&D Policy Framework

A particularly challenging issue is how to identify which technologies need to be promoted, and this underscores the need for a comprehensive energy RD&D policy framework. Suitable energy RD&D policy frameworks are a cornerstone of energy technology promotion. A coherent and co-ordinated RD&D energy strategy — with clear prioritization in line with national energy policy goals — is the most important feature of a good practice energy RD&D framework (Fulton and Mellquist, 2011). In addition, a strong commitment from governments to make RD&D a sustainable and attractive proposition for all stakeholders is important (IEA, 2011a, b; Pandey *et al.*, 2014; Kammen *et al.*, 2004). This is achieved when clearly defined energy production goals and realistic targets — and not *ad hoc programmate* or fiscal interventions — guide medium-term to long-term direction of energy innovation (Pandey *et al.*, 2014; Kammen *et al.*, 2004; IEA, 2011a, b; Fulton and Mellquist, 2011). For instance, countries with small grid capacities may need to set targets which would reflect constrained grid capacities and, hence, may initially promote distributed generation over centralized generation. In the case of both wind and photovoltaic (PV) technologies, the promotion of power storage technologies could dramatically enhance their effectiveness.

According to IEA (2011a, b), the components of an RD&D policy framework based on good practices comprises:

- coherent energy RD&D strategy and priorities;
- adequate government RD&D funding and policy support;
- coordinated energy RD&D governance;
- strong collaborative approach, engaging industry through public–private partnerships (PPPs);

- effective RD&D monitoring and evaluation; and
- strategic international collaboration.

4 Drivers for Promoting Low-Carbon Energy Technologies

In general, there exist at least six specific drivers or energy development goals, either individually or in combination with each other, that shape the energy development pathways (IRENA, 2013). These are: (i) reducing GHGs and their impact on the environment, (ii) energy security (reducing dependence on vulnerable energy supplies), (iii) energy access (reducing energy poverty and expanding access to secure, reliable, and low-cost energy), (iv) energy cost (reducing exposure to persistently costly energy services), (v) international competitiveness (maintaining competitiveness in international energy markets and trade), and (vi) modernization (modernizing national energy systems).

5 Barriers to Development and Adoption of Low-Carbon RETs

A clear understanding of the barriers faced by different low-carbon technologies is required to develop appropriate and effective policies.

While the standard characterization of market failures is the inability of the markets to fully internalize the social costs/benefits in the pricing mechanisms, the market barriers are disincentives that adversely impact the market entry and/or adoption/use of solutions/devices/products and services (Groba and Breitschopf, 2013). Further, while market failures, as the term suggests, are necessarily linked to the poor functioning/absence of markets, market barriers could be linked to the functioning of the markets, distorting regulatory and fiscal policies, social and cultural factors, and asymmetric information etc. Selected market failures and barriers are listed in Table 1 and discussed in what follows. The discussion draws upon Groba and Breitschopf (2013).

The most common form of market failure takes the form of *unpriced social costs* of emissions, that is, prices of fossil fuels may not adequately reflect a variety of associated social costs. This would result in these goods being consumed at a level higher than what is socially desirable (Brown, 2001; Gillingham and Sweeney, 2010). Another negative externality is *supply vulnerability, price volatility and national security risks,* especially those pertaining to oil and gas imports (Bohi and Toman, 1996). Costs associated with these risks, such as increased military and diplomatic expenditures, are not adequately reflected in fossil fuel

Table 1. Selected market failures and barriers to RE innovation, adoption and diffusion.

Market failures	
Un-priced costs and negative externalities	**Economies of scale and market power**
• Un-priced social costs of emissions	• Un-priced benefits of learning-by-doing (LBD)
• Un-priced social costs of supply vulnerability, price and national security risks	• Marginalization of new technologies due to market power exerted by conventional energy companies
Un-priced benefits and positive externalities	**Information market failures and distortions**
• Un-priced benefits of innovation/knowledge	• High transactions cost of information
	• Principal-agent problems
	• Policy coordination problems
Market barriers	
Low priority and awareness of energy issues Capital market barriers	**Distortionary fiscal and regulatory policies**
• Uncertainty of future energy prices	• Subsidies for conventional energy sources
• High discount rates	• Administrative project approval procedures
• Capital-intensive investments in RET	• Unfavorable standards for RE

Source: Groba and Breitschopf (2013).

energy prices. Both of these would entail that the substitutes for fossil fuels, such as RETs, will be rendered uncompetitive and under-utilized unless incentives to invest in alternatives are provided by mitigating these external costs (Owen, 2006).

Unpriced social benefits in the form of knowledge creation and spillover in clean energy technologies creates a source of positive externality. Being non-rival and sometimes non-excludable (in the absence of patent and copyright protection), knowledge generating firms fail to capture the full economic benefit of their investment, thus causing it to be under provided. The concerns of market failure due to absence of full *appropriability* (AP) and LBD are also closely linked to the issue of unpriced benefits. Most technological developments face the difficulty of protecting research, especially basic research. This is tantamount to the inability of innovating firms to fully capture the benefits of R&D. In particular, other firms might copy, legally imitate, or use the knowledge about the new technology to advance their own research (Goulder and Parry, 2008). Empirical studies suggest that the (marginal) social return to innovation in general might be greater than the (marginal) private return (Griliches, 1992; Mansfield, 1985; Levin *et al.*, 1988; Jones and Williams, 1998). This is referred to as the concern of AP. While AP issue may arise in all three phases of the innovation, R&D spillovers may be much more important for very early stage R&D, rather than for technologies at the pilot or implementation stage (Nordhaus, 2010). Further, it is argued that LBD is necessary in bringing down the costs of technologies. This is supported by empirical evidence (Ek and Söderholm, 2010; IEA, 2010; Isoard and Soria, 2001; Junginger *et al.*, 2010; Kahouli-Brahmi, 2009; Klaassen *et al.*, 2005; Neij, 2008; Söderholm and Klaassen, 2007) though actual size of learning rates may vary widely for specific technologies (Lindman and Söderholm, 2012). However, competitors may benefit from the external benefits of the efforts of early adopters. Consequently, investments in learning will be sub-optimal in stimulating the efficient levels of cost reduction. Similar to the R&D spillovers, the lack of full AP of the gains is a positive externality and thus forms the basis for the market failure in LBD. While empirical analyses are scant, the econometric analysis of Braun *et al.* (2010), which is based on patent data, shows that innovation in wind and solar technologies is strongly driven by knowledge spillovers.

Economies of scale and market power constitute yet another source of market imperfection. With increasing returns and learning-by-using effects, the competition between the conventional energy sources and new RETs is tilted in favor of the former, especially since, in the absence of policy, innovators/investors in RETs are unable to capture the gains of future cost reductions induced through learning-by-using (Neuhoff, 2008). Thus, traditional vertically integrated utilities tend to wield market power against the small or renewable energy (RE) facilities with special characteristics such as decentralized production and intermittency (Neuhoff, 2005; Jamasb and Pollitt, 2008). Additionally, conventional energy companies exhibit organizational strength that might allow them to use their bargaining strength and lobbying power with the regulators against RE policy design and implementation (Hughes, 1986; Mitchell *et al.*, 2011).

Finally, *information market failures and distortions* render the adoption and diffusion of fossil fuel saving technologies at sub-optimal levels (Jaffe and Stavins, 1994; Levine *et al.*, 1995). Neoclassical frameworks attain efficiency based on the assumptions of free and perfect information situations. In reality, the transactions costs associated with information collection and decision-making intricacies are high, especially with regard to RE investment and consumption (Brown, 2001). Information is important in case of budding technologies, as uncertainty associated with the return on investment in innovation is often large and constitutes a barrier to innovation efforts (Young, 2010; Scherer *et al.*, 2000). Furthermore, the principle-agent problem looms large in case of RE dissemination. For example, landlords and tenants tend to have differing incentives to invest in distributed RE generation and energy efficiency, in that, although tenants are likely to benefit from investment, landlords are not compensated for the costs they bear, which results in considerable underinvestment (Levinson and Niemann, 2004; Murtishaw and Sathaye, 2006).

Key *market barriers* for RET D&D stem from low interest and awareness of policy makers, producers and consumers with regard to energy concerns, capital market barriers, and distortionary fiscal and regulatory policies (Brown, 2001; Henriques and Sardorsky, 2008; van den Bergh and Bruinsma, 2008; IPCC, 2011). Presence of consumer myopia causing undervaluation of benefits of energy efficiency/low-carbon energy poses a significant market barrier. In addition, poor information and cultural and social barriers to do things differently presents strong resistance to adoption. Innovation in low-carbon energy technologies often has very high upfront capital requirements, and involves long time horizon for recovery. Like any R&D it involves substantial economic, technical and regulatory risks that hamper access to finance.

While the identification of specific barriers that limit the progress in RE technology innovation and diffusion in general is required, it is necessary to differentiate the barriers by different RE technologies, which is attempted by Gillingham and Sweeney (2012) (Table 2).

6 Choice and Design of Complementary Instruments for Technology D&D and Criteria for Comparison

In what follows, we discuss the guiding principles that underlie the choice and design of instruments with emphasis on relative merits of specific instruments on identified performance criteria. These discussions draw from the theoretical literature as well as from select literature on recent country experiences and thus serve as a lesson for designing and implementing a policy instrument. Notably, these discussions ought to be seen in light of the fact that there may be a large number of other policy and general business environment related factors in individual countries informing as well as influencing both the design and the performance of a policy.

6.1 Choice of policies

Several considerations, with significant overlap among them, determine the choice and design of technology policies. However, there are some general rules at the conceptual level that guide the choice, as enumerated below.

- Enhancement of economic efficiency is the primary criterion to rank policy choices as policies would have to address the identified externalities. Although, some technologies may require special consideration. For instance, breakthrough technologies such as CCS that may have the potential to produce dramatic results are highly capital intensive with a lot of uncertainty about their long-term impacts (Fischer and Newell, 2007). Therefore, a policy mix

Table 2. Market failures and barriers in RE by technologies.

Technology	Market failure	Remarks	Barrier	Remarks
Central generation	AP, LBD	The evidence on the extent of the R&D and LBD, AP remains very limited. Quantifying this is very difficult. Similarly, quantifying LBD separately from the economics of scale and exogenous technologies change is a difficult empirical challenge.	Capital constraints, simultaneous coordination problem.	A simultaneous co-ordination problem has some similarities to a public goods problem, and may provide motivation for either government co-ordination of different agents or possibly government provision of the good or service.
Distributed RE	AP and LBD may be relevant		These technology may face the same barriers as in central generation.	The only major difference is that in this case, consumers (and sometimes firms) are the purchasers of the technology, rather than electric utilities as in the case of centralized generation.
CCS Technologies	Theoretically same AP issues are likely to apply in the case of CCS	However, since much of the research in this area is being done by the Public Sector the AP would not apply.	The most fundamental barriers to CCS are high cost (early stage technology which is highly energy intensive).	Concerns of leak out of carbon, risk of abrupt release of CO2 and the consequent liability risk and public acceptance.

Source: Based on Gillingham and Sweeney (2012).

incorporating preferential capital, international collaboration, among others, will need to be designed (IRENA, 2013).

- The choice of appropriate policy instruments will also depend on how optimal are the emissions policies in dealing with GHG emissions reduction. For instance, in the presence of a sub-optimal emissions policy — such as when emissions pricing is just a token (e.g., the tax on carbon emissions that has no link to emissions reduction targets in a country) and/or covers only a few sectors of the economy — the role of complementary policy instruments can be seen as a way of correcting negative environmental externalities resulting from the use of fossil fuels as well as of addressing market failures in the low-carbon energy technology market. Moreover, present an optimal emissions policy along with a clear roadmap to fossil fuel subsidy reform, the role of policy instruments can be seen as a way of achieving dynamic efficiency by stimulating technical change (Fischer *et al.*, 2012).
- Even with a strong emissions policy, certain technologies, which require large capital investment and must be scaled up to realize cost reduction, are likely to face barriers, if there are capital constraints or a simultaneous coordination problem. Capital constraints are more significant in emerging economies that lack venture capitalists and private equity institutions (Gillingham and Sweeney, 2012).

In addition, a number of other factors determine the choice of instruments, namely,

- Status of many critical factors such as skilled manpower, R&D capability, strong supporting institutions and capacity for developing systems for price discovery (e.g., auctions, reverse bidding) significantly influence both the choice of complementary fiscal instruments and their impact.
- Also critical is the availability of empirical evidence on the contribution of specific market failures (relative importance and magnitude of AP and LBD) on technology development/penetration/adoption (e.g., despite a vast empirical literature, considerable uncertainty remains regarding LBD for a wide range of technologies (Doner, 2007).
- Policies enacted at the sub-national/state level should be in agreement/coordinated and consistent with national policies and goals.
- The maturity of clean energy market, regulatory provisions (such as long-term policy and financial commitment), and targets for clean energy are some of the other important determinants of choice of policy instruments.

An important concern in deciding policy instruments for D&D of clean technologies is the choice of quantity (Q) vs. price (P) instrument. Some discussion on this can be found in Box 1.

Box 1: Quantity vs. price instrument

As a general point, in the case of pollution control methods, price-based (P) and quantity-based (Q) schemes produce similar outcomes when all the necessary information is available. However, the outcome of these two approaches will tend to differ when information is incomplete (Cropper and Oats, 1992). One or the other of these will be preferred depending upon the relative slopes of the marginal abatement cost curve and the damage curve (Weitzman, 1974). In applying these concepts to stimulate low-carbon energy generation, a simplified argument would be that a Q-based approach is preferred when the slope of the MC is relatively flat. Conversely, a P instrument such as feed-in-tariff (FIT) may lead to significant increase in supply and, consequently, in subsidies. It can then be argued that the Q-based approach is more effective in controlling the cost of government incentive policies, whereas in the P-based systems, production cannot be anticipated with any precision because of the uncertainty regarding cost curves. Therefore, if the emphasis is on fast pacing the RE generation, and also keeping a check on the cost of subsidies, the policy maker should choose a combination of Q (e.g., renewable portfolio standard(RPS)) and P instrument (such as competitive bidding (CB) system) which provides the incentive to reduce costs *vis-a-vis* FIT alone, since competing producers must reflect lower costs in prices in order to win subsidies. However, this may or may not work for all types of technologies. Dong (2012) finds that FIT has better long term effects in promoting wind energy, although in the short-run RPS could also provide some incentives to developers.

However, a cautious approach would be required. For, it may be argued that the bidding approach may lower the price and the cost of RE, though this price reduction may not be due to technical change but may happen due to systematic effort to reduce costs through economies of scale and use of the very best sites available (low hanging fruit argument). In terms of efficiency, in the P vs. Q debate, whichever system is chosen, the main objective in the medium- to long-term in most cases is to stimulate technical progress, such that the gap between the costs of low-carbon energy and existing technologies continuously narrows down.

Empirical research shows that the technological learning effects have been much greater for manufacturers in countries that have opted for FIT (Dong, 2012). An explanation would be that the surplus that goes to the producers in Q-based approach is limited whereas technical change tends to increase the producers' surplus in the case of P-based approach (e.g., FIT), thus encouraging them to innovate more.

(*Continued*)

Box 1: (*Continued*)

According to Menanteau *et al.* (2003), if social preference is attached to climate change prevention and reflected in a high quantitative objective for RE, FIT is a good compromise in order to promote technical progress. The quota/certificate system also presents a number of advantages in terms of static efficiency, but its ability to stimulate innovation has still to be confirmed by experience. They also derive that in terms of installed capacity, from an empirical point of view, P-based approaches yield better outcomes than the Q-based approaches. This is ascribable to the strong incentive effect of fixed prices that induce greater stability and predictability in the incentive systems for the investors. However, in terms of control over costs, the system of fixed FITs renders it difficult to anticipate the level of RE production of electricity on account of uncertainties of cost curves. Thus, in this respect, Q-based approaches induce lower costs as bidding for successive quotas provides an indirect way of controlling overall costs.

Madlener *et al.* (2010) considers a perfectly competitive market with the possibility of technological innovation, and contrasts guaranteed FIT for electricity from renewables with traded green certificate from the point of view of social welfare as well as dynamic efficiency. The main finding is that subsidy policies are preferable in terms of dynamic efficiency. However, the P approach dominates the Q approach in terms of social welfare if the assumption of perfect competition is relaxed.

6.2 Design of policies

The most important aspects of designing complementary fiscal policy instruments are the determination of the support level and the duration of the support. Notably, policy instruments that would effectively promote basic R&D are different from those needed to stimulate a dynamic learning process and bring down the cost of technology. This emphasizes the need for differentiating technologies by the stage of technology development. Further, as the RE technologies evolve, markets mature and the costs of RE are lowered, the financial support to renewables will have to be gradually phased out, with the exception of the support for R&D expenditure to immature new technologies on the anvil with good long-term potential. Incentive/support schemes will have to be flexible enough to adjust as technologies evolve on the global market, mainly due to learning curves and technological innovation that lead to cost reductions. This would require that the design of the support scheme has the built-in flexibility in level and time frame to accommodate changes in the development of costs and technologies without any adverse impact on the momentum of potential innovation, pace of RE generation targets and other drivers. That is, these schemes should include automatic tariff degressive characteristics and built-in revision mechanisms. Some key considerations in designing this would be: an understanding of market dynamics, interactions among policy instruments, an understanding of entry points both in scale and magnitude, a slowing/course correction strategy (by incorporating feedback loops, LBD, information diffusion) and an exit strategy as market dynamics change. Moreover, the importance of making policies predictable, stable in medium to long-term to reduce the risk and uncertainty that investors and consumers face has been emphasized in the literature. In this context, first a brief discussion on policy mechanisms available to policy makers is in order. This is followed by a brief distinction between market-pull and technology-push instruments (Pandey and Mehra, 2015).

7 Public Policy Mechanisms Available to Policy Makers

Broadly, fiscal policies commonly refer to tax and public expenditure based measures such as accelerated depreciation, tax holidays for initial years of the project (post-commissioning), tax rebates through waiver/reduction of import duties and excise duty (tax on production of goods), and capital subsidy (grants, soft loans). They are, invariably, based on the size of the investment/actual installation of the equipment, are generally not linked to the use or performance of the equipment, and there may be some (e.g., tax incentives and subsidies for projects in designated areas/special economic zones etc.) that are not even linked to the actual activity and/or use of specific technology or quantity of power generation.

Financial incentives, on the other hand, are (mostly) directly linked to the actual amount of generation and, in some cases, to the amount of investment, e.g., policies such as FITs, generation-based incentives (GBI) etc. Financial instruments are often designed to address financial barriers, such as access to capital, high perceived risk to the sector, etc.

UNEP (2011) defines public finance mechanisms (PFMs) as financial commitments made by the public sector that alter the risk-reward balance of private sector investments by reducing or removing barriers to investment. It further states that while policy instruments that set the overall economic framework conditions for investment in low-carbon technology such as FITs, carbon taxes and *renewable portfolio standards* (RPS) are not regarded as PFMs, their presence has a significant effect on the success of a given PFM. They should, therefore, be taken into account when evaluating the context in which successful PFMs operate.

In this chapter, complementary policy instruments are taken to be a combination of supporting regulatory policy and tax mechanisms, and PFMs to support investment in low-carbon energy technologies. This is because of the interdependencies (e.g., presence of RPS can enhance the effectiveness of FIT) between them and the fact that different types of instruments are required along the low-carbon technology continuum.

7.1 Fiscal policy instruments differentiated by market-pull and technology-push policies

This differentiation is helpful in identifying the right instrument and its appropriate design. Table 3 presents a broad categorization. While the demand-pull policies aim to increase the RE demand by addressing environmental externalities or reducing market barriers, technology-push policies primarily aim at increasing the incentives to generate new knowledge and further work on the available knowledge to improve upon its performance and cost.

Technology-push policies can be classified into fiscal measures (e.g., grants, rebates, tax credits), financial measures (e.g., direct investment, soft loans, credit risk guarantees etc.), institutional support (government funded research facilities, support for getting patents) and stricter patent rules to reduce the upfront costs and risks of investments (Mitchel *et al.*, 2011). These directly target and incentivize the private investment in various stages of technology development and diffusion. Technology-push policies are especially important in pushing investment in early stages of innovation due to various risks and uncertainties around the chances of success and the time taken in reaching the commercial stage.

Market pull policies include both Q-based (e.g., carbon trading mechanism, RPS) and the P-based (e.g., carbon tax, FIT) instruments that can be either technology neutral (e.g., carbon tax, carbon trading mechanism) or target specific technologies (e.g., FIT, RPS).

As a general rule, policies such as R&D support, financial incentives, and procurement incentives are more suitable for stimulating commercialization and initial market creation for new technologies, which can create a technology push. Once a technology is established in the market, further growth can be stimulated by policies such as FIT, RPS and other financial incentives.

An important issue, however, is to strike a balance between technology- push and market-pull measures from the beginning. To do so, policy makers need to understand how these measures interact under and respond to different market conditions. Although some discussion on this is available in Dong (2012) that points toward more empirical research on the structural reasons for a country to

Table 3. Strategies and selected policies for promotion of RE.

		Technology-specific (direct)		Non-technology-specific (indirect)
		Price-driven	**Quantity-driven**	
Market-pull policies				
Market-based	Investment incentives	• Investment subsidies • Tax credits • Supportive tax policy • Tenders (prices)	• Tendering systems for investment grants (quantity) • Quotas (capacity)	• Environmental taxes • Emission trading
	Generation incentives	• FITs • Premium FITs	• Energy portfolio standard (quotas) in combination with tradable green certificates (TGCS) • Tendering systems for long-term contracts	
Command-and-control		• Technology and performance standards • Authorization procedures		
Voluntary	Investment Promotion	• Shareholder programs • Contribution programs		• Voluntary agreements
	Generation promotion	• Green tariffs		
Technology-push policies				
• Public R&D spending (direct funding, grants, prices) • Tax credits to invest in R&D • Capacity enhancement for knowledge exchange • Support for education and training • Financing demonstration or pilot projects • Market engagement/incentive programs/public procurement • Strategic development policies • Technology exhibitions/fairs • Network creating/building				

Source: Groba and Breitschopf (2013).

adopt a given policy, this area remains to be explored in detail. This should be done in a technology-specific, country-specific and a case specific manner.

7.2 The comparative efficiency of different policies

The deployment of policy instruments for RE programs requires choice based on several criteria, namely, effectiveness in terms of stimulation of RE deployment, cost of deployment for the economy, incentives to reduce costs and prices and incentives to innovate/technological learning or market maturation. Select country experiences regarding these aspects provide important lessons on how the deployment of select policy instruments for RE technologies have performed on these accounts (Mehra and Pandey, 2016).

Mainly, the following three key sets of support schemes will be taken up for more detailed analysis:

- *Price-based market instruments such as FITs and feed-in-premiums (FITPs)*: FITs/FITPs are price-based regulatory instruments wherein producers are assured a set price or premium per unit by the government for the electricity produced, irrespective of the amount generated. An important difference between FIT and premium payment is that the latter induces competition between producers in the electricity market, while the former may not directly induce competition. The public utility is obligated to connect the RE generator to the grid and pay a pre-determined rate/premium for the life of FIT/FITP contract, usually 10–20 years, to lower market risks to investors. Both FITs and FITPs are structured to stimulate specific technologies and cost reductions (latter though a phased reduction in tariff/premium).
- *Quantity-based market instruments called RPSs or quota obligations*: RPS is a form of quantity regulation in which a target or quota obligation is set by the government in order to ensure that a set market share of energy (say, in the form of electricity) comes from RE sources (Dong, 2012). Here, a retailer is obligated to include energy generated by renewable sources into his portfolio. Generally, RPS use tradable/non-tradable renewable energy certificates (RECs) or TGCs to create a market for environmental attributes (as in the UK) although this is not always the case (as in California, US). A TGC is an official record certifying that a particular amount of RE has been generated. Quota obligations with TGCs are generally technology-neutral support mechanisms, aiming at promoting most cost efficient technology options. Since an RPS relies on the private market for its implementation, it allows for competition among different types of RE. It also permits RE sources to compete with the cheaper fossil fuels in the long run due to efficiency and innovation.

- *Tendering/competitive bidding*: A tender is announced for providing a certain quantity of electricity from a specific technology source, and the bidding process ensures that the lowest offer is accepted. The structuring of competitive bidding can range from a single bid to multiple rounds of bidding. Under the single bid arrangement, power producers bid for providing a fixed amount of RE level, and the lowest price-bidder wins the bid. Under multiple rounds of bidding, there are multiple winners and with each successive round of bidding, the price quoted by the bidder gets reduced, thereby reducing the cost of RE provision (Beck *et al.*, 2004). Tendering allows for incorporation of additional conditions, e.g., mandated local manufacturing of technology.

8 Conclusion

The issue of design and implementation of support measures for RE technologies is complex and requires a nuanced, case-by-case approach. However, some broad conclusions can be drawn from a review of design and implementation of such measures discussed in the foregoing sections.

Foremost, the design of the support instrument needs to be placed in a specific policy context (e.g., energy and climate policies), with clear identification of drivers for and barriers to its design and deployment. The role of the regulatory, institutional and political environment needs to be emphasised, especially as the level and structure of the instrument have to be benchmarked against the prices of conventional energy, besides other advantages that conventional energy sources enjoy (e.g., supporting infrastructure, consumer acceptability, established technology and such like). The cost of RE, as much as the grid-based prices (and more recently the presence of carbon taxes), has a bearing on the viability of RETs. There is widespread recognition of availability and connectivity to grid infrastructure as a constraint to diffusion of solar and wind power across a range of country studies.

In general, it has been found that price-based instruments have worked better as compared to quantity-based instruments, and amongst various RES, wind technology has had the maximum potential for cost reduction and dissemination. It is also commonly suggested that incentives/support measures need to rely, as much as possible, on market-based instruments, e.g., quota obligations coupled with tendering and/or green certificates, such that the true costs get revealed. A caveat in this regard is that reliance on market forces will circumscribe the ability of the producers to reap the sufficient rent that can otherwise help spur innovation. Thus, incentives for dynamic efficiency for less mature technologies (in particular) should not be ignored.

None of the instruments offer an optimal solution in all the evaluation criteria. As a consequence, governments will have to select an instrument and sustain it in the long run in accordance with the relative importance of its objectives. In a complementary way, conditions of a successful instrument *vis-à-vis* the regulatory risk include long-term government's commitment, foreseeability of the instrument and ex ante flexibility to capture decreasing RE cost and correct redistributive effects. The level of the support must not be abstracted from the incurring risks and transaction cost.

The costs of RETs tend to fall as there is LBD and market maturation. Thus, the instrument design needs to have in-built flexibility in the price or quantity domain so as to adapt to the changing market situation. In this regard, a smooth phasing out/exit policy for the RE technology is also prescribed as the levelised cost of the technology is lowered to approach that of conventional energy in the limit.

References

Azuela, G.E. and L.A. Barroso (2011), Design and Performance of Policy Instruments to Promote the Development of Renewable Energy: Emerging Experience in Selected Developing Countries, Energy and Mining Sector Board *Discussion Paper no. 22*. The World Bank, Washington, DC.

Beck, F. and E. Martinot (2004), *Renewable Energy Policy and Barriers. Encyclopedia of Energy*, Vol 5, Ed. Cutler Cleveland, Academic Press/Elsevier Science: San Diego.

Bohi, D. and M.A. Toman (1996), *Economics of Energy Security*, Kluwer Academic Publishers, Norwell. M.A.

Braun, F.G., J. Schmidt-Ehmcke and P. Zloczysti (2010), Innovative Activity in Wind and Solar Technology: Empirical Evidence on Knowledge Spillovers using Patent Data, *CEPR Discussion Paper no. DP7865*. Available from SSRN: http://ssrn.com/abstract=1640387. (Accessed on 15 June 2015).

Brown, M.A. (2001), Market Failures and Barriers as a Basis for Clean Energy Policy, *Energy Policy*, 29(14), 1197–1207.

Cropper, M.L. and W.E. Oates (1992), Environmental Economics: A Survey, *Journal Economic Literature* 30, 675–740.

Doner, J. (2007), *Barriers to Adoption of Renewable Energy Technology*. Illinois State University, Institute for Regulatory Policy Studies.

Dong, C.G. (2012), Feed-in Tariff vs. Renewable Portfolio Standard: An Empirical Test of their Relative Effectiveness in Promoting Wind Capacity Development, *Energy Policy*, 42, 476–485.

Downing, P.G. and L.J. White (1986), Innovation in Pollution Control, *Journal of Environmental Economics and Management*, 13, 18–29.

Ek, K. and P. Söderholm (2010), Technology Learning in the Presence of Public R&D: The Case of European Wind Power, *Ecological Economics*, 69, 2356–2362.

Fischer, C. and R.G. Newell (2007), Environmental and Technology Policies for Climate Mitigation, *Journal of Environmental Economic Management*, 55, 142–162.

Fischer, C., A. Torvanger, M.K. Shrivastava, T. Sterner and P. Stigson (2012), How Should Support for Climate-Friendly Technologies Be Designed? *Ambio*, 41, 33–45.

Fulton, M. and N. Mellquist (2011), *The German Feed-in Tariff for PV: Managing Volume Success with Price Response*. DB Climate Change Advisors, Deutsche Bank Group.

Gillingham, K. and J. Sweeney (2010), Market Failures and the Structure of Externalities, in: Padilla, A. J. and R. Schmalensee (Eds.) *Harnessing Renewable Energy*, RFF Press, Washington, DC.

Gillingham, K. and J. Sweeney (2012), Barriers to Implementing Low Carbon Technologies, *Climate Change Economics*, 3(4),1250019.

Goulder, L.H. and I.W.H. Parry (2008), Instrument Choice in Environmental Policy. *Review of Environmental Economics and Policy*, 2(2), 152–174.

Griliches, Z. (1992), The Search for R&D Spillovers. *Scandinavian Journal of Economics*, 94, 29–47.

Groba, F. and B. Breitschopf (2013), Impact of Renewable Energy Policy and use of Innovation — A Literature Review. *Discussion Paper no 1318*, DIW Berlin, German Institute for Economic Research.

Henriques, I. and P. Sardorsky (2008), Oil Prices and the Stock Pieces of Alternative Energy Companies, *Energy Economics*, 30(3), 998–1010.

Hughes, T. (1986), The Seamless Web: Technology, Science, Etcetera, Etcetera, *Social Studies of Science*, 16(2), 281–292.

IEA (2010), Global Gaps in Clean Energy RD&D: Update and Recommendations for International Collaboration, Paris. Available from: https://www.iea.org/publications/freepublications/publication/global_gaps.pdf.

International Energy Agency (IEA) (2011a), *Good Practice Policy Framework for Energy Technology Research, Development and Demonstration (RD&D)*. Energy Technology Policy Division, IEA Paris. Available from: https://www.iea.org/publications/free publications/publication/good_practice_policy.pdf. (Accessed on 20 December 2015).

IEA (2011b), *Deploying Renewables, Best and Future Policy Practice*. Paris, France.

IPCC (2011), AR5, WGIII. Technical Summary. Availablc from: http://www.ipcc.ch/pdf/assessment-report/ar5/wg3/drafts/ipcc_wg3_ar5_fd_comments_summary-for-policymakers.pdf.

IRENA (2013), Renewable Energy Innovation Policy: Success Criteria and Strategies. *Working paper*. Available from: https://www.irena.org/DocumentDownloads/Publications/Renewable_Energy_Innovation_Policy.pdf.

Isoard, S. and A. Soria (2001), Technical Change Dynamics: Evidence from the Emerging Renewable Energy Technologies, *Energy Economics*, 23(6), 619–636.

Jaffe, A.B., R.G. Newell and R.N. Stavins (2005), A tale of two market failures: Technology and Environmental policy. *Ecological Economics*, 54(2–3), 164–174.

Jaffe, A.B. and R.N. Stavins (1994), The Energy-Efficiency Gap, *Energy Policy*, 22(10), 804–810.

Jaffe, A.B. and R.N. Stavins (1995), Dynamic Incentives of Environmental Regulations: The Effects of Alternative Policy Instruments on Technology Diffusion, *Journal of Environmental Economics and Management*, 29, 43–63.

Jager, D. and M. Rathman (2008), *Policy Instrument design to reduce financing costs in renewable energy technology projects*. ECOFYS and IEA. Available from: http://www.ecofys.com/files/files/report_policy_instrument_design_to_reduce_financing_costs_in_renewable_energy_technology_pro.pdf (Accessed on 20 October 2015).

Jamasb, T. and M. Pollitt (2008), Liberalisation and R&D in Network Industries: The Case of the Electricity Industry, *Research Policy*, 37(6–7), 995–1008.

Jones, C.I. and J.C. Williams (1998), Measuring the Social Return to R&D, *Quartery Journal of Economics*, 113, 1119–1135.

Junfeng, L., S. Pengfei and G. Hu (2010), China Wind Power Outlook 2010. Beijing: CREIA, GWEC, Greenpeace. Available from: http://www.greenpeace.org/eastasia/Global/eastasia/publications/reports/climate-energy/2010/2010-china-wind-power-outlook.pdf. (Accessed on 3 June 2015).

Junginger, M., W.V. Sark and A. Faaij (2010), *Technological Learning in the Energy Sector — Lessons for Policy, Industry and Science*. Cheltenham, UK.

Kahouli-Brahmi, S. (2009). Testing for the Presence of Some Features of Increasing Returns to Adoption Factors in Energy System Dynamics: An Analysis via the Learning Curve Approach, *Ecological Economics*, 68(4), 1195–1212.

Kammen, D.M., K. Kapadia and M. Fripp (2004), Putting Renewables to Work: How Many Jobs Can the Low-Carbon Technology Industry Generate? RAEL Report. Energy and Resources Group Goldman School of Public Policy, University of California, Berkeley.

Klaassen, G., A. Miketa, K. Larsen and T. Sundqvist (2005), The Impact of R&D on innovation for wind energy in Denmark, Germany and the United Kingdom, *Ecological Economics*, 54(2–3), 227–240.

Levin, R.C., A.K. Klevorick, R.R. Nelson and S.G. Winter (1988), Appropriating the Returns from Industrial Research and Development, *Brookings Papers on Economic Activity*, 3, 783–820.

Levine, M.D., J.G. Koomey, J.E. McMahon, A. Sanstad and E. Hirst (1995), Energy Efficiency Policy and Market Failures, *Annual Review of Energy and Environment*, 20, 535–555.

Levinson, A. and S. Niemann (2004), Energy Use by Apartment Tenants when Landlords Pay for Utilities, *Resource and Energy Economics*, 26, 51–75.

Lindman, A. and P. Söderholm (2012), Wind Power Learning Rates: A Conceptual Review and Meta-Analysis, *Energy Economics*, 34(3), 754–761.

Mansfield, E. (1985), How Fast does New Industrial Technology Leak Out? *Journal of Industrial Economics*, 34, 217–233.

Mehra, Meeta K. and Rita Pandey, (2016), Emerging Experience with Design and Implementation of Policy Instruments for RET D&D across Countries, in: Agarwal, Manmohan, Jing Wang and John Whalley (Eds.). *The Economics of China and India: Cooperation and Conflict. Volume 3: Economic Growth, Employment and Inclusivity: The International Environment*. World Scientific. Forthcoming.

Menanteau, P., D. Finon and M.L. Lamy (2003), Price versus Quantities: Choosing Policies for Promoting the Development of Renewable Energy, *Energy Policy*, 31(8), 799–812.

Millimen, S.R. and R. Prince (1989), Firm Incentives to Promote Technological Change in Pollution Control, *Journal of Environmental Economics and Management*, 17(3), 247–265.

Mitchell, C., J.L. Sawin, G.R. Pokharel, D. Kammen, Z. Wang, S. Fifita, M. Jaccard, O. Langniss, H. Lucas, A. Nadai, R. Trujillo Blanco, E. Usher, A. Verbruggen, R. Wustenhagen and K. Yamaguchi (2011), Policy, Financing and Implementation, in: O. Edenhofer, R. Pichs-Madruga, Y. Sokona, K. Seyboth, P. Matschoss, S. Kadner, T. Zwickel, P. Eickemeier, G. Hansen, S. Schlomer and C. Von Stechow (Eds.) *IPCC Special Report on Renewable Energy Sources and Climate Change Mitigation*, Cambridge University Press, Cambridge, New York.

Murtishaw, W. and J. Sathaye (2006), *Quantifying the Effect of the Principal-Agent Problem on US Residential Energy Use*, Lawrence Berkley National Laboratory, Berkley. C.A.

Neij, L. (2008), Cost Development of Future Technologies for Power Generation — a Study Based on Experience Curves and Complementary Bottom-up Assessments, *Energy Policy*, 36(6), 2200–2211.

Neuhoff, K. (2005), Large-Scale Deployment of Renewables for Electricity Generation, *Oxford Review of Economic Policy*, 21(1), 88–110.

Neuhoff, K. (2008), Learning by Doing with Constrained Growth Rates: An Application to Energy Technology Policy, *The Energy Journal*, 29(2), 165–182.

Nordhaus, W.D. (2010), Designing a Friendly Space for Technological Change to Slow Global Warming, *Energy Economics*, 33(4), 665–673.

Owen, A.D. (2006), Renewable energy: Ecternality costs as market barrier, *Energy Policy*, 34(5), 632–642.

Pandey, R., S. Bali and N. Mongia (2014), *The National Low-carbon Technology Fund of India: A Framework for Promoting Effective Utilization*. Springer Briefs in Energy.

Pandey, R. and M.K. Mehra (2015), Role of Fiscal Instruments in Promoting Low-carbon Technology Innovation. *GGKP Working Paper No. 06*, November 2015. Available from: http://www.greengrowthknowledge.org/sites/default/files/downloads/resource/Role_of_Fiscal_Instruments_in_Promoting_Low-carbon_Technology_Innovation_GGKP_0.pdf

Popp, D., R.G. Newell and A.B. Jaffe (2010), Energy, The Environment, and Technological Change, in: Hall, B.H. and N. Rosenberge (Eds.) *Handbook of the Economics of Innovation. Vol 2*.

Scherer, F., D. Harhoff and J. Kukies (2000), Uncertainty in the Size Distribution of Rewards from Technological Innovation, *Jounral of Evolutionary Economics*, 10(1), 175–200.

Söderholm, P. and G. Klaassen (2007), Wind Power in Europe: A Simultaneous Innovation Diffusion Model. *Environmental and Resource Economics*, 36(2), 163–190.

United Nations Environment Programme (UNEP) (2011), Evaluating Clean Energy Public Finance Mechanisms. UNEP on behalf of UNEP Sustainable Energy Finance (SEF) Alliance. UNEP SEF Alliance Secretariat, Montpelier, VT. Available from: http://www.cleanegroup.org/wp-content/uploads/Evaluating-Clean-Energy-PFM.pdf. (Accessed on 26 May 2015).

UNEP (2012), Feed in Tariffs as a Policy Instrument for Promoting Renewable Energies and Green Economies in developing Countries. Available from: http://www.unep.org/pdf/UNEP_FIT_Report_2012F.pdf.

Van den Bergh, J.C.J.M. and F.R. Bruinsma (2008), *Managing the Transition to Renewable Energy: Theory and Practice from Local, Regional and Macro Perspectives*, Edward Elgar Publishing Limited, Cheltenham, UK.

Weitzman, M.L. (1974), Prices vs. Quantities, *The Review of Economic Studies*, 41(4), 477–491.

Young, P. (2010), Innovation and Diffusion in Heterogeneous Populations: Contagion, Social Influence and Social Learning, *The American Economic Review*, 99(5), 1899–1924.

Part III

Employment

Chapter 9

Wages and Earnings of Marginalized Social and Religious Groups in India: Data Sources, Scope, Limitations and Suggestions

Vinoj Abraham

Centre for Development Studies
Thiruvananthapuram, Kerala, India
vinoj@cds.ac.in

Abstract: Understanding wage and earnings discrimination, its composition, its causes and its effects is crucial to decipher the position and mobility of individuals in marginalized social groups. This paper is an attempt to survey the database available for understanding wages and earnings discrimination, and to suggest directions for the statistical systems to answer emerging issues of research in this area. Firstly, it provides an overview of existing databases that deal with these issues and underscores their limitations. Secondly, it analyzes the trends in wage inequality followed by a literature review on attempts towards explaining these observed trends. Drawing from the literature and analysis of data, we identify emerging issues of research but are limited by data constraints. Finally, a few suggestions are attempted towards improving the statistical system available for understanding wage discrimination.

1 Introduction

Discrimination against marginalized groups, be it social groups such as deprived castes, or minority religious communities, or subjugated genders, labor market is one of the prominent institutions through which this social action has been manifested. This particular social action of discrimination in the labor market manifests both as a source of inequity and as an expression of inequality. While there are many ways in which labor market discrimination occurs, the most important one is of course the age-old and conventionally practiced entry and exit barriers based on ascriptive status (Thorat and Newman, 2007) into particular labor markets in the country. While these institutional rigidities have been dismantled through constitutional provisions, still the practice of discrimination persists. Discrimination in the labor market occurs through three important modes, one is through barriers to entry into particular labor markets, the other is through restrictive occupational mobility within the internal labor markets and third is by way of discriminating on returns to work for same occupation. While social exclusion into labor markets acts as a direct entry barrier into particular labor markets, wages and earnings discrimination provides a 'premia for tastes' and acts as a signaling mechanism towards discouraging marginalized communities to participate in particular labor markets.

Understanding wage and earnings discrimination, its composition, its causes and its effects is crucial to decipher the position and mobility of individuals in these social groups. The depth of this understanding depends crucially on the statistical data that is available for analysis. This paper is an attempt to survey the database available for understanding wages and earnings discrimination, and to suggest directions for the statistical systems to answer emerging issues of research in this area.

The chapter is organized in the following manner. After the introduction, Section 2 summarizes the major databases available in India for analyzing wage inequality. This is followed by a description of the availability of data on wages of social groups, and religious minorities and their limitations in Section 3. Section 4 provides an overview of the trends in wage discrimination followed by a literature review on attempts towards explaining these observed trends in Section 5. Drawing from the literature and analysis of data, we identify emerging issues of research but are limited by data constraints in Section 6. Finally, in the last section, a few suggestions are attempted towards improving the statistical system available for understanding wage discrimination.

2 Major Data Sources on Wages and their Scope

The workforce in the country can be classified as wage labor and self-employed workers. In India, 51% of the workers are self-employed while the remaining are in wage labor, of which 33.5% are casual wage workers and 15.5% are regular employees as per 2009–2010 NSS employment unemployment survey. We get wage information of the regular and casual workers, but we don't get any information on earnings of the self-employed from any data source. Hence, the discussion in this chapter is mostly relevant to the wage workers only, except in the last section on suggestions.

Estimates on wages per person-day are arrived at mainly through two methods. One is a direct survey of workers on wages and earnings, and the other is an estimate of wages generated from the total wage bill of a firm, divided by total person-days of work. Estimates using the second method mentioned are arrived from firm level data with minimal worker characteristics. For the indirect methods of estimation of wage from wage bill, a number of surveys are available such as the Annual Survey of Industries, Census of Small Scale Industries, NSSO rounds on unorganized manufacturing and services. In all of these surveys the unit of data collection is the firm and not the worker, but all these surveys collect data on total wage bill, total workers including classification of total males and females. So it is possible to estimate average wage per worker. Though some surveys do provide some details of the labor composition such as gender composition, yet it is not possible to make any estimation of wage differentials across gender, social groups or religious groups since these surveys do not collect wage bills separately for these groups. For the purpose of understanding, wage discrimination these surveys cannot contribute much. Hence, I shall stick to a discussion on the direct survey sources that are relevant to this chapter. The following is a discussion of the major data sources on wages in India. Table 1 below summarizes the major data sources and their features.

Table 1. Sources of information on wages.

Name of Data Source	NSS EUS	OWS	RLI	WRRI
Publisher	NSS-CSO	Labor Bureau	NSS-CSO	NSS-Labor Bureau
Setting of Market information	National estimates	Particular industry in organized sector	Rural Sector	Rural Sector
Data collection process	Two stage random Sampling	Two stage random Sampling	Two stage random Sampling	600 sample villages in 66 NSS regions
Periodicity	Once in five years approximately	Irregular intervals of many years	Once in five years approx	Yearly
Information on caste, gender, religion	Caste, gender, religion	Gender	Caste, gender, religion	Gender
Unit of data collection	Household/ individuals	Firm/workers	Household/ individuals	

2.1 The employment–unemployment surveys of the NSSO

The single most important data source on wages is available from the quinquennial employment and unemployment surveys undertaken by the National Sample Survey Organization of Central Statistical Organization (NSS-EUS). The reports of the survey are available from 1973, though the unit level information is available only from 1983. The data is taken from the current weekly status data on wages and is usually represented as wages per week or wages per day. The data is available for regular workers and casual workers. The sample is drawn based on a stratified random sampling procedure. The survey covers an entire year divided into four sub-rounds of three months each. Estimates can be generated at the sub round level as well as for the country as a whole. A wide degree of disaggregation is possible at the unit level data. The data can be analyzed at the NIC industrial classification and/or at the NCO classification for rural/urban sectors. Since the data is at the individual level, it can be used to explore individual characteristics associated with wages.

2.2 Rural labor enquiry

The rural labor enquiry is the successor of the Agricultural Labor Enquiry (ALE) in 1950–1951 and 1956–1957, which was specific to agricultural workers. Thereafter, the scope of the subsequent enquiries was enlarged to cover all rural labor households and was rechristened as Rural Labor Enquiry (RLE) with the survey in 1963–1965 and 1974–1975. However, in 1977–1978, the RLE was integrated with the quinquennial surveys of the NSS-EUS. So, currently RLE is a subset of information from the NSS-EUS specific to manual work in the rural areas following the same methodology as that of NSS for employment–unemployment and wages. To provide comparability with previous rounds of RLE, the RLE, gives information for both rural workers and agricultural workers separately.

2.3 Occupational wage surveys (OWS)

The objective of OWS was to support building of wage index for major industries. It provides information of occupation wise wage, employment, earnings, DA, HRA and other perks for the industries from different geographic regions chosen for the survey. The average wage information is provided for males, females, adolescents and children. The Labor Bureau has been entrusted with the conducting of these surveys ever since the first round in 1958–1959. Till date six rounds have been completed. The OWS first round in the year 1958–1959 covered 44 industries comprising 37 manufacturing, 4 mining and 3 plantation industries. The second Occupational Wage Survey was during the period 1963–1965 and the third OWS in 1974–1979 in 81 industries. The fourth round was in 1985–1992 covering 53 industries. The Fifth Round was undertaken in 1993–2001 covering all the 53 selected industries of the Fourth Round. The Sixth Round was taken up in the year 2002 and 56 selected industries was covered during this round under different sectors (45 Manufacturing, 4 Mining, 3 Plantation and 4 Service Sectors).

The survey is done for firms in the organized sector, i.e. firms that are registered under the Factories Act 1948. Occupation-wise wage data are collected for those workers who conform to the definition of worker defined under the Factories Act, 1948. However, managerial, technical and clerical staff, though may be covered by the Act as workers, is excluded from the scope of the survey. Yet, if the supervisory personnel, whose duties besides supervision, generally involve considerable element of manual work then they are covered under the survey. Similarly, regular, badli and casual workers who have worked continuously for a period of at least one month preceding the reference date have also been covered under the survey. Contract workers working in the premises of the unit are also taken into consideration. As per recommendation of the Study Group on Labor Statistics, part-time workers and apprentices have also been included in the survey.

2.4 Wage rates in rural India

This data is collected by NSSO and compiled by the Labor bureau. The main objective of the collection of this database is to work out the cost of cultivation for the purpose of fixation and revision of support/procurement prices of Kharif and Rabi crops. The wage rate data for rural workers who are doing daily manual work (implying casual workers) are collected on a continuous monthly basis for 11 agricultural and 7 non-agricultural occupations from a fixed set of 600 sample villages spread over 66 N.S.S. regions of 20 states since July, 1986. These data are being compiled and published from the year 1995–1996 annually, the latest being in the year 2009–2010. The data collected is presented as average occupation wages for each month for males and females across different states.

3 The Data on Marginalized Groups in the Major Data Sources and their Limitations

Though there are multiple sources of information for wages in India, there is limited information in understanding wage differentials of marginalized groups. The most detailed information is available with the NSS-EUS surveys.

The NSS-EUS collects household level information of the social group status such as SC, ST and OBC. It also provides the household level information of religious categories of Hindus, Muslim, Christians, Sikh, Jain, Buddhists, Zoroastrianism and others. Further it collects individual information of gender as well. Given that this information is available at the unit records level of household and individual level, it is possible to isolate the wage estimates of each of these groups separately and in combinations of these groups. While the religious groups and gender classification had been consistent throughout all quinquennial surveys the social groups classification has undergone various changes that creates inter-temporal comparison problematic.

Firstly, the data on NSS marginalized groups, especially castes are not consistent across different rounds. The Scheduled Castes(SC) and Scheduled Tribes (ST) categories have stayed on since earliest quinquennial surveys, but an additional classification that remained was neo-Buddhists till 1987–1988. Thereafter with the amalgamation of Buddhists as a social group with the SC in 1990[1] this as an analytical category lost relevance and it was dropped, with the neo-Buddhist being added to SC. So the SC categorization prior to the 50th round does not include neo-buddhists, while since 50th round neo-buddhists are largely accounted within SC category. Therefore, the aggregate wages of SCs before the 50th round and after the round are affected by the inclusion of wages of neo-buddhists. As can be seen in Table 3 the neo-Buddhists had an average daily wage rate lesser than the SC and ST in the rural areas, while in the urban areas it was higher for male neo-Buddhists as per the 38th round. Now it can be expected that the inclusion of this category since the 50th round has downwardly biased the average wages of SCs in rural areas, while it has upwardly biased that of the urban SCs.

Secondly, the problem we have at hand is the inclusion of OBC in 'others' since 1983 to 1993–1994. Based on The Second Backward Classes Commission report known as the Mandal Commission report identified socially and educationally backward communities to be included in the new list of Other Backward Classes (OBC). The OBC list is declared at the state level and can vary across different states. A large share of the SC that converted to Islam and Christianity are also included within this group. Within the NSS questionnaire the OBC as a separate category

[1]Neo-Buddhists were accorded SC status through an amendment of Para 3 of Article 341 in 1990 to include them in the Presidential Order of SC and ST Order 1950.

Table 2. Marginalized groups: Data availability and comparisons from NSS.

1983	1987–1988	1993–1994	1999–2000	2004–2005	2009–2010
Social groups					
SC	SC	SC	SC	SC	SC
ST	ST	ST	ST	ST	ST
			OBC	OBC	OBC
Neo-Buddhists	Neo-Buddhists				
Others (OBC included)	Others (OBC included)	Others (OBC included)	Others	Others	Others

Table 3. Average daily wages of social groups and growth rates in current.

	1983			2009–2010			CAGR 1983–2009–2010		
	Male	Female	Total	Male	Female	Total	Male	Female	Total
Rural									
ST	48.9	29.2	41.5	208.2	127.5	187.7	4.90	4.99	5.11
SC	46.6	28.5	41	155.8	92.1	140.9	4.07	3.95	4.16
OBC	NA	NA	NA	184.4	102.7	163.0	NA	NA	NA
Neo-Buddhists	43.9	21.3	34.3				NA	NA	NA
Others	67.7	33.3	57.9	244.9	170.8	231.8	4.34	5.55	4.69
Total	59.3	31.1	50.7	195.1	115.5	176.3	4.01	4.43	4.20
Urban									
ST	99.5	48.6	87.6	336.3	272.8	321.6	4.10	5.86	4.39
SC	92.5	48.1	82.1	220.3	135.2	201.4	2.91	3.47	3.01
OBC	NA	NA	NA	256.6	182.0	242.5	NA	NA	NA
Neo-Buddhists	114.8	50.1	104.2				NA	NA	NA
Others	135.7	74.5	125.9	380.4	349.1	375.0	3.46	5.23	3.67
Total	128.7	68.1	118.2	305.5	238.8	292.7	2.90	4.23	3.04
Total									
ST	58.6	31.2	48.9	246.4	167.2	226.8	4.86	5.70	5.20
SC	58.3	32.3	50.8	180.3	107.8	163.7	3.80	4.06	3.94
OBC	NA	NA	NA	218.0	131.6	198.1	NA	NA	NA
Neo-Buddhists	72.8	25.7	56.6	NA	NA	NA	NA	NA	NA
Others	103	47.4	90.5	326.8	277.0	318.1	3.89	6.00	4.24
Total	89.4	41.1	77.2	246.7	165.2	229.1	3.41	4.70	3.66

appeared in the 55th round in 1999–2000 following the implementation of the Mandal Commission recommendations. Prior to the 55th round the deprived caste converts from Hinduism to other faiths was excluded from SC lists and hence probably continued to report as part of “Others”. Since the others category also included these communities during this period, it is not possible to compare “Others” of period 1999–2000 and later to the earlier period of 1983 to 1993–1994. The available option is to include OBCs in “Others” for later years too at the severe cost of losing disaggregation and that too of a group of people of very relevant social categorization. Table 2 shows the data availability from EUS surveys across social groups and the changes in social group classification over the years.

Thirdly, even the commonly available comparison of inter-group earnings disparity is also problematic. As Deshpande (2005) states the benchmark group of “others” is again a heterogeneous group of jatis, some of whom are very close to SCs in economic and social position. Others is a residual term which renders underestimation of the gap between the top and bottom end of the caste hierarchy. Therefore, sub classification of ‘Others’ is also a necessity to make meaningful comparison of the SCs with Others.

Finally, With regard to religious groups Hindus account for about 80% of the labor force while Muslims account for another 14%. The balance is made up of a variety of religions including Sikhs, Christians and Buddhists. Since each of these other religious groups individually account for a small share of the labor force — no more than 2% — they have limited representation within the samples (Table A3). For purpose of disaggregated analysis at various stages (like industry and occupation) this would imply very few samples available from each religious group. Since wages are averages that would be based on this poor size of sample for this religious groups, we may end up with biased figures than a true representation of the relevant population group.

Despite the inter-temporal comparability problems present in the NSS-EUS on marginalized groups, this survey continues to be used as the single most popular database for wages and earnings, along with employment patterns. This is so because, none of the other surveys mentioned above provide information on caste and religion, apart from the RLE, but since RLE is generated from the NSS surveys the problems discussed above on NSS would be equally relevant for RLE as well. OWS and WRRI do collect information on gender, but not on caste or religious groups.

4 Trends in Wage Inequality

Keeping in mind the unavailability of any other reliable source than the NSS-EUS on wages for the social and religious groups, here I take stock of what have been the trends in wages for the various social and religious categories using NSS-EUS.

Here only the two end periods of the data available is taken to provide a cursory view of wage movements. It is not the intention of the paper to get into a detailed analysis of wages; rather it is to provide a background to the discussion on the data requirements for further research. The daily wages is calculated by dividing total wages reported during the week divided by the number of days of work in the weekly activity intensity given in the current weekly status, and is reported in current prices without converting to real prices.

As can be seen from Table 3, the average daily wages for SC, ST and neo-Buddhists in 1983 was much lower than 'Others' for both males and females in urban areas and rural areas. This trend is reflected in totals as well. Since OBC classification was not available for the period it is not accounted. It may be noted that the wages were lowest for neo-buddhists as a category in 1983, followed by SC, in rural areas. While in Urban areas the neo-buddhists had higher wages than both SC and ST. Also, the wages for SC and ST were more or less similar in both rural and areas, the SC wages being marginally lower than the ST wages.

After more than a quarter century, in 2009–2010 the wage discrimination is still visibly large. Clearly the wages of SC, ST and the new category OBC is much lower than that of Others. The SC still continue to have the lowest average daily wage compared to ST and the new category of OBCs in rural areas and urban areas.

More interesting to note is the fact that compared to the others, the growth rate of daily wages has been higher for the ST in rural males, urban males and urban females, while for SCs the growth rates had been lower than the Others in all the categories. This essentially has meant that there is a tendency towards convergence of wages in case of STs while there is a case of divergence in case of SC from the Others.

As an indicator towards convergence the ratio of daily wages of each social category to Others is calculated. Table 4 shows that while the SC wages was 71% that of Others in 1983, in 2009–2010 the gap widened and was only 61%. On the other hand, the ST gap declined from 72% to 81% in rural areas. Similarly in the urban areas, the ST gap declined from 70% to 86%, while for SCs the gap widened from 65% to 54% in 2009-10 For OBCs, the gap with others was 70% in 2009–2010 in rural areas and 65% in urban areas.

Now, within each of these social groups there is considerable wage gap between males and females. The male wages across all social groups were considerably higher than female wages. Table 5 shows female wages as a proportion of male wages in their respective social groups. Overall the gender gap declined from 52% in 1983 to 59% in 2009–2010 in rural areas and from 53% to 78% in urban areas. It is also noted that in 1983 among all categories, Others had the widest gender gap in rural areas, while in urban areas it had the least. The least gap in

Table 4. Ratio of daily wages of marginalized social groups to "others".

	1983			2009–2010		
	Male	**Female**	**Total**	**Male**	**Female**	**Total**
Rural						
ST	0.72	0.88	0.72	0.85	0.75	0.81
SC	0.69	0.86	0.71	0.64	0.54	0.61
OBC	NA	NA	NA	0.75	0.60	0.70
Others	1	1	1	1.00	1.00	1.00
Urban						
ST	0.73	0.65	0.7	0.88	0.78	0.86
SC	0.68	0.65	0.65	0.58	0.39	0.54
OBC	NA	NA	NA	0.67	0.52	0.65
Others	1	1	1	1.00	1.00	1.00
Total						
ST	0.57	0.66	0.54	0.75	0.60	0.71
SC	0.57	0.68	0.56	0.55	0.39	0.51
OBC	NA	NA	NA	0.67	0.48	0.62
Others	1	1	1	1.00	1.00	1.00

gender ratio was for the SC and ST in 1983 in rural areas, but during the period 1983 to 2009–2010 the gender wage gap declined marginally from 60% to 61% for STs and for SCs it deteriorated from 61% to 59%. This trend is similar in the case of urban regions as well. The fact that gender gap was high in Others in 1983 may be also partially be due to inclusion of OBCs in the others. Evidence for this comes from the fact that in 2009-10, while the gap for Others declined to 65%, for OBCs was 54%, highest among all groups in 2009–2010.

A classification of the workers further into socio-religious groups provides a more disaggregated view of social groups within religious communities (for wage differences across religious communities see Table A1 in Appendix). The ST is a group with no particular religious connotations, implying that tribal people of all religious persuasions may be included as STs, but, for SCs the constitution allows only deprived caste members of Hindu, Buddhists or Sikhism to be included in the SC list. The OBC again is a marker for socially and educationally backward, implying that such people of all faiths may be included in this list.

Though the constitutional provisions does not allow members of any other religious groups than Hinduism, Sikhism or Buddhism to be accounted as SCs, there do exist a large number of low caste converts from Hinduism to other faiths,

Table 5. Gender ratio of daily wages by social groups.

	1983	2009–2010
Rural		
ST	0.60	0.61
SC	0.61	0.59
OBC	NA	0.56
Neo-Buddhists	0.49	NA
Others	0.49	0.70
Total	0.52	0.59
Urban		
ST	0.49	0.81
SC	0.52	0.61
OBC	NA	0.71
Neo-Buddhists	0.44	NA
Others	0.55	0.92
Total	0.53	0.78
Total		
ST	0.53	0.68
SC	0.55	0.60
OBC	NA	0.60
Neo-Buddhists	0.35	NA
Others	0.46	0.85
Total	0.46	0.67

largely to Islam and Christianity. There are very strong popular movements that have taken up the cause of "Dalit Muslims" and "Dalit Christians", to be included within the SC list but there is very little empirical evidence of these groups as there is no statistical data collection of them as a social group.

Even though there is no constitutional standing for such groups, since the NSS collects data on the basis of self reporting, large number of people do report themselves as SC from all other faiths as well than stipulated by the constitution. For instance, from the NSS sample, we get a few samples of SC, ST and OBCs from all religious groups (See Appendix Tables A2 and A3). However, it is often the case that there are self-reporting errors as well. Deshpande (2008) remarks that it is possible that a large number of the 'Dalit' groups in other faiths report themselves as OBCs though they may not have been officially included in their state list for OBCs. Nevertheless as Deshpande (2008) suggests NSSO is the only data

Table 6. Average daily wages by socio-religious groups and CAGR in current prices rupees.

	Hinduism	Islam	Christianity	Sikhism	Buddhism	Others	Total
1983							
ST	46.72	105.45	69.68	64.59	99.38	74.50	48.88
SC	49.99	53.23	53.42	71.18	58.28	46.94	50.79
OBC	NA	NA	NA	NA	NA	NA	NA
Others	91.83	72.75	99.91	147.34	106.43	77.37	90.46
Total	76.31	72.81	92.58	112.32	62.68	71.58	77.16
2009–2010							
ST	148.4	351.7	302.4	754.8	326.9	398.7	222.9
SC	162.9	132.8	185.1	163.0	181.6	277.5	163.8
OBC	199.0	179.3	253.0	193.0	224.4	290.1	198.6
Others	346.9	202.5	332.4	382.6	233.5	251.7	315.8
Total	223.4	197.6	294.7	248.0	240.3	375.4	228.1
CAGR							
ST	3.89	4.06	4.97	8.46	4.01	5.70	5.14
SC	3.98	3.07	4.19	2.77	3.82	6.04	3.94
OBC	NA	NA	NA	NA	NA	NA	NA
Others	4.49	3.44	4.05	3.20	2.63	3.97	4.22
Total	3.61	3.35	3.90	2.65	4.54	5.63	3.64

source that can give any information about socio-religious groups. So here we attempt to explore the wage differences across socio-religious groups.

As can be seen from Table 6 there are considerable variations in wage rates across socio-religious groups. For instance, in 2009–2010 among Hindu others, the average daily wage was Rs. 346.9, while for SC Hindus it was less than half at Rs. 148. Another feature in specific is that while the Sikh Others recorded the highest wages across all groups in 2009–2010, the Sikh SC groups recorded one of the lowest among all socio-religious groups in 2009–2010, and also the lowest wage growth among all SC religious groups during 2009–2010. Also, even while Christian community records high wages the wages of SC Christians is very low and comparable to other SC groups, but the lowest SC wages is that of Islam SC groups, which is much lower than that of even Hindu SC groups. Moreover, as a group they have very low growth in wage during the period 1983 to 2009–2010.

From the above brief analysis, what comes out clearly is that wage discrimination exists and persists for a long period of time across social groups. However, wage discrimination is not uniformly felt across different social groups. The worst affected are the SCs. The STs are affected but they seem to be on a path of mobility, unlike SCs. Moreover, gender based wage discrimination within social groups are rampant and worsening. Further social groups are not a homogenous set but heterogenous, as seen in the analysis of socio-religious communities. Also, we find that though SC of different religious persuasions and faiths do exist, they seem to have similar experiences of wage discrimination.

Now we proceed to review the literature on wage discrimination and wage inequality across social and religious groups in a view to apprise about the composition and factors that explain away this aggregate picture of wage discrimination.

5 A Summary of Literature on Earnings and Wage Discrimination and Inequality

Studies in India on wages and earnings discrimination or inequality had focused on two sets of issues, namely the existence of inequality, which gives a static dimension of the problem. The second issue is the persistence of inequality, which is a comparative static or dynamic dimension. A number of studies have repeatedly marked the existence and persistence of wages and earnings discrimination in India against these marginalized sections of the country as has been explained in the previous section. Most studies using secondary data on wages across marginalized groups have been done till now using data from the NSSO Employment unemployment survey rounds.

The questions that are often answered in the static analyzes are; to identify the extent of earnings discrimination across caste and religious groups; to decompose the earnings discrimination into discrimination in wage, employment opportunities and occupational choices that explains earnings discrimination; and to analyze the factors that affect wage discrimination, the most prominent being education, though studies do attribute other causes such as geographical isolation and spatial segregation, presence of upper caste population, etc.

Madheswaran and Attwell (2007) analyze the caste discrimination in urban labor market by examining inequalities in employment, occupation and earnings between SC/ST, OBC and forward caste Indians using the NSS-EUS. They take OBC as a separate category from 1999 to 2000 and before this period the category is included in Others. They use the Blinder_Oxaca decomposition to partition the observed wage gap to "endowment effect' and "discrimination" or "coefficient" effect with a refinement to allow for occupational discrimination and wage discrimination in same jobs. They conclude that earnings differentials do exist and a large share of that come from differences in human capital endowments, while about 15% is also due to discrimination in market place. Further, occupational discrimination is more pronounced than wage discrimination.

Das and Dutta (2007) similar to Madheswaran and Attwell (2007) conclude that caste is still a determining factor in how individuals are remunerated in the wage labor market. They identify that amongst regular workers the extent of the wage gap is substantial at about 0.37 log points, of which between a third is attributable to unequal treatment of scheduled caste workers relative to general caste workers. The wage gap among casual workers is very low and almost entirely accounted for by differences in characteristics.

Deininger *et al.* (2011) use a nationally representative household survey conducted by NCAER to quantify the magnitude of discrimination, both caste based and gender based, in casual labor markets. To seek answers for the future course of discrimination they compare between high income and low income villages. They conclude that discrimination in the informal labor market is more severe than formal market, however, this is entirely concentrated in gender based relations while there is no evidence of caste based discrimination in informal labor market. Discrimination do express in occupational choices and wages for same occupation. Further, the study also notes that higher income levels do not diminish gender based discrimination.

Dutta (2004) using the NSS-EUS studied the caste and religion effect on wage inequality and measured the extent of wage discrimination during the period 1983–1999–2000 in the Indian labor market. She too finds that wage discrimination does exist across categories and religious categories. She takes support from other literature that probably this discrimination is more occupation based earnings differences rather than wage differences for same occupation. Interestingly, this study makes contrary claims of that of the previous study. She concludes that belonging to a SC (or tribe) or being Muslim significantly decreases the wage received by regular workers (formal sector workers to a large extent) in all three periods while the opposite is the case for casual workers (informal sector workers to a large extent).

Bhaumik and Chakraborty (2009) use National Sample Survey household-level data for 1987–1988 to 2004–2005 to study earnings differential between Hindus and Muslims and their causes. They conclude that substantial earnings differential exist between the two groups, but this is not because of differences in returns to education, rather it is due to differences in education itself.

On the question of persistence of discrimination, the studies have mostly analyzed wage discrimination in a comparative static form.

Jacob (2006) using NSSO data again does the familiar exercise of decomposing wage gaps of different social groups based on Blinder–Oxaca decomposition. However, here she finds that the wage gap attributable to discrimination has decreased over time and also within discrimination gap itself wage discrimination component has decreased over time and the job discrimination component is statistically insignificant.

Majumdar (2007) using NSS data states that the relative earnings of the excluded group (SC/ST) has been decreasing over the years, with the worst affected year being 2004–2005. Also upward mobility to higher wage class had been slower for these workers compared to other workers, rendering widening earnings differentials with the others. The lack of mobility has been mainly due to preponderance of excluded workers in low wage occupations, rather than wage difference in same occupations.

Hnatkovska *et al.* (2010) is the only study that deals with the issue of inter-generational mobility using NSS data from 1983 to 2004–2005 to analyze patterns of occupation choices, education attainment and wages of both SC/ST and non-SC/ST households. They conduct a time series evolution of SC/STs vs. non-SC/STs in terms of education, occupation and industry choices and wages in the same age cohorts. They also look into inter-generational persistence of education, occupation, industry of employment and wage levels of SC/ST and non-SC/ST households. In general, they conclude that though difference does exist in occupation, education and wages, there seems to be convergence in the 20-year period. Specific to wages, the median wage premium of non-SC/STs relative to SC/STs declined systematically from 17% in 1983 to 3% 2004–2005. Also, correspondingly, the elasticity of wages of children with respect to the wages of their parent has also declined relatively faster for SC/ST.

In summary, though there are not many studies on earnings or wage discrimination the overwhelming evidence tend to affirm that wage discrimination against SC/ST is real. Further, the role of wage discrimination for same occupation seems to be lower while it is the occupational discrimination that is generating the wage discrimination. However, we get contra-indications from different studies with regard to the presence of caste based discrimination in the formal vs. informal sector. Further, there is contra-indications on the question of wage convergence of SC/ST to others, some studies indicating a convergence while the other studies claim widening inequality.

6. Issues that Needs Further Research Attention for Policy Intervention

It has been established from available data sources beyond doubt that wages discrimination across caste groups and some religious groups does exist, but understanding caste discrimination at this generalized broad level conceals more than it reveals. Again the issue that needs to be addressed can be conceptualized as three types, depending on their analytical structure, namely static, comparative static and dynamic. The static analysis provides with greater insights into the nature of discrimination. The comparative static largely would give us the effects of different external shocks such as policy intervention, trade liberalization etc. Dynamic analysis would provide us the paths of mobility.

First we discuss that needs to be addressed from a static point of view.

Group heterogeneity: The castes, tribes and OBC are treated as if they are homogenous groups, while in reality they are heterogeneous. The SC largely consists of many *jati* and *upajati* within the fourth *varna*, *Shudras*, and the large number of communities that are excluded from the *varna* system itself. The ST on the other hand consists of a large number of communities that were spatially excluded from development. The OBC is a much more fluid term that refers to socially and educationally backward classes, determined by their relative position in their community. While the clubbing of these numerous castes, tribes and classes into the three fold division of SC, ST and OBC makes it empirically tractable, it has also suppressed the intra-group differences within these broad groups. A number of issues remain unaddressed due to this homogenous treatment of heterogeneous groups.

Firstly, a relevant question that needs to be answered on the issue is that of inter-group vs. intra-group inequality. It is of immense policy relevance to address this issue to identify target groups for intervention. Micro level studies such as that of Swaminathan and Rawal (2011) does address this question. They do a comparison of dalit and non-dalit households across eight Indian villages. While the study identifies that income inequality is substantial between dalits and non-dalits the more relevant aspect for this paper is the manuevatiblity that they achieve by breaking into different dalit groups within the SC itself. They are able to identify within group inequality and between group inequality distinctly and argue clearly on the dominance of between group inequality share as up to 50% of the total inequality index using entropy measures.

Secondly, while caste mobility[2] may not be possible economic mobility has been successfully achieved by many castes and tribes (Srinivas, 1962). So, while still the overwhelming majority of these groups are suffering lack of mobility some communities seems to have achieved economic mobility. It is important to know the means of economic mobility of these smaller groups. Who are these groups? How did they overcome the barrier of caste to achieve economic mobility? Research into these issues would throw light on the possible policy strategies that could be imbibed to enable other poor communities to achieve economic mobility. There is need to understand economic mobility of these groups using large scale datasets.

[2] Srinivas also has argued that lower castes do indeed strive for caste mobility as well through the now famous sanskritization process (Srinivas, 1962)

Understanding wage inequality in socio-religious groups: The second set of issues pertain to understanding earnings and wage discrimination within socio-religious groups. Our current understanding of wage discrimination within social groups within religious groups is rather scanty due to two reasons. One we do not have any other database than the NSS-EUS that look into this aspect. Two, within the NSS-EUS database the sample size of some of the social groups within religious groups are too thin and hence subject to sample biases, but this is an important dimension that needs attention. There has been mounting pressure on the government to include non-Hindu SC groups in policy interventions for the SCs. Earnings inequality within the labor market is considered as a telltale sign of social discrimination. Table 6 demonstrates that substantial wage inequality exists across social groups within religious communities. Hence studies that address issue of wage inequality within socio-religious groups would throw light on caste practices within other religious groups as well.

Understanding gender dimensions of socio-religious groups: Another dimension of importance, but less attended is the issue of gender discrimination within different social groups. As has been shown in Table 5, gender discrimination within social groups is high, but more interesting is the aspect that while Others and ST categories have achieved substantial progress in reducing gender based wage discrimination in case of SCs this aspect seems to persist and worsen in some cases. It is important to understand how this mobility was achieved in case of ST and others, while how it eluded the SCs. Is it policy intervention? If so, how did it have differential impact? Was it that women in some social groups achieved greater occupational mobility and hence wage mobility? Answering these issues would help unravel the multiple and overlapping effects of the institutions of gender and caste.

Next, we discuss a set of issues that needs to be addressed from a comparative static analysis. Comparative Static analysis would provide us a picture of what happened before and after an external shock in the system. We take up two relevant cases that affect wages and earnings of individuals, namely, policy interventions and new economic policies of the economy.

Policy interventions: Policy interventions for the uplift of the deprived social groups have been mainly in the areas of education and employment, by providing reservations in public funded institutions. Firstly, the expectation is that socially deprived groups would be able to achieve earnings mobility through both these interventions. Reservation in education would provide them with the skills for occupational mobility while reservation in employment would insure against wage discrimination and facilitate occupational mobility within public institutions.

While reservations in employment would be implemented only through public funded institutions, reservations in education would have an economy wide effect, by supplying skilled labor in both public and private sector. Secondly, it is also expected that the benefits of reservations in education and employment provides for inter-generational earnings mobility.

Impact of Reservations: Now the questions of relevance are: *Firstly,* did reservations in education and employment help in reducing the earnings and wage discrimination? Micro studies indicate persistence of wage inequality. For instance, Chakravarty and Somanathan (2008) studied the 2006 batch of IIM-Ahmedabad MBA graduates and found that SC/ST graduates get significantly lower wages than those in the general category. However, the wage discrimination is attributable to the lower GPA scores that they achieved suggesting that the large wage difference is due to the weaker (on average) academic performance of SC/ST candidates and hence suggests stronger policy intervention for educational attainment among the deprived groups.

Again, Table 4 shows that wage discrimination seems to have declined for the STs while it seems to have widened for the STs and for OBCs discrimination exists. Now if wage discrimination among STs declined is it due to reservations? How it is that wage mobility was achieved by the STs, through educational reservation and occupational mobility, or through declining wage discrimination, or through gender parity in wages. If STs achieved mobility through reservations why did reservation not have the same effect on SCs and OBCs?

Inter-generational transfer of benefits: *Secondly,* does reservation provide for transfer of its benefits to the next generation and if so at what rate? Hnatkovska *et al.* (2010) using NSS data had concluded, using a wage cohort study, that the elasticity of wages of children-generation with respect to the wages of their parent-generation has also declined relatively faster forSC/ST compared to others during the period 1983 to 2004–2005. However, whether this was an effect of reservation is not known. Does education and employment reservations have differential effects on generational transfer of reservation benefits? What transfers the benefits the best? Is it education, or employment, or a combination of both? Answering this set of questions would give the policy makers on where to put the resources most efficiently to achieve the goal of reduction in disparity.

Economic liberalization and privatization: Ever since the liberalization and privatization of the economy, the issue of wage discrimination has come to occupy a more important dimension. With the emergence of private sector as the dominant player in the economy, and the relative reduction of the role of public sector, the possibilities of employment based reservations would also shrink. On the other hand, it is possible that reservations in education would have a greater role to play, by eliminating skill differences and potential occupational differences; but experimental studies do show (Thorat, Attewell and Rizwi, 2007; Deshpande and Newman; 2007) that entry to the private sector is rift with discriminatory practices. Similarly new employment opportunities are opening in new sectors that have emerged due to the globalization of the economy. However, entry to certain occupations in such sectors is restricted by not only educational discrimination, but also employer preferences. Moreover, recruitment in private sector is encouraged through social networks, hence more prone to such practices. Further, studies on these aspects would open up dimensions of discriminatory practices that are newly emerging within the economy.

The third set of issues relate to earnings mobility of individuals and groups over a period of time.

Earnings mobility: While the comparative static approach could tell us the aggregate effects of external shocks, their effects have a time dimension. The effects reveal over a period of time. Moreover, these effects are played within the board parameters of the macro-economy that are ever changing. Hence, the changes in earnings and their effects may not be similar for different social groups. Hence, the need to track households and individuals within these social groups over a period of time so that all other effects on these households are controlled. For instance, Lanjouw and Rao (2010) using repeat sample data identified that in Palanpur village, while in general, all castes achieved income mobility, the largest caste group did not. They also remark in this study that it is the panel structure of the data that help unravel this within group effect.

7 Some Suggestions for Improvement of Database for Further Research on the Area

While there are very pertinent issues that are of impending policy relevance, at present the research in the area based on large scale secondary data has been limited mainly due to the limitations of the available data and unavailability of data. Policy decisions have also been constrained owing to the unavailability of information on issues of national relevance in this area. In the light of this background the following suggestions are made.

1. Case for a longitudinal Panel

Some of the most important questions on wages and earnings of social groups pertain to their mobility, both in terms of occupation and wages. Currently there are very limited studies of this type done in India due to the lack of reliable data. To quote Gary Fields (2011), a pioneer in the study of earnings mobility.

> *"A newer approach in the development literature is to study the distributional consequences of economic growth (or non-growth) by using data for the same recipient units for two or more points in time to analyze changes in total income ("income mobility") and in income from paid employment and self-employment ("earnings mobility")".*

Micro level studies of longitudinal panel data such as the SPARC data used by Swaminathan (1998) in Mumbai, or the ones by Djurfeldt *et al.* (2008) in Tamil Nadu are an indication in this direction. Also there are larger longitudinal sample databases in India such as the ICRISAT village studies, the NCAER data sets on Rural Economic and Demographic Surveys, etc. Large sample data for Income in US is being collected by the University of Michigan since 1968, called The Panel Study of income Dynamics. Studies on racial discrimination and race mobility have been one of the core dimensions of the PSID survey. Since this survey, a number of countries, both in the developed world and developing world, have adopted this model of household panels for studying mobility across social and religious groups. It is time that we develop a panel data that can explore the issues of earnings and occupational mobility across social and religious groups. A large sample panel data would answer a number of questions related to effectiveness of policy interventions, inter-group mobility, intra-group mobility.

2. Accounting for self employment

Almost 50% of working population are self-employed. There is no earnings information for this part of the working population in the NSS data or any other data source, but for the marginalized religious groups and workers in OBC self-employment consists of a larger share of workers than that of general category workers. The only information that is available from NSS is the perception of satisfaction of self-employed workers, but the veracity of this information is doubtful, due to the fact that the response would be subjective and also there may be tendency to over-report on the query on the "amount to be considered as satisfactory" and under-report on "whether you are satisfied". So essentially all the discussion on wage inequality using the NSS data is restricted to wage employment, while a larger segment of the population lie outside the purview of wage labor. Any discussion of earnings discrimination cannot be but made without including this large population, largely dependent on small and marginal farming in the rural areas and retail trade and informal services in the urban areas. While wage information may not be available for such workers, it is possible to arrive at some measure of their earnings either through assets/wealth accumulated or through consumption expenditure, which is available in the NSS data, but again we may not get any mobility information from this data. This could again be achieved through a longitudinal survey to capture earnings mobility as suggested earlier.

3. Suggestions on NSS data

a. Account for caste heterogeneity both within the deprived social groups and others. Bringing in further caste and tribe categories within the broad SC, ST, OBC and Other categories would allow accounting at least partially for the vast heterogeneity that is masked in the NSS data set now. This is certainly a very sensitive issue as we had seen in the case of census data collection. May be the NSS can use the same list of castes and tribes as identified in the Census list of SC/ST, but the census does not have an entry on OBCs, which needs to be rectified in case of NSS.

b. To understand the effect of reservation on wages, additional queries on reservations may be included for both education and employment. Additional information eliciting information on whether the individual has enjoyed the benefits of reservation either in education or employment could render capturing the effects of reservation possible from the NSS data. This would also enhance the understanding reservations, especially within public sector employment and also differences in reservation on private and public sector.

4. Suggestions on OWS and WRRI

Two other data sources that collect data on wages are the OWS and WRRI. OWS pertains to the various industries and occupation within the organized sector. However, the OWS does not collect information on the social group or religion. Since the survey is conducted at the firm level with individual workers as units it is possible to address these questions. Additional queries on social groups in this data set could bring better understanding of occupational and wage discrimination within the organized sector. The OWS can provide us with important information on occupational segregation and also can help us answer issues on wage differentials across same occupations in the formal sector, but there is need to bring in some uniformity in the scope of survey with regard to industries and geographical coverage and periodicity. Similarly WRRI can also include additional categories of social groups.

References

Bhaumik, S. K. and M. Chakrabarty, (2009). Is education the panacea for economic deprivation of Muslims?: Evidence from wage earners in India, 1987–2005. *Journal of Asian Economics*, 20(2), 137–149.

Chakravarty, S. and E. Somanathan (2008), Discrimination in an Elite Labor Market? Job Placements at the Indian Institute of Management — Ahmedabad. *Discussion Paper 08-01*, Ahmedabad: IIM.

Das, M. B. and P. V. Dutta (2007), Does caste matter for wages in the Indian labor market?

Deshpande, A. (2005), Affirmative Action in India and the United States, background papers to EQUITY & DEVELOPMENT, World Development Report, 2006.

Deshpande, A. and K. Newman (2007), Where the Path Leads: The Role of Caste in Post-University Employment Expectation, *Economic and Political Weekly*, October.

Deshpande, S. (2008), Dalits in the Muslim and Christian Communities: A Status Report on Current Social Scientific Knowledge prepared for the National Commission for Minorities, Government of India. Available from: www.ncm.nic.in/pdf/report%20 dalit%20%20reservation.pdf. (*Accessed February 14th, 2012).*

Djurfeldt, G. V. Athreya, N Jayakumar, S. Lindberg, A. Rajagopal and R. Vidyasagar (2008), Agrarian Change and Social Mobility in Tamil Nadu. *Economic & Political Weekly*, November.

Dutta, P. V. (2004), The Structure of Wages in India, 1983–1999. *PRUS Working Paper No. 25*, Scisson: Poverty Research Unit at the University of Sussex.

Government of India, *Agricultural Wages in India.* Directorate of Economics and Statistics, Ministry of Agriculture, New Delhi. (Various Issues)

Government of India, *Rural Labor Enquiry*, Labor Bureau, Shimla (Various Issues)

Government of India, *Report on Employment and Unemployment*, National Sample Survey Organisation (NSSO). (Various Issues)

Guhan, S. (2001), Comprehending Equalities, Reprinted in S. Subramanian (Ed.) India's Development Experience, New Delhi: Oxford University Press.

Feilds, G. S. (2011), What We Know (and Want to Know) About Earnings Mobility in Developing Countries. http://digitalcommons.ilr.cornell.edu/cgi/viewcontent.cgi?article=1153&context=workingpapers.

Himanshu (2005), *Indian Journal of Labor Economics*, 48(2).

Hnatkovska, V., A. Lahiri and S. B. Paul (2010), Castes and Labor Mobility, UBC. Departmental Archives, UBC Department of Economics. (Revised October 22. 2010).

Jacob, M. (2006). Changes in the wage gap of gender and caste groups in India. PhD Dissertation. College Park. MD: University of Maryland.

Klaus, D., S. Jin, H. Nagarajan (2011), Wage Discrimination in India's Informal Labor Markets: Exploring the Impact of Castes and Gender. *NCAER Working Papers on Decentralisation and Rural Governance in India No. 6.*

Lakshmanasamy, T. and S. Madheswaran (1995), Discrimination by Community: Evidence from Indian Scientific and Technical Labor Market. *Indian Journal of Social Sciences*, 8(1), 59–77.

Lanjouw, P. and V. Rao(2010), Revisiting Between-group Inequality Measurement: An Application to the Dynamics of Caste Inequality in Two Indian villages. *Policy Research Working Paper 5337*, World Bank.

Madheswaran, S. and P. Attewell (2007), Caste Discrimination in the Indian Urban Labor Market: Evidence from the National Sample Survey. *Economic and Political Weekly*, October.

Majumder, R. (2007), Earnings Differentials Across Social Groups : Evidence from India. *Indian Journal of Labor Economics*, 50(4).

Sethi, R. and R. Somanathan (2010), Group Identity and Social Mobility in India.

Srinivas, M. N (1962), Caste in Modern India and other essays, Asia Publishing.

Appendix

Table A1. Average daily wages per capita by religious categories.

	1983			2009–2010			CAGR 1983–2009–2010		
Religion	**Male**	**Female**	**Total**	**Male**	**Female**	**Total**	**Male**	**Female**	**Total**
Rural									
Hinduism	58.1	30.4	49.3	185.8	105.9	165.9	3.9	4.2	4.1
Islam	59.3	30.3	53.8	186.9	106.7	175.3	3.9	4.2	4.0
Christianity	69	51.8	63.4	277.4	204.6	259.6	4.7	4.6	4.8
Sikhism	93.9	56.9	90.4	189.9	152.0	185.1	2.4	3.3	2.4
Buddhism	46.3	20.2	35.4	273.4	164.6	243.9	6.0	7.2	6.6
Others	55.1	27	46.8	342.5	213.8	316.4	6.2	7.1	6.5
Total	59.3	31.1	50.7	195.1	115.4	176.3	4.0	4.4	4.2
Urban									
Hinduism	132.1	66.5	120.7	312.3	228.2	295.8	2.9	4.2	3.0
Islam	100.4	47.1	92.6	223.4	203.1	220.9	2.7	4.9	2.9
Christianity	137.7	105.9	128.5	358.1	326.5	350.1	3.2	3.8	3.4
Sikhism	159.6	136.8	156.2	349.0	361.6	351.0	2.6	3.3	2.7
Buddhism	115.6	66.2	105.5	245.4	196.8	231.9	2.5	3.7	2.6
Others	106.8	48.1	99.6	487.3	385.1	463.1	5.1	7.1	5.2
Total	128.7	68.1	118.2	305.4	238.7	292.6	2.9	4.2	3.0
Total									
Hinduism	89.5	39.5	76.3	244.5	153.6	224.0	3.4	4.6	3.6
Islam	80	37.4	72.8	206.0	153.0	198.9	3.2	4.8	3.4
Christianity	100.8	74.4	92.6	313.5	260.6	300.4	3.8	4.2	4.0
Sikhism	114.8	92.6	112.3	250.5	245.8	249.9	2.6	3.3	2.7
Buddhism	78.4	31.1	62.7	262.2	177.8	239.1	4.1	5.9	4.5
Others	82.2	32.7	71.6	399.5	289.3	375.6	5.4	7.5	5.6
Total	89.4	41.1	77.2	246.7	165.2	229.1	3.4	4.7	3.7

Note: For Females the sample size for all other religions than Hinduism is less than 250. Hence the averages need to be inferred cautiously. For Jainism and Zoroastrianism, the sample size is negligible hence aggregated to "Others" category.

Table A2. Sample size for wage workers as socio-religious groups.

HHreligion	ST	SC	OBC	Others	Total
Hinduism	5,739	14,492	23,209	15,162	58,602
Islam	269	140	3,067	4,851	8,327
Christianity	3,353	282	764	973	5,372
Sikhism	6	742	194	525	1,467
Jainism	4	0	8	118	130
Buddhism	387	552	57	21	1,017
Zoroastrian	2	1	0	9	12
Others	446	18	55	32	551
Total	10,206	16,227	27,354	21,691	75,478

Table A3. Sample size of households as socio-religious groups.

HHreligion	ST	SC	OBC	Others	Total
Hinduism	6,526	14,687	31,681	24,029	76,923
Islam	277	130	4,882	7,141	12,430
Christianity	4,738	226	771	1,207	6,942
Sikhism	19	654	337	1,142	2,152
Jainism	4	0	20	258	282
Buddhism	532	455	63	49	1,099
Zoroastrian	2	2	0	17	21
others	828	27	116	67	1,038
Total	12,926	16,181	37,870	33,910	100,887

Chapter 10

Is Disinvestment Detrimental to Employment? Firm Level Evidence from Indian Central Public Sector Enterprises

Ritika Jain

Assistant Professor, Center for Development Studies, Thiruvananthapuram, Kerala, India

ritika@cds.ac.in

Abstract: The employee strength in central public sector enterprises (CPSEs) in India has been plummeting since the late 80s. This period overlaps with the inception and evolution of disinvestment since 1991 as a remedial policy tool to improve the performance of the CPSEs. Disinvestment is defined as the transfer of ownership of public sector enterprises (PSEs) from the government to the private sector. Against this background, the current study aims to explore the effect of disinvestment on the size of employment in CPSEs. Using an instrumental variable approach, the study focuses on the employment decisions of all CPSEs (approximately 230) from 1991–1992 to 2011–2012. The study recognizes and accounts for the political influence in public sector enterprises and disinvestment decisions. The results suggest that disinvestment has, in fact, had a positive influence on employee strength. Further, ideology of the state where the enterprise is located not only affects employment directly but also conditions the influence of disinvestment on employee size.

1 Introduction

In India, the early decades of the post-independence era marked the reservation of specific industries exclusively for central public sector enterprises (CPSEs). The motivating idea was to establish a strong industrial and manufacturing base, to invest in projects with long gestation periods, provide employment to the masses and reduce income inequalities.[1] Nevertheless, CPSEs in India were characterized by surplus employment, underutilization of assets, political interference and by huge losses in most units (Gupta, 2005).[2] This poor performance of CPSEs was accompanied by several factors like increasing fiscal deficits and a sinking foreign exchange rate in the late 80s which led to a set of reforms in 1991 that marked a turning point in Indian economic history. The policy aimed at reducing the massive presence of the state in manufacturing to selected sectors. Disinvestment, defined as the transfer of ownership and/or control of public sector enterprises (PSEs) from the government to the private sector, has been identified as one of the important goals in almost every annual budget, since then.

Against this background, this study aims to examine the effect of disinvestment policy on the employment in CPSEs in India since 1991. Employing approximately 1.4 million people, the 'gross value addition' in CPSEs stood at 6.3% of GDP in 2012–2013. However, there has been a massive decline in average employee size (total employee size divided by the number of CPSEs) from 1991–1992 to 2011–2012 (Figure 1). According to Gupta (2005), this trend may be explained by two things — auxiliary services (security, transport, canteen, etc.) being contracted out and natural attrition on retirement: with gradual slowdown in fresh employment

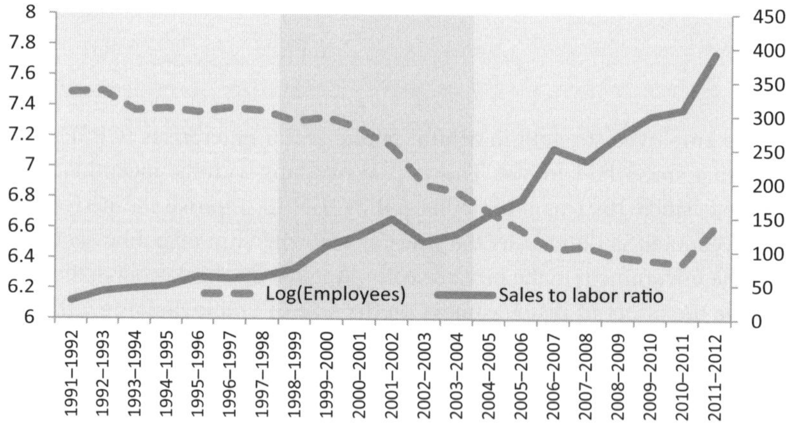

Figure 1. Total employee size and sales to labor ratio in CPSEs in India.

Source: Data from Public Enterprise Survey. The political background denotes the Central Government regimes under the two main political parties in India (Pink — Indian National Congress, Blue — Bharatiya Janata Party). Total employee size is plotted in the primary axis and sales to labor ratio in the secondary axis.

[1] Planning Commission, The First Five Year Plan, Government of India Publication, New Delhi, p. 28.
[2] Industrial Policy Statement, 1980. Department of Industrial Policy and Promotion, p. 6.

in recent years, majority of the employees had reached retiring age thus contributing to the declining total employee strength.

This reduction in employment at CPSEs overlaps with the period of inception and evolution of disinvestment in India which may tempt one to expect some relation between disinvestment and employment. Dinc and Gupta (2011) argue that disinvestment of CPSEs in India is an unbalanced policy option in the benefits infused and the costs it carries. The benefits from the proceeds of sales add to the Central exchequer's funds but the political costs (perceived job loss and wage cuts) of an unaccepted policy option are borne by people in the region where the enterprise is located. This can make the respective state governments averse to such a policy making the pace of implementation slow (approximately 25% of the enterprises have been selected for disinvestment). Figure 2 shows the

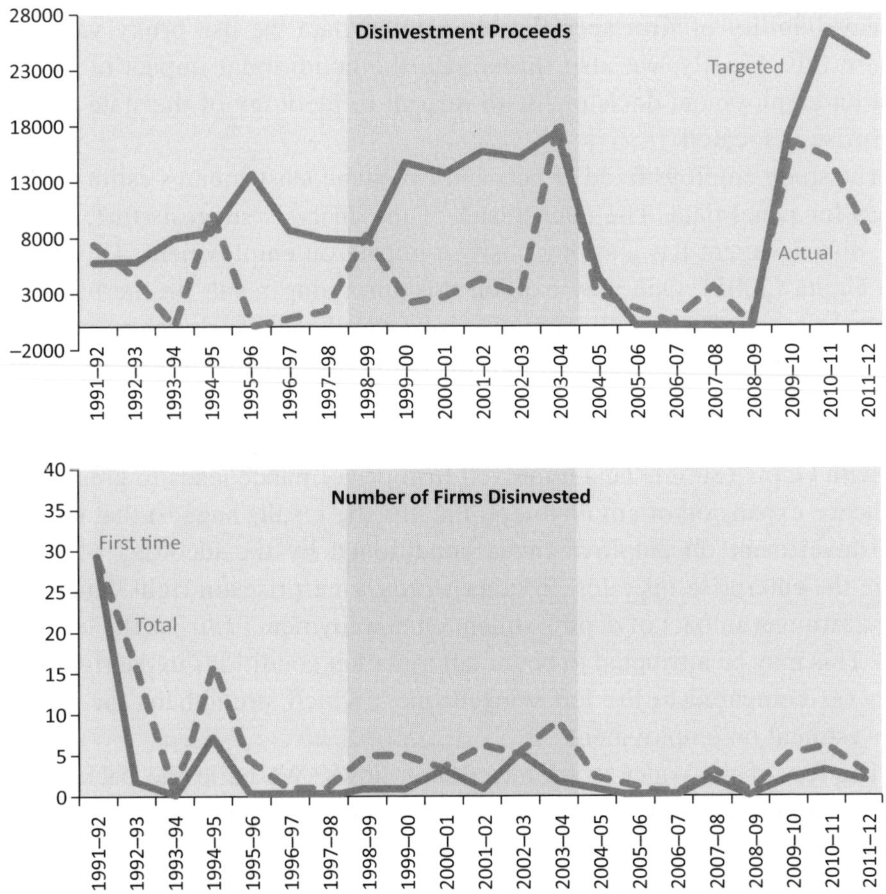

Figure 2. Disinvestment trend in India against the political timeline.

Source: Same as Figure 1.

trend followed by the disinvestment proceeds and number of firms selected for disinvestment respectively against the political background.

Against this background, the current study aims to explore the influence of disinvestment on firm employment. The basic rationale behind this is that disinvestment is a policy option that reduces the government's role in these enterprises through reduced state ownership. With reduced ownership of the state, the enterprises move slightly away from the multidimensional objective function which emphasizes the social mandate of providing employment in a situation of considerable unemployment and poverty. This should imply that disinvestment reduces employment. While examining this relationship empirically for India, we incorporate the importance of political factors in disinvestment decisions related to India. In particular, we capture the local political factors that may influence employment decisions in public enterprises. CPSEs in India have a strong labor union presence. However, due to unavailability of firm specific labor union data we use proxy variables to capture this. Finally, we also investigate the conditional impact of disinvestment on employment decisions with respect to ideology of the state where the enterprise is located.

The study employs fixed effects and two stage least squares estimation techniques for panel data. The main result of the analysis suggests that, unexpectedly, disinvestment has a strong positive impact on employment. This is in line with Gupta (2005). One may explain this surprising result on the basis of the following points. First of all, employee size shrinkage was driven by contracting out of services and natural attrition. Secondly, the positive effect of disinvestment on employment may be driven through the efficiency channel. Jain (2014) finds that disinvestment has a positive impact on firm performance. This is in line with Gupta (2005). This improved firm performance leads to greater output and hence expansion of employment. Finally, the results suggest that the impact of disinvestment on employment is conditioned by the ideology of the state where the enterprise operates. In other words, enterprises in right winged states have a stronger impact of disinvestment on employment *vis-à-vis* the left winged ones. This may be attributed to better labor market conditions in the right winged states (as compared to the left winged ones) which strengthens the impact of disinvestment on employment.

The rest of the paper is organized as follows. We build the background of CPSEs, employee trends and disinvestment policy in the next section. In Section 4, we discuss the basic hypotheses that we test and move to the definitions of variables and dataset. Finally, we discuss the empirical strategy and the results obtained. Section 9 concludes.

2 Background on the Role of CPSEs in India: A Brief Overview

According to the Indian Labour Market Report, 2008 the growth of the public sector in India can be divided into three phases: *First phase (1951–1966), Second phase (1967–1991) and Third Phase (1991 onwards).*[3]

First Phase (1951–1966): The first phase of the growth of (CPSEs) started with *The First Plan (1951–1956)* that marked the beginning of planning for a strong industrial sector. In the face of the massive unemployment and the limited stock of capital, the government adopted an industrial strategy under which the industrial base across various sectors would be in the public sector because of the required huge investments and long gestation periods. Thus, *The Second Plan (1956–1961)* focused on the active role of the public sector in developing heavy and capital goods industries. *The Third Plan (1961–1966)* outlined the strategy of strengthening the role of the public sector over major economic activities and sectors. As a result, the first phase of CPSE growth had all the elements to ensure a dominant public sector driven industrial growth in India. However, the growth rates of GNP were not sustained with the agricultural crisis, rising defense expenditure and the aid cutback in the mid-1960s.

Second Phase (1967–1991): The second phase, marked by *The Fourth, Fifth and Sixth Plans,* witnessed major nationalization of banking, insurance and the coal sectors. The second phase saw a substantial rise in the number of CPSEs which had surged to 244 by *The Seventh Plan* (from 5 in *The First Plan*). With an emphasis to provide employment, the fifth and sixth plans envisaged enormous widespread investment by the public sector. In the 1980s, the average employment grew only 1.55% per annum, although GDP grew at over 5% (Papola, 1991). However, the high GDP growth rate in the 80s may be attributed to over borrowing and over spending which led to a swift rise in the debt service ratio by approximately 25%. In addition, the plummeting of foreign exchange reserves to $1 billion in 1991 (insufficient to last three weeks) led to a massive crisis which pushed India to initiate economic reforms.

Third Phase (1991 onwards): In contrast to the first two phases, the final phase witnessed structural change in the public sector with a rising tendency towards reduced state ownership. Amidst a crisis, *The New Economic Policy* was

---

[3] The present study focuses on the *Third Phase*.

announced in 1991. It threw open to the private sector many industrial sectors hitherto reserved for the public sector, dispensed with industrial licensing, and announced measures to encourage foreign investment and technology transfers. Disinvestment, transfer of ownership and/or control, of state owned enterprises (SOEs) to the private sectors was also initiated in 1991. Subsequently, this wave of deregulation was further accentuated. Since 1991, disinvestment has received considerable attention of the policymakers in India, as in many other countries across the world.

2.1 Employment in CPSEs

According to the Economic Survey, 2009–2010, the total employment in CPSEs in India has an inverted U shape (Figure 3). This is consistent with the growth story of CPSEs in India. Figure 3 depicts total employment in CPSEs India against the different phases in CPSE growth.[4] As the figure suggests, employment increased in the first and second phases of CPSE growth. However, since the late 80s there has been a sharp decline in total employment in CPSEs. The initial rise in employment was driven by the inception of building a strong industrial base with a dominant state presence. However, with natural attrition and contracting out several services, the recent years marked a decline in employee size. The current study focuses on the third phase of CPSE growth and examines if disinvestment had a role to play in the shrinkage of employment.

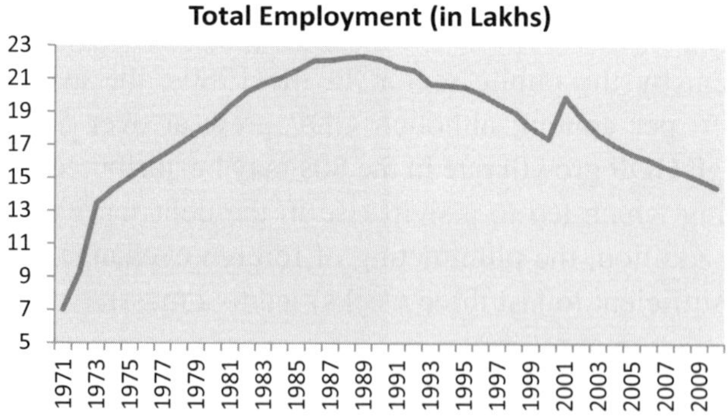

Figure 3. Total Employment in CPSEs between 1971 and 2010. The background color denotes before and after liberalization periods.

Source: Economic Survey, 2009–2010.

[4] Data on employment is available from 1970–1971.

3 Testable Hypotheses

PSEs are not as profitable as their private counterparts because these enterprises have a multidimensional objective function and hence might pursue goals other than profit maximization, such as employment increase, investment in certain sectors, subsidized pricing policy or high but unsustainable dividend payouts. The lack of a clearly defined objective function affects performance and employment in PSEs. Hence, transferring the ownership to private investors can make the objective faced by the management more focused (towards profit maximization and away from the different dimensions mentioned previously) implying that disinvestment as an intervention will reduce surplus labor. Based on this, the first hypothesis may be formulated as:

Hypothesis I*: *Disinvestment reduces employment of PSEs.

Despite being owned by the Central government, CPSEs in India are spread in different states that are run by a range of ideologically diverse parties. Traditionally, left winged governed states have a more pronounced presence of labor unions[5] and other labor market rigidities which makes implementation of disinvestment difficult. Hence, the effect of disinvestment on labor may be conditioned by the states where these enterprises are located. The second testable hypothesis is:

Hypothesis II*: *Effect of disinvestment on employment of PSEs will be stronger for enterprises operating in right-winged states.

4 Data and Methodology

The studied dataset is created by compiling the information on all the central government owned manufacturing and non-financial services firms (approximately 240 for each year) from 1991–1992 to 2011–2012. We have not considered the three strategic cognate groups in our dataset, which, the Department of Disinvestment had excluded from disinvestment in 1995. Data on CPSEs has been hand collected from various issues of Public Enterprise Survey. Further, data on disinvestment, political parties running state governments and other policy variables has been collected from various government documents and websites. Data on ideology of parties at the state level is borrowed from two past studies

[5] According to the "Trade Unions in India–2008" Report (Labor Bureau, Ministry of Labor and Employment), the highest number of state labor unions is highest in the states of West Bengal and Tamil Nadu, p. 21. Further, according to the "Statistics on Industrial disputes, closures, Retrenchments and Layoffs Year 2012" Report (Labor Bureau, Ministry of Labor and Employment), the number of labor disputes was highest in West Bengal, p. 35.

Table 1. Description of data and data sources.

Categories of variables	Broad source	Brief information on variables
Disinvestment transactions	1. Public Enterprise Survey 2. Department of Disinvestment website 3. www.bsepsu.com	Selection of disinvestment and percentage divested
CPSE financial performance and employment size	Public Enterprise Survey	Firm size, age, profitability, productivity, ratna status, firm location
Political variables	Election Commission of India, Press Notes and other published studies	Ideology score, ideology difference, coalition dummy
Industry variables	Public Enterprise Survey, Annual survey of industries, policy documents	Industry type, Ratna Status, profitability of the industry
Changes in policies	Government policy documents	MOU, Deregulation

(Chhibber and Nooruddin, 2004; Dash and Raja, 2014). Table 1 summarizes a brief overview of the dataset used.

5 Variables

Dependent variable: The dependent variable for the analysis is the natural logarithmic transformation of employee size of each CPSE.[6]

The independent variables comprise of disinvestment, political, firm, industry and state specific economic factors. The variable of interest is disinvestment and an interaction of disinvestment and ideology of the state where the enterprise is located.

(i) Disinvestment

To capture disinvestment the study uses a multivariable approach instead of a single dummy variable.

- *First time disinvestment*: First time disinvestment is defined as a dummy variable that takes the value one when a firm is selected for disinvestment for the first time. This essentially captures only the effect of first time selection and ignores later disinvestment selection.

[6] Using natural logarithmic transformation to capture employee size is in line with Gupta (2005), Brown *et al.* (2005) and Amess *et al.* (2009).

- *Occurrence of disinvestment*: We capture the occurrence of disinvestment where a dummy variable takes the value 1 each time a firm is selected for disinvestment. This variable treats first and repeated disinvestment to be of equal importance and assigns a value 1 to both.
- *Extent of disinvestment*: We use the amount disinvested (proportion transferred) in a firm as the extent of disinvestment.

(ii) Political factors

We use three variables to capture the political scenario prevailing in the state in which each enterprise or plant is located. Although state level politics is dominated by coalitions as much as in the center, the retrieval of data for all state level government coalitions for the period of analysis (20 years) is beyond the scope of this study. However, we use three variables to capture specific political features in the respective states.

- *Ideology score*: For every state, we identify the party that had won the most recent Vidhan Sabha elections or was the dominant party in a coalition. Irrespective of whether the party made a single party government or was a part of a coalition government, we use the party's ideology to be the government's ideology during the term. Also, we deviate from the standard practice of using a left–right dummy variable and use an ideology scale developed by Chhibber and Nooruddin (2004) and Dash and Raja (2014). This study has coded major national and regional political parties in India based on the objectives and policies that these parties have espoused to and implemented in the past. The study covers all the major parties. For the few remaining ones, the information has been collected from media reports. The ideological strand, as described, spans from 1 to 5 where right is coded 1, right center 2, center 3, left center 4 and left 5.[7]
- *Ideology difference*: Ideological difference is captured as the difference in ideology between the Center and the state where the public enterprise is located. For this we use the previous table and as a final step we take the absolute difference between the ideologies of the Center and the state. We do this for all the enterprises during our period of analysis. It is represented as follows:

$$State\ Index_j^s = \left| I_j^s - Index_j \right|,$$

[7] We assume that the ideology orientation of a party does not change over time.

where i is the ith party in a coalition of n parties at the Center and s denotes the state in which the enterprise is located. Index_j, I_j^s is the ideology of the coalition at the Center[8] and ideology of the main party in state s in the jth year respectively. *State* $\textit{Index}_j^S$ is the ideological difference between the sth state and center in the jth year. The index captures the absolute ideological difference between the two governments. It ranges from 0 to 5 and is a continuous variable.[9] A value 0 indicates that the two governments have exactly the same ideological orientation. On the other hand, a value 5 indicates that the two governments' ideologies are diametrically opposite to each other.

- *Single party dummy*: To capture whether the government in question is part of a coalition or is a single party government, we use a dummy variable. Due to the limitation of the data on composition of coalitions, we follow Sridharan (2010) which reports data on the presence of coalition governments in state elections. So, single party government is a categorical variable that takes the value 1 when the party with majority seats forms a single party government and the value 0, when it is part of a coalition government. This variable acts as a useful control in accounting for the coalition driven political era in Indian states.

(iii) Labor market rigidity

The employment decision of a CPSE depends on the labor market rigidities prevailing in the state. Rigidity of labor market depends on the bargaining strength and dominance of labor unions which play a critical role in CPSE decisions related to attrition and employment. We define it as the ratio of total man days lost in a state due to strikes and lockouts to the total workforce in a state. The direction of the effect of labor market rigidity on employment may not be unidirectional. A state with high labor market rigidity is expected to have higher employment (due to hindrances in layoffs) as compared to their counterparts. However, a state with a rigid labor market may affect efficiency of enterprises negatively since operations are hindered and indirectly it may have a negative externality on employment as a whole.

(iv) Policy variables

We use two policy variables — deregulation and Memorandum of Understanding (MoU). Disinvestment decisions are dependent on the prevailing competition in a particular industry. To capture the competitiveness in a particular industry and

---

[8] This is the weighted average of all parties in the center coalition with seat shares as the weights.

[9] Since the data on coalitions is not available at the state level, we take the ideology of the ruling party (assuming it is a single party) at the state level.

to check the overall changing competitiveness in an industry we construct a variable — delicensing. For every 2 digit NIC industry, we calculate the proportion of 4 digit NIC industries that were delicensed in a particular year. For the manufacturing sector, we get a time series of the delicensing variable. For the services sector, we collect information from government websites and documents for similar reforms and add it to the variable. We refer to it as 'deregulation' variable. Also, to check whether the public enterprise has signed an MoU with the central government or not we use a dummy variable. Additionally, we incorporate the previous years MoU score to capture the autonomous position of the enterprise. Besides these important controls, we include dummies to control for industries, overtime effect, geographical location and ratna status of each public sector enterprise.

(v) Firm specific variables

We use an array of firm specific variables which may be broadly classified into firm profile specific variables. Specifically, we consider firm age and firm size as the most basic factors. Firm age is the number of years that a firm has been operating since inception. It captures the experience of a firm. Firm size has been identified as one of the most important control factors when considering firm employment (Gupta, 2005). We also control for debt size. The variables are computed as follows:

$$Age_{ij} = (Current\ Year - Incorporation\ year),$$
$$Size_{ij} = \log(Total\ Assets_{ij}),$$
$$Debt\ size_{ij} = \frac{Total\ loans_{ij}}{Total\ Assets_{ij}},$$

where i denotes the firm and j denotes the year.

5.1 Econometric method

The descriptive statistics of all the variables is in Appendix A.

We estimate the impact of disinvestment and local political and economic factors on the employment of state owned enterprises using two specific econometric models. We first use a fixed effects regression to obtain the baseline regression results. The fixed effects are considered at the industry and time level. The regression equation is given by

$$y_{ijkt} = \alpha_{ijkt} + \beta_j + \chi_t + \sum_{i=1}^{n} \delta_{it} x_{it} + \sum_{k=1}^{K} \varepsilon_{kt} z_{kt} + \sum_{j=1}^{J} \phi_{jt} w_{jt} + e_{ijkt},$$

where y_{ijkt} is the employment of the ith firm belonging to the jth industry situated in k^{th} state and in the tth year. The term α_{ijkt} captures the intercept for the regression and β_j and χ_t capture the industry and time fixed effects, respectively. The rest of the three sets of factors capture the firm level, industry specific and state level economic and political factors. Model I of each part in results capture this sort of a regression framework. Model II includes interaction terms between the state specific political and institutional variables with disinvestment policy.

However, it may be naive to rule out the possibility of potential endogeneity between the firms selected for disinvestment and the effect of disinvestment. For example, if the government is more likely to select firms with abundance of labor, then comparing employment of divested firms to firms that remain government-owned may overstate the impact of disinvestment. So, one needs to tease out the effect of employment on disinvestment decisions and then examine the impact of disinvestment on firm employment. The instrumental variable analysis allows us to distinguish the impact of disinvestment on firm employment from the endogenous selection of firms with a surplus of labor for disinvestment. Hence, we use two stage least squares technique for capturing the effect of disinvestment on performance.

Following Wooldridge (2002), in the first stage, we focus on capturing the disinvestment decision. It is imperative to note here that these enterprises are owned by the Central government and hence decisions pertaining to disinvestment are taken by that wing of the government. So, political conditions prevailing at the Center will directly influence the decision of disinvestment, but this does not seem to have a direct effect on employment decisions of the enterprises. Employment of enterprises is driven by local labor market conditions, firm specific factors and political scenarios prevailing in the states. So, in the first stage we use the Central government specific political variables as instrument variables. This is similar to Dinc and Gupta (2011). Specifically, we use the ideology of the central government, the stability of the government and political fragmentation.[10]

---

[10] Ideology of the center: Weighted average of the ideology scores of all parties forming the Center coalitions with weights as the seat share that each party has in the coalition. Stability of the government: We use two measures of stability of the Center coalition. The first captures the instability in terms of number of seats won by the coalition and the deviation of this from the magical number 272. The second measure captures the number of days the government has been in power. These two measures deal with two different aspects of stability. The first is an ex-ante measure of stability where as the other is ex-post. Political fragmentation of the government: It is captured by the effective number of parties in the center coalition. It is a measure of the level of concentration in political life which assigns more influence to large parties and screens out very small parties in its computation. It can be simply defined as the inverse of the sum of the squared proportion of seats won by each electoral party.

Finally, we use the estimated values from the first equation and include that in the second step of the regression. Model III in each regression analysis is the result of this model. The model is very similar to Model I except that we use estimated disinvestment variables instead of the actual disinvestment variables. This enables us to tease out the effect of performance on disinvestment and just focus on the actual effect of disinvestment on firm performance. Finally, in Model IV we include the interaction terms between disinvestment and state specific political and economic factors.

6 Results

6.1 First time disinvestment

First of all, we capture disinvestment as the selection of a firm for disinvestment for the first time. The variable is a binary variable taking unit value only in case of first time selection and zero otherwise. The results are summarized in Table 2.

Table 2. Effect of first time disinvestment on employment of CPSEs.

Variables	Model I	Model II	Model III	Model IV
First time disinvestment	0.623***	0.161	11.541***	53.322***
	(0.164)	(0.744)	(2.594)	(13.396)
Ideology of the state	0.053	0.052	0.027	0.186***
	(0.035)	(0.035)	(0.046)	(0.065)
Ideology Difference	0.004	0.001	0.035	0.124**
	(0.029)	(0.029)	(0.035)	(0.048)
Single Party Dummy	−0.223***	−0.226***	−0.141	−0.124
	(0.050)	(0.050)	(0.086)	(0.083)
Labor Market Rigidity	−0.002	−0.002	−0.002	0.003
	(0.002)	(0.002)	(0.003)	(0.003)
First time* Id Score		0.018		−17.024***
		(0.257)		(4.289)
First time* Id Difference		0.231		−11.149***
		(0.232)		(2.849)
MOU Dummy	0.220**	0.219**	0.002	0.057
	(0.097)	(0.097)	(0.151)	(0.138)

(*Continued*)

Table 2. (*Continued*)

Variables	Model I	Model II	Model III	Model IV
Cognate group Profitability	−4.488***	−4.527***	1.920*	1.509
	(0.865)	(0.865)	(1.055)	(1.533)
Delicensing	−0.974***	−0.965***	0.694**	−0.713**
	(0.193)	(0.195)	(0.320)	(0.333)
Firm Size	0.536***	0.536***	0.119**	0.087**
	(0.016)	(0.016)	(0.049)	(0.044)
Debt Size	−0.655***	−0.653**	−0.228**	−0.189**
	(0.148)	(0.147)	(0.091)	(0.087)
Firm Age	0.709***	0.712***	−0.586***	−0.313**
	(0.048)	(0.048)	(0.146)	(0.155)
Firm Liquidity	−0.012	−0.012	−0.001	0.015
	(0.009)	(0.009)	(0.020)	(0.019)
Constant	−4.459***	−4.478***	6.103***	10.226***
	(0.430)	(0.433)	(1.188)	(1.359)
Year Dummies	Yes	Yes	Yes	Yes
Industry Dummies	Yes	Yes	Yes	Yes
Ratna Status Dummies	Yes	Yes	Yes	Yes
Number of Observations	3723	3723	3723	3723
Number of CPSEs	230	230	230	230
R-squared	63.27	63.30	—	—

Note: The table presents results obtained from the regression analysis for determinants of firm employment with the first time selection of firms for disinvestment. Standard errors are reported within parentheses. *, ** and *** indicate significance at 10%, 5% and 1% respectively. Models I and II are OLS regressions and Models III and IV are the second stage results of the 2SLS regressions. Models II and IV include interaction terms between first time disinvestment and state specific political and economic factors.

As the table suggests, selection of firms for disinvestment has a positive effect on employment of CPSEs. This is in sharp contrast to our initial hypothesis that disinvestment has a detrimental impact on employment. There may be two reasons explaining this result. Keeping in mind, one of the main objectives of disinvestment to improve efficiency of CPSEs, there has been a rise in the efficiency of firms selected for disinvestment (Jain, 2014). This rise in efficiency boosts employment in CPSEs. This may seem contradicting to the declining trend in total employment over the years. However, this decline in employment trends is not because of disinvestment. Instead, this trend is driven by two specific features — auxiliary services (security, transport, canteen, etc.) being contracted out and natural attrition, on retirement: with gradual slow down in fresh employment in the recent years, majority of the employees had reached retiring age thus contributing to the declining total employee strength. In fact the positive effect of disinvestment on employment has been documented by Gupta (2005). The study emphasized that partial privatization does not cause the government to abandon the political objective of maintaining surplus employment. In the Indian context this result is not too surprising, since company law restricts layoffs in companies, and most state-owned enterprise employees belong to well-organized labor unions that are directly affiliated with major political parties.

Besides disinvestment, ideology score of the state has a positive impact on employment decisions of the firm. Left-winged states (with higher ideology scores) are characterized by stronger labor unions and hence lesser attrition. So, firms located in left-winged states have higher employment as compared to their counterparts. Besides, the direct political effect, the effect of disinvestment on employment is strongly conditioned by the political situation prevailing in the state. Specifically, the effect of disinvestment on employment is stronger in right-winged states as compared to left-winged ones. In other words, disinvestment raises employment in right-winged states via a rise in the efficiency which boosts employment eventually which is not as present in left-winged states.[11]

Besides, low debt size of the enterprises, more experienced and large sized firms have a positive influence on employment. We control for the labor market differences across different states. We have also controlled for two main policy tools available to the government — memorandum of understanding and delicensing. We have also included industry and time dummies to control for unknown time and industry specific effects. The results confirm that first time disinvestment is not significant in the fixed effects Model II. However, when we use the 2SLS technique in Models III and IV, disinvestment of firms for the first time has a very strong positive influence on employment.

In Model IV, we have included the interaction terms between the two ideological variables and disinvestment. The interaction term is positively significant suggesting that first time disinvestment of enterprises conditions the effect of the political variables on firm employment. It is seen that although left-winged governments are favorable for employment as compared to their right-winged counterpart,

[11] The total employee size for public sector enterprises in left-winged states is 25%, higher than those in right-winged states. Hence, the effect of disinvestment on employee size is higher in right-winged states because, the scope of increase in employee size is also higher.

disinvestment reverses the effect. More specifically, the effect of disinvestment on firm employment is stronger when the firm is operating in the right-winged state as compared to left-winged ones because of better policies, by virtue of its ideology, being implemented to support disinvestment to affect firm employment.

6.2 Disinvestment occurrence

Occurrence of disinvestment is defined as the event in which disinvestment takes place in an enterprise at a particular time. In other words, first time disinvestment and repeated disinvestment is considered to be of equal importance. The results obtained by using occurrence as the disinvestment indicator and other political and state specific choice variables have been presented in Table 3.

Table 3 suggests that disinvestment occurrence has similar impact as first time disinvestment. All other variables continue to behave as expected. The political ideology variables affect firm employment similarly. The pattern exhibited by occurrence of disinvestment is similar to first time disinvestment. Disinvestment occurrence has no impact on firm employment directly when modelled by OLS techniques with interaction terms. However, the 2SLS framework captures the effect of disinvestment by controlling for endogeneity and occurrence of disinvestment becomes highly significant.

Table 3. Effect of disinvestment occurrence on employment of CPSEs.

Variables	Model I	Model II	Model III	Model IV
Occurrence disinvestment	0.350***	0.508	7.454***	58.073***
	(0.095)	(0.410)	(1.147)	(15.331)
Ideology of the state	0.053	0.056	0.007	0.706***
	(0.035)	(0.036)	(0.046)	(0.202)
Ideology Difference	0.003	0.006	–0.004	0.470***
	(0.029)	(0.030)	(0.035)	(0.139)
Single Party Dummy	–0.226***	–0.239***	–0.326***	0.064
	(0.050)	(0.051)	(0.091)	(0.157)
Labor Market Rigidity	–0.002	–0.001	–0.002	–0.005
	(0.002)	(0.002)	(0.003)	(0.006)
Occurence* Id Score		–0.104		–17.932***
		(0.145)		(–12.797)

(*Continued*)

Table 3. (*Continued*)

Variables	**Model I**	**Model II**	**Model III**	**Model IV**
Occurence* Id Difference		–0.076		3.386***
		(0.132)		(4.725)
Occurence* Single Govt		–0.104		–12.566***
		(0.145)		(3.442)
MOU Dummy	0.222**	0.224**	0.068	0.276
	(0.096)	(0.097)	(0.147)	(0.236)
Cognate group Profitability	–4.569***	–4.571***	–0.784	–2.165
	(0.863)	(0.863)	(0.973)	(1.570)
Delicensing	–1.008***	–1.026***	0.085	–1.078**
	(0.194)	(0.195)	(0.297)	(0.496)
Firm Size	0.532***	0.531***	0.142***	0.1827**
	(0.016)	(0.016)	(0.048)	(0.075)
Debt Size	–0.649***	–0.645***	–0.175*	–0.324**
	(0.147)	(0.146)	(0.094)	(0.151)
Firm Age	0.709***	0.709***	0.025	–0.365**
	(0.048)	(0.048)	(0.172)	(0.164)
Firm Liquidity	–0.012	–0.012	0.004	0.0213
	(0.009)	(0.009)	(0.020)	(0.032)
Constant	–4.310***	–4.273***	3.518***	5.355***
	(0.432)	(0.435)	(1.129)	(1.674)
Year Dummies	Yes	Yes	Yes	Yes
Industry Dummies	Yes	Yes	Yes	Yes
Ratna Status Dummies	Yes	Yes	Yes	Yes
Number of Observations	3723	3723	3723	3723
Number of CPSEs	230	230	230	230
R-squared	63.1	62.79	—	—

Note: The table presents results obtained from the regression analysis for determinants of firm employment with disinvestment occurrence. Standard errors are reported within parentheses. *, ** and *** indicate significance at 10%, 5% and 1% respectively. Models I and II are OLS regressions and Models III and IV are the second stage results of the 2SLS regressions. Models II and IV include interaction terms between first time disinvestment and state specific political and economic factors.

6.3 Extent of disinvestment

In the third part of the analysis we try and capture disinvestment as the proportion of shares transferred from the government to the private sector, referred to as the disinvestment extent. The rest of the explanatory variables are the same as before. The results are compiled in Table 4. Most of the factors behave as before.

Table 4. Effect of disinvestment extent on employment of CPSEs.

Variables	Model I	Model II	Model III	Model IV
Extent disinvestment	1.112***	0.641	5.791***	55.198***
	(0.362)	(1.497)	(1.077)	(11.010)
Ideology of the state	0.053	0.053	0.005	0.090**
	(0.035)	(0.035)	(0.024)	(0.036)
Ideology Difference	0.003	0.003	–0.000	0.071**
	(0.029)	(0.029)	(0.018)	(0.028)
Single Party Dummy	–0.225***	–0.230***	–0.141***	–0.119**
	(0.050)	(0.050)	(0.045)	(0.059)
Labor Market Rigidity	–0.002	–0.002	0.001	0.001
	(0.002)	(0.002)	(0.001)	(0.002)
Extent* Id Score		–0.052		–18.793***
		(0.464)		(3.688)
Extent* Id Difference		–0.241		–18.283***
		(0.690)		(3.750)
Extent* Single Govt		–0.052		–8.106***
		(0.464)		(1.950)
MOU Dummy	0.231**	0.232**	0.172**	0.109
	(0.097)	(0.097)	(0.076)	(0.096)
Cognate group Profitability	–4.645***	–4.630***	–0.426	–0.710
	(0.862)	(0.863)	(0.479)	(0.639)
Delicensing	–1.005***	–1.005***	0.049	–0.004
	(0.194)	(0.194)	(0.150)	(0.194)
Firm Size	0.536***	0.536***	0.039	0.075**
	(0.016)	(0.016)	(0.024)	(0.031)

(Continued)

Table 4. (*Continued*)

Variables	Model I	Model II	Model III	Model IV
Debt Size	–0.654***	–0.653***	–0.226***	–0.226***
	(0.147)	(0.147)	(0.048)	(0.061)
Firm Age	0.705***	0.706***	–0.853***	–0.194*
	(0.048)	(0.048)	(0.069)	(0.109)
Firm Liquidity	–0.012	–0.012	–0.005	0.010
	(0.009)	(0.009)	(0.010)	(0.013)
Constant	–4.392***	–4.380***	9.519***	9.462***
	(0.429)	(–0.430)	(0.464)	(0.665)
Year Dummies	Yes	Yes	Yes	Yes
Industry Dummies	Yes	Yes	Yes	Yes
Ratna Status Dummies	Yes	Yes	Yes	Yes
Number of Observations	3723	3723	3723	3723
Number of CPSEs	230	230	230	230
R-squared	63.22	62.99	—	—

Note: The table presents results obtained from the regression analysis for determinants of firm employment with disinvestment extent. Standard errors are reported within parentheses. *, ** and *** indicate significance at 10%, 5% and 1% respectively. Models I and II are OLS regressions and Models III and IV are the second stage results of the 2SLS regressions. Models II and IV include interaction terms between first time disinvestment and state specific political and economic factors.

7 Conclusion

Indian CPSE employment has been dropping since the late 80s. This coincides with the adoption of various major reforms undertaken in 1991 — disinvestment being one of them. On one hand, disinvestment is perceived to carry benefits like infusing efficiency and competitiveness in industries and inducing better performance of public firms. On the other hand, it is linked to higher unemployment, which in turn may have detrimental effect on the chance of re-election. Against this backdrop, using a comprehensive dataset of all enterprises owned by the Central government of India for the period of 1991–1992 to 2011–2012, the paper aims to explore the factors affecting the employment in public sector enterprises.

We explore factors that may affect employment size of firms- the internal capacity of a firm driven by firm specific characteristics and external factors (disinvestment policy, political and institutional factors) in the states where the enterprises operate. We use a multidimensional approach to capture the effect of ideology and disinvestment policy instead of a standard dummy variable approach. Using two stage least squares technique and instrumental variable approach we find that it's a combination of both internal and external factors that influence the employment size of enterprises. The results suggest that ideology of the state plays a very important role in explaining employment in firms. Employment is driven by a more right-winged coalition and low ideological difference between the center and the state where the public enterprise is located. Further, it is found that selection, repeated occurrences and higher extent of disinvestment improves the employee strength of public sector enterprises. It is seen that firm level, industry specific and policy variables affect firm employment significantly. We also find that the effect of disinvestment on firm employment is stronger in right-winged states as compared to the left-winged ones.

There are a few caveats in the study. Most of the states in India are governed by more than one party. However, gathering data on parties forming coalitions at the state level for 1991–2011 is beyond the scope of this study. Hence, the study is based on the simple assumption that the ideology of the party in the state with majority seat share is the representative of the government ruling that state irrespective of the fact that it might be a part of a coalition. Also, we assume that ideology of a party does not change over time. This may be taken care of in future works.

References

Amess, K., J. Du and S. Girma (2009), Full and Partial Privatization in China: The Labor Consequences. University of Nottingham Research Paper Series, Number 2009/11, UK: University of Nottingham, GEP.

Brown, J.D., J.S. Earle and A. Telegdy (2005), Does Privatization Hurt Workers? Lessons from Comprehensive Manufacturing Firm Panel Data in Hungary, Romania, Russia and Ukraine. Upjohn Institute Working Papers, No.-05–125, Michigan, United States: Upjohn Institute.

Chhibber, P. and I. Nooruddin (2004), Do Party Systems Count? The Number of Parties and Government Performance in the Indian States, *Comparative Political Studies*, 37(2), 152–187.

Dash, B.B. and A.V. Raja (2014), Do Political Determinants Affect Revenue Collections? A Study of the Indian States, *International Review of Economics*, 3(61), 253–278.

Dinc, I.S. and N. Gupta (2011), The Decision to Privatize, Finance and Politics, *The Journal of Finance*, 66(1), 241–269.

Gupta, N. (2005), Partial privatization and firm performance, *The Journal of Finance*, 60(2), 987–1015.
Indian Labor Market Report (2008). ATLMRI, Tata Institute of Social Sciences, Mumbai. Available from: http://www.cosv.org/download/centrodocumentazione/ATLMRILabour MarketReport(1).pdf. September 21, 2015.
Jain, R. (2014), Economic and Political Interactions in explaining the Performance of Public Sector Enterprises in India: The Disinvestment Experience. Revise (2015), Trivandrum. Centre for Development Studies.
Papola, T.S. (1991), Industry and Employment: Recent Indian Experience, Institute for Studies in Industrial Development, ISID Foundation Day lecture.
Sridharan, E. (2010), 'The Party System' in Gopal Jayal, N. and P. Bhanu Metha (Eds.): The Oxford Companion to Politics in India, Delhi: Oxford University Press, 117–135.
Wooldridge, J. (2002), Econometric Analysis of Cross Section and Panel Data. MIT Press, Massachusetts.

Appendix A

The summary statistics of all the important variables are shown below:

Category	Variable	# Observation	Mean	Standard deviation	Minimum	Maximum
Dependent Variable	Total Employee size	3723	8052.00	20884.57	0.00	189193.00
	Log of employee size	3723	7.29	2.01	−2.30	12.15
State specific political variables	Ideology of the state	3723	2.82	1.33	1.00	5.00
	Ideology difference	3723	−0.30	1.56	−3.58	2.08
	Coalition dummy\	3723	0.54	0.41	0.00	1.00
Disinvestment Variables	Disinvestment Extent	3723	0.00	0.04	0.00	1.00
	First time disinvestment	3723	0.01	0.11	0.00	1.00
	Occurrence of disinvestment	3723	0.04	0.19	0.00	1.00
State labor market conditions	Labor market rigidity	3723	5.02	10.09	0.00	56.43

(*Continued*)

(*Continued*)

Category	Variable	# Observation	Mean	Standard deviation	Minimum	Maximum
Firm specific variables	Firm Age	3723	29.57	16.93	2.00	110.00
	Return on Assets	3723	0.00	0.57	−3.84	32.02
	Debt Size	3723	0.42	0.37	0.00	8.81
	Log of age	3723	3.25	0.55	0.69	5.36
	Firm Size	3723	21.73	2.29	15.80	27.90
Policy variables	Delicensing extent	3723	0.92	0.17	0.00	1.00
	MOU Score	3723	0.44	0.50	0.00	1.00
	MOU Dummy	3723	0.91	1.25	0.00	5.00
Industry specific dummy variables	Cognate Group Profitability	3723	0.04	0.04	−0.05	0.24
	Miniratna I dummy	3723	0.19	0.39	0.00	1.00
	Miniratna II dummy	3723	0.06	0.23	0.00	1.00
	Maharatna dummy	3723	0.01	0.11	0.00	1.00
	Navratna dummy	3723	0.08	0.27	0.00	1.00
Center specific political variables	Ideology score of the Center	3723	2.52	0.71	1.42	3.08
	Stability in seat share	3723	0.74	0.17	0.58	1.00
	Stability in days	3723	2.31	1.35	0.48	4.22
	Effective Number of Parties	3723	5.26	1.08	3.70	6.50

Chapter 11

Migration Policies, Employment Choices and the Vulnerability of South Indian Domestic Workers in the Middle East

Praveena Kodoth
Centre for Development Studies,
Thiruvananthapuram, Kerala, India
praveena@cds.ac.in

Abstract: Emigrant domestic workers from South India are found in two broad categories of employment in the Middle East, i.e. full-time live-in jobs with employers, who have sponsored them as mandated by the system, or informal employment, where the sponsor and the employer are separate and workers take up full time, part time or irregular jobs that are outside the purview of the system. The regulatory system in the Middle East introduces friction in the relationship between sponsor-employers and domestic workers. The legal obligation of sponsors to pay for the emigration and subsistence of domestic workers imparts a sense of entitlement over the latter and shapes violation of rights. The benefit of this provision, however, is usually absorbed by intermediaries. Thus, South Indian domestic workers invest large sums of money on emigration and are under tremendous pressure to tolerate exploitation and abuse in order to continue employment with the sponsor. In this context, India's emigration policy, which relies on barriers to prevent the flow of domestic workers to the Middle East and denies them support in the destination pushes the latter to depend on informal support networks and heightens their vulnerability in overseas employment. Severe ill treatment by sponsors or aspirations for better jobs could motivate domestics to seek informal employment, which is illegal in the Middle

East. This paper draws attention to how Indian policy undermines the ability of emigrant domestic workers to combat the ill effects of the regulatory framework in the Middle East and induces them instead to make precarious employment choices.

1 Introduction

The employment choices of migrant domestic workers (MDWs) in the Middle East are structured substantially within a regulatory environment generated by the *Kafala* system of sponsorship and recruitment, which regulates all immigrant workers in the Middle East. The sponsorship system vests all legal and economic responsibility over MDWs in their sponsors who are expected to employ them, provide for their subsistence during the tenure of their visas, and to pay for their emigration and return. Domestic workers go to the Middle East on a separate category of visas, meant exclusively for workers employed in households, and unlike other migrant workers are excluded from the purview of labor laws.[1] Reform of the *Kafala* system in the recent past has altered its severity in some of the Middle Eastern countries, but has excluded domestic workers. Thus, the system continues to pose hurdles in the way of domestics who wish to change their employers during the tenure of their visa. Effectively, sponsor-employers may terminate the employment of a domestic worker and send her back home or may contrive to have her deported even when the worker may aspire to remain in the destination.

The extent of power that sponsor-employer's wield over migrant workers has been compared to which only states wield over citizens (Gardner, 2012), but employment choices of MDWs are constrained additionally by the emigration policy of the sending country and the extent of their non-state support networks in the destination. The Indian state has reinforced the vulnerability of its emigrant domestics in the Middle East by adopting a protectionist policy since at least the 1990s and strengthening barriers against the migration of women domestics in the past decade. Policy disincentives have failed to stem the flow of domestics from India, but the experience of South Indian domestics in the Middle East suggests that protectionism renders their employment precarious because it drives aspirants to rely on informal/illegal means to access overseas jobs and throws them upon their individual resources in the struggle to cope with structural constraints.

Emigrant domestics in the Middle East are found in two broad categories of employment i.e. in full-time live-in jobs with their sponsor-employers as mandated by the system and in informal employment where the sponsor and the employer are separate and workers may take up full-time or part-time jobs that are outside the purview of the system. I characterize the latter form of employment as

[1] About 99% of all domestic workers in the Middle East are outside the scope of labor legislation (ILO, 2013).

informal because though the *Kafala* system renders it illegal, an "open" market for paid domestic work, where workers and employers negotiate diverse and multiple work arrangements, is well entrenched. Depicting the informal market as illegal in this context merely diverts attention from its institutionalization.

Informality in paid domestic work is a fallout of the regulatory framework in the Middle East as nationals, recruiters, employers and workers seek to profit from it. The development of a wider informal market in the Middle East is linked to the large-scale demand for workers in the region, which generated competition among recruiters and made way for a system of visa trading.[2] Work visas referred to variously as "private" visas, "free" or "azad" visas are made available through a manipulation of the sponsorship system, wherein nationals, entitled to sponsor a specific number of domestic workers sell these visas to intermediaries or directly to workers. More affluent migrant workers, like nurses and other professionals, who form a fairly big section of employers of domestics in the Middle East may prefer informal workers on mutually beneficial terms as it allows them to avoid the responsibilities of sponsorship.

Workers, however, enter the informal market through different routes. They may obtain private visas and take up a variety of jobs while living in rented accommodation or take up a full-time job and live with an employer. Another category of workers who seek employment on the informal market are undocumented, who have run away from their sponsor–employers owing to ill treatment or in search of more remunerative work or who have overstayed their visas.

The regulatory system introduces sharp tensions in the relationship between sponsor employers and MDWs. Sponsors are able to violate the rights of MDWs with impunity because they are almost never punished within the regulatory system. The obligation of sponsors to pay emigration and subsistence costs of workers imparts a sense of entitlement over domestics and an urge among sponsors to make good their investment. Sponsors may also fear that workers will run away to tap better opportunities on the informal market. Thus, they may withhold or delay payment of salaries in order to prevent workers from running away or to reduce their losses if they do. MDWs invest large sums of money on emigration as the benefit of the sponsor's obligation to pay for their emigration is usually absorbed by intermediaries. Thus, MDWs may be under tremendous pressure to tolerate exploitation and abuse in order to continue employment with the sponsor, but ill treatment compounded by non-payment of salaries, could drive domestics to run away.

---

[2] Immigrants constitute an overwhelming majority of the labour force in the GCC countries (Bahrain, Kuwait, Qatar, Oman, Saudi Arabia and the United Arab Emirates), averaging about 77% in 2008 (Baldwin-Edwards, 2011). Informality is widespread. In 2004, the Saudi Minister of Labor said that 70% of the visas issued by the government are sold on the black market (Shah, 2009).

The structuring of legal employment relations could render informal employment attractive to workers because they have greater space to negotiate beneficial terms of employment and may exit jobs when the terms agreed upon are not honored, but workers may be forced on to the informal market because of severe violation of rights which renders them vulnerable. In either case, to survive on the informal market, emigrant domestics need the ability and sufficient connections to evade detection and deportation. In this chapter, I use the experiences of MDW from the states of Kerala and Andhra Pradesh (AP) to draw attention to the effects of the regulatory framework in the Middle East on employment choices and explore the nature of relationships these choices entail. Drawing on this analysis, I also ask, given the specificities of the regulatory system in the Middle East how appropriate is Indian regulation to secure better outcomes for MDWs.

The chapter is in six sections. I provide a brief description of the fieldwork that generated the material used in this chapter in Section 2. In the next two sections, I first map the emigration rules, scale of migration and the social context in the sending regions and then provide an overview of the regulatory environment in the Middle East. In Section 5, I probe employment choices of Indian MDWs, the conditions that shape them and the vulnerabilities associated with them. Drawing on the experiences of Indian MDWs, the conclusion directs attention to the appropriateness of Indian regulation.

2 Fieldwork

Andhra Pradesh (AP) and Kerala, where fieldwork was undertaken, are considered to be major sending regions of emigrant domestics from India, according to scattered references in the literature and limited official information. Official information suggests that migration of domestics from AP has grown significantly in the past decade and according to activists/NGO representatives, domestics from AP form the majority of Indian women seeking refuge shelter homes in destination countries.

Fieldwork was conducted over four sites, two in each state. A sample survey, of 502 emigrant women or those who returned not earlier than 2008, was conducted in one taluk each in East Godavari and Kadapa districts in AP and four taluks each in Trivandrum and Malappuram districts in Kerala.[3] Over 340 emigrant and returnee women were interviewed, irrespective of when they had

[3] For the purpose of administration, districts are divided into taluks. The sample was distributed unevenly across sites on account of logistical constraints and the ease with which respondents could be located — 202 in East Godavari, 94 in Kadapa, 150 in Trivandrum and 54 in Malappuram.

returned. Interviews were conducted also with government officials concerned with emigration, recruiting, emigration and travel agents, representatives of migrant rights/domestic workers' organizations and representatives of migrants' associations. Non-structured interactions with family members of emigrant workers and members of the local community provided useful insights into perceptions about emigrant domestic work and the women who take up such employment. Fieldwork was more intensive in East Godavari and Trivandrum where interviews covered a wider spectrum of emigrant and returnee women and probed the context of women's emigration from the 1960s to the present.

The sample for the survey and interviews was drawn up through snowballing from a wide base in the selected areas. In Trivandrum and Malappuram, MDWs were scattered over the coastal region and the highland taluks.[4] In East Godavari, women's migration was concentrated in a taluk adjoining West Godavari, also a major sending region of women domestics and in Kadapa, one of two taluks believed to have a concentration of MDWs was selected. Local field investigators in the field sites in AP identified survey respondents and most of the interviewees.[5] In all the field sites, effort was made to identify diverse categories of respondents distributed as widely as possible across the talukas.

3 The Sending Context: Regulation and Practices

Since the 1990s, Indian governments have successively tightened regulations. MDWs are likely to have Emigration Check Required (ECR) passports, reserved for people who have not completed 10 years of education, and therefore require emigration clearance from the Protector of Emigrants (POE) in order to migrate. At present, to be eligible for emigration clearance, domestic workers must be at least 30 years old and must present themselves personally before the POE in possession of a work contract attested by the Indian embassy at the destination, which is contingent on payment of a security deposit of $2500 by the sponsor-employment. The security deposit is slated to be used by the embassy for repatriation of the worker

[4] In Kerala, the Kudumbasree network, a state-wide micro finance network of women, a micro finance organization of the Catholic Church, the Self Employed Women's Association and the National Domestic Workers Movement helped identify emigrant and returnee women.

[5] Project staff of the Azim Premji Foundation in field work area in East Godavari helped locate field investigators. The Migrant Rights Forum in Hyderabad helped organize my initial visit to East Godavari, where I spoke to returnee women the organization had helped to repatriate and families of deceased domestic workers. In Kadapa, a project staff of the Migrant Forum Asia helped to identify field investigators and to conduct the survey.

if the need arises.[6] To qualify for a visa, aspirants must pass a medical test, conducted by accredited hospitals in select cities specifically for the Gulf countries, and for emigration clearance they must get a certificate of clearance from the police.

In the absence of official interest in this stream of migration and support for it, the flow of domestics is poorly documented at the source. The two available sources of data — the statistics on ECR granted by the POE offices and sample surveys on migration undertaken from time to time at the state level — tend to underestimate the scale of migration.

The ECR data tells us only about workers who observe the due legal process in a context where there are indications that there may be considerable irregular migration. Emigration Check Not Required (ECNR) endorsements are granted to less skilled migrants who have completed three years of overseas employment. Thus, repeat migration obviates the need for emigration clearance, though ECNR passports are otherwise reserved for more educated persons whose mobility is not scrutinized by the state. A small proportion of domestic workers, particularly those from Kerala, possess the minimum education required for ECNR passports.[7] Irregular/illegal migration, which official statistics do not account for, is believed to range from 10% to 40% in this segment.

Sample surveys undertaken at the state level underestimates the scale of MDW, who are more spatially concentrated than all migrants. Surveys undertaken in regions with high intensity of migration do worse because, they do not necessarily correspond to the sending regions of women domestic workers. Besides, MDWs and their families are likely to underreport their presence because of the stigma associated with overseas domestic work.

According to a recent estimate, 2.1 million workers in the Middle East were employed as domestic workers in 2010, nearly double the 1.1 million in 1995 (ILO, 2013). India is not considered a major sending country, but collation of scattered information mostly from the destination suggests that India may be a significant source of MDWs in the Middle East. India is considered to be the largest supplier to Kuwait after Sri Lanka. Out of 294,000 Indian residents in Kuwait in 2000, 113,000 were domestic workers and 49,000 were women (MOIA, 2001). A sample of 300 domestic workers studied in Kuwait in 2001 was constituted of 25% Indians and 42% Sri Lankans, but among the 322 domestic workers employed

[6] All applications to the POE for emigration clearance are made online. The information is used to generate the emigration clearance granted sticker that is fixed onto the passport after verification of documents produced personally by the aspiring domestic worker.

[7] One-third of 43 Indian women domestic workers had matriculate or higher levels of education according to a survey in Kuwait in 2001 (Godfreys *et al.*, 2005).

by a sample of 200 employers, 37% were Indian (Godfrey *et al.*, 2005). According to the POE in Hyderabad, over 90% of the emigrations granted to women domestic workers from his field office were to Kuwait (Interview, February 22, 2013).

India had a head start with respect to migration of domestic workers to Kuwait, the UAE and Bahrain owing to British interests in oil installations which drew upon Indian semi-skilled labor. In Bahrain, some of the wealthy families hired Indian domestic workers, from Kerala, Goa and AP, as a sign of social prestige even before the oil boom (Sabika al-Najjar, 2005). Indian women MDWs are estimated to be between 12,000 and 15,000 in Bahrain (Pradhan, 2009). India is among the largest suppliers of domestics to Oman, where they were estimated to be over 30,000 (Deffner and Pfaffenbach, 2011). India is among the relatively smaller suppliers of domestic workers to Saudi Arabia, which accounts for the largest number of domestic workers in the Middle East (HRW, 2010). Nevertheless, a media source put the figure at 50,000 in 2013.

The sustained flow of MDWs from India in the face of barriers owes as much to the demand in the Middle East as to the context in the sending regions. The openness to migration within the sending communities, forged through previous labour mobility to South East Asia, and a proactive migration industry have been crucial factors. The sending regions of Kerala and AP also had in common a dense web of connections leading to Bombay, which until recently was the nodal centre for recruitment to the Middle East.

A restrictive migration policy has served to narrow the social and spatial base from which MDWs are drawn. The sample from Kerala was overwhelmingly from the Other Backward Classes (OBC) (Latin Catholic, Muslim and Hindu) (82%) followed by Scheduled Castes (SC) (10%). The sample from Trivandrum was almost evenly divided among the three religious affiliations but was predominantly Muslim in Malappuram. Information from local networks suggests that MDWs in Trivandrum and Malappuram were concentrated in localities marked by uncertain livelihoods and/or resource scarcity. Density of emigrant women was highest in the coastal villages, though women were by no means evenly distributed. In Trivandrum, coastal villages with a history of migration in the colonial period had witnessed migration of domestics from OBC Latin Catholic families to the Middle East since the late 1960s. OBC women in other coastal villages, and OBC and SC women in highland villages and urban slums were drawn to migration since the 1980s. A few Scheduled Tribes (ST) women from the highlands had returned and several were currently working overseas. MDWs from the higher castes were few and far between and were dispersed.

The survey sample in AP comprised 47% each from SC and OBC. The region in East and West Godavari districts with a concentration of MDWs was prosperous agriculturally, having benefited from the construction of the Godavari canal system. SC families did not own land but had witnessed the possibility of upward mobility through migration to Burma since the late 19th century (Adapa, 2002). Women respondents from East Godavari who migrated in the early 1970s were all SC and connected to a single mandal,[8] where a few SC families had prospered through previous migration to Burma. In recent decades, women from OBC and a small number of upper caste (Kapu) families had taken advantage of migrant opportunities in the Middle East. One-third of respondents in the sample survey from East Godavari were OBC, 1% was upper caste and 65% SC. Though it is believed that emigration from Rayachoty taluk in Kadapa is mostly of Muslim women, recent years had seen OBC and SC/ST women joining their ranks in increasing numbers. Only a third of the respondents in our sample were Muslim, whereas 73% were OBC, including Muslim, 15% was SC/ST and 11% was upper caste (Reddy). In recent years interior villages in both sites had witnessed a rush for overseas jobs by women from agricultural labor families motivated by the easy access to visas.

MDWs in Kerala and AP were subject to stigma but had internalized it differently. Women's emigration as domestics breached the male breadwinner norm which found wide acceptance in Kerala. It also removed women from the everyday scope of family and local patriarchy and raised suspicion of breach of sexual codes. More intensive investigation showed that stigma was more intense and widespread in Trivandrum compared to East Godavari. A strong aversion was expressed within sending communities in Trivandrum and wider society to emigrant domestic work whereas in East Godavari, the SCs, the major sending social group, underlined the desirability of overseas employment as a remunerative form of livelihood and considered it less demeaning than agricultural labor or domestic work at home. However, it was associated with pejorative meanings in wider society, and upper caste emigrant domestics were subject to stigma within their communities.

The effects of stigma were apparent in the significantly lower proportion of currently married women emigrants at the time of the first journey from Kerala (53%) compared to AP (85%). Breakdown of marriage on account of widowhood, divorce or separation was highest (60%) among emigrants on their first journey from Malappuram. Notably, emigrant women from Kerala underlined the failures of marital provisioning, irrespective of marital status, to legitimize their mobility, whereas emigrant women from AP saw their migration as mutually beneficial and rarely spoke of resistance from their spouses. Spouses of MDWs were not subject to ridicule among the SC as were the spouses of upper caste women in East Godavari.

---

[8] Administrative sub-division below the taluk level.

Social networks and the migration industry were a key influence in promoting migration from the sending regions. Emigrant workers channelized visas for their relatives and acquaintances. Two and sometimes three generations of women from the same families in East Godavari had worked in the Middle East as domestics when there was not sufficient upward mobility. This was less prevalent in Trivandrum but there were instances of two generations of women having worked in the Middle East as domestics. First generation emigrants who made good had paved the way for their daughters to access slightly more respected jobs in schools and hospitals usually after arranging their marriages to men with jobs in the Gulf.

At the source, the use of networks produced clusters of extended kin groups: the migration of a woman enabled her siblings, more distant kin and the next generation of relatives to go. The influence of personal connections and networks is borne out by the clustering of MDWs in particular destinations and connections between a specific source and destination. Kuwait was the most frequently reported destination of emigrant and returnee women from Trivandrum, East Godavari and Kadapa, but the major destinations from Malappuram were the UAE and Saudi Arabia.[9] Notably, Saudi Arabia was among the principal destinations from places with a sizeable proportion of Muslims in the sample.[10]

MDWs are relegated systematically to seek the services of non-state and mostly not licensed intermediaries because they are abjured by public sector and licensed private agencies. The distinction between social networks and commercial intermediaries were blurred as emigrant workers acted as middle men, supplying visas for a fee. Agents were referred to as simply "travels" in Kerala because travel agents sourced visas for aspiring workers, whereas in AP, a distinction was made between "office" visas supplied by recruiting/travel agents and those supplied by individuals. Intermediaries raised aspirations among women, provided visas, accompanied women to Bombay, Chennai or Hyderabad and assisted them to navigate emigration procedures and to make their way to the destination.

Government restrictions have bred a complex nexus between aspiring migrants and agents, who are perceived as facilitators. Agents assist aspirants to travel overseas even when they do not qualify for emigration clearance. They manipulate the emigration process by engineering an overstated age on prospective migrants' passports, when they are below the minimum age, or by bribing emigration officials to get the required clearance. Our sample survey showed that 42.6% of

[9] Considering all journeys undertaken by the sample, Kuwait accounted for 35% of all journeys by the survey respondents from Trivandrum, 40% from East Godavari and 70% from Kadapa. UAE accounted for 41% of journeys from Malappuram and Saudi Arabia for 27%.

[10] Saudi Arabia accounted for 17% of journeys from Trivandrum and 12% from Kadapa, where it was second to Kuwait in terms of principal destinations.

workers who took up their first overseas jobs after 2000 were below 30 years, the minimum age required for emigration clearance.[11] Aspirants may fail to get emigration clearance because they are underage or because they lack the documents necessary for it. They are sent through an informal arrangement brokered by agents through emigration officials at airports.

4 Regulation in the Middle East

The *Kafala* system takes its name, ironically, from the Bedouin custom of granting hospitality to strangers for as long as they stayed. As a modern-day mechanism for managing labour inflows into the Middle Eastern countries, it binds immigrant workers to their sponsors (*kafil*). Sponsors may be individuals, placement agencies or corporations but in the case of domestic workers they are always individuals. The first three months of employment for domestic workers is considered a probationary period when the employer or employee may seek a replacement (Manseau, 2006) and the agency is expected to bear the cost of return of a domestic during this period. However, in reality 'when disputes arise the domestic worker is forced to continue working with a sponsor regardless of the situation' (Sabika al-Najjar, 2005).

In the face of persistent demands from human rights agencies and the effort under the aegis of the ILO to provide a framework for the employment of domestics, Middle Eastern countries have made small moves to reform the system. Sponsors routinely take possession of the legal documents of workers to gain a measure of control over workers (Godfrey *et al.*, 2004; Sabban, 2005; HRW, 2008). Kuwait prohibited employers from withholding workers' passports and enabled domestic workers, in certain cases, to change their employers without the approval of the previous employer through ministerial decisions in 2010 and 2011 respectively (IHRC, 2013). Legislative reforms in the UAE and Bahrain, respectively in 2005 and 2009 allowed workers to change their employers with the latter's consent but excluded domestic workers from their purview.

Qatar, Kuwait, UAE, Oman and Saudi Arabia continue to exclude domestic workers from the scope of the country's labor laws — there being no limitation on their weekly working hours, no provision for annual paid leave and no statutory minimum wage (ILO, 2013). Domestic workers are barred from joining a trade union. The contract of an employee is usually for two years but not all countries

[11] More than half the workers in our sample (307) had migrated since 2000. About 53% of all workers were below 30 years at the time of their first journey.

insist upon signed contracts. The possession of contracts by workers varied between destination countries.[12]

Though Kuwait has a mandatory standard employment contract, domestic workers have little access to the justice system to seek enforcement of their contracts (IHRC, 2013).[13] The UAE and Oman have introduced a standard contract for domestic workers (Esim and Kerbage, 2011). The UAE did so in 2007 to require "adequate breaks" but does not limit working hours or provide for a weekly rest day, overtime pay, or workers' compensation (Human Rights Watch, Country Reports, 2012).[14] A regulation adopted by Saudi Arabia in 2013 provides domestic workers a weekly day off and a month's paid vacation every two years. Notably, it requires rest of nine hours a day for a worker, which however is less than the provision for eight hour work days in other sectors (HRW, 2014: 15).[15]

In 2012, Bahrain extended coverage of provisions relating to labor contracts, wage calculation, annual leave and dispute settlement to domestic workers, but did not include limits to hours of work, weekly days off, and ability to leave their employers. A decree issued in Qatar in 2008 stipulates that domestic workers should not be forced to work in any way that insults them physically or mentally and that the sponsor must provide them with suitable accommodation and health care and must maintain proof of payment of the agreed upon salary (Breslin and Jones, 2010: 402).

Jordan restricts entry of domestics to countries with which it has bilateral agreements and India is not one of them. However, it has gone further than other Middle Eastern countries in securing the rights of domestic workers. Jordan's labor laws

---

[12] In the UAE, domestic workers did not have legally binding contracts governing their employment (Sabban, 2005); the contracts signed at home were replaced in Saudi Arabia, where contracts were mandatory to get work permits, by a different one (HRW, 2008) and in Bahrain less than half the workers in a survey had contracts (Sabika al-Najjar, 2005).

[13] In Kuwait, domestic workers are excluded from a new private sector labor law passed in February 2010 that sets maximum working hours, requires a weekly rest day and annual leave, and sets end-of-service bonuses.

[14] In May 2012, a local newspaper obtained a copy of a new draft law for domestic workers, which the authorities are yet to make public. The draft reportedly provides for one weekly day off, two weeks of paid annual leave and 15 paid sick days while also making a domestic worker liable for prosecution and sanctions of up to six months in prison and a fine of 100,000 Dirhams (US$27,000) if she reveals the "secrets" of her employers. Also apparently the draft law also imposes harsh criminal sentences on those who "encourage" a domestic worker to quit her job or offer her shelter. Authorities have not made the draft law public.

[15] The approximately 1.5 million migrant domestic workers in Saudi Arabia are excluded from the 2005 labor law, which provides limits to working hours and restrictions on salary deductions, rest days and mechanisms for resolving labor disputes (Human Rights Watch, Country Report, 2012).

which are partly general laws and partly specific or subordinate laws entitle domestic workers to weekly rest from work, annual leave to the same extent as other workers and to minimum wage provisions (ILO, 2013: 133). In a significant move, in October 2011, a court in Jordan ordered the employers of a domestic worker to pay her fines for being in the country without documented residency status creating a judicial precedent in favor of migrant workers (HRW, Country Reports, 2013).

Under the *kafala* system, the sponsor undertakes to inform the immigration department of any change in the labor contract such as expiry, renewal or cancellation, and pledges to repatriate the employee upon termination of the contract, but in practice may seek to evade its legal responsibility by deliberately not renewing the workers residency permit. In such situations, migrant workers may be slapped with false charges of theft or absconding and jailed under the law (Chammartin, 2005: 21). Workers are rendered vulnerable because enforcement is poor, even where provisions exist, and it is very difficult for them to access the justice system. In this context, support from sending states is imperative for workers to take advantage of provisions for their protection and to signal to employers that they will be called to account for violations.

5 Employment Choices and Vulnerability

Contrary to representations that stereotype MDWs in their sending regions as either abjectly seeking overseas employment in dire circumstances, thus incapable of making a choice, or motivated to make money through illicit sexual activities, thus invested with sexual agency, respondents expressed their preference for overseas employment in coherent and sober terms (Kodoth, 2014). Rarely, in their own perspectives, did women go passively. Yet, once in the Middle East, their employment choices are constrained by tensions introduced by the regulatory frameworks in the Middle East and the dearth of support from the Indian state. Nevertheless, MDWs advance strong rationale for wanting to continue in employment, even when they choose a particular type of job under pressure. The regulatory environment shapes distinct vulnerabilities for MDWs depending upon the choice of employment. In this section, I analyze the nature of employment choices, the contexts in which they are made and workers' vulnerability in four broad categories of employment in the Middle East — stable employment with sponsors, precarious employment with sponsors, stable informal employment and precarious informal employment.

i. *Stable Employment with Sponsors*

In the weak regulatory environment of the Middle East, stable employment of MDWs is characterized usually by patronage relations, which involves the exchange of loyalty for protection and serves to obfuscate exploitation. Within a framework of patronage, however, MDW may negotiate and bargain in explicit or subtle ways and even resist violence. Beena, a former fish vendor from Trivandrum, had worked in Kuwait for 12 years with a single sponsor-employer. Her trajectory as an MDW shows the terms on which patronage relations are established. In the first six months of employment, her sponsor subjected her to physical violence and paid her salary only intermittently. Beena could not follow instructions as she did not understand Arabic which raised the sponsor's ire. As patronage relations are a means of gaining a foothold in the employer's household, MDWs may constitute violation of rights not as dead ends but as part of everyday struggles to hold on to employment. Looking back at how she survived the early period of employment, Beena observed that ill treatment by her sponsor was aggravated by her inability to communicate in Arabic and lack of training.

The first three years were the most difficult. Beena was made to work in three households, that of her sponsor and her sponsor's two children. Overworked and with little rest, she looked forward to her vacation, which her sponsor delayed on one pretext or other. When three years had passed she confronted her sponsor. "In that situation I said to her, if you don't send me home I will consume something and die. Once I learnt the language, I got the courage to speak back to them, to match word for word" (Trivandrum, OBC, Interview, July 2013). Beena returned to Kuwait after a year and a half. At first she looked for a new sponsor but her former sponsor learnt through the agent in Kuwait that Beena was looking for a visa and persuaded her to return. She agreed to go back to the former sponsor on the condition that she would not be made to work in multiple households.

As the only domestic in the household, Beena worked long hours when the family got together at the weekends and during Ramzan, but Beena's salary rose from KD 35 in 1997 to KD 90 (Rs. 18,000) in 2012 and her sponsor had promised to increase her salary to KD 100 if she returned. She could cook her own food, had a relatively free reign over the kitchen and had even provided food to emigrant workers who were in difficult situations. Beena did not have a regular weekly holiday but was not prevented from going out.

She underlined the affection she was held in. Referring to her sponsor's daughter, she said: 'She would hug me and plant a kiss on each cheek when she came home even if I was soiled from work in the kitchen.' With a wide circle of acquaintances in Kuwait, Beena had declined several overtures to work on the informal market because she believed it could tarnish her reputation. In 2013, Beena felt she was not strong enough anymore for the strenuous work that was demanded of her but her sponsor-employer, an older woman, was keen to retain her services. The sponsor had sent her money to treat her aching shoulder, according to Beena, a result of years of giving body massages to her sponsor and her sponsor's daughter.

MDWs value patronage relations when it establishes strong reciprocity associated with affective ties with the sponsor's family coded usually in terms of fictive kinship, gifts on special occasions and assistance during crisis in their families. Those who made repeated efforts to go overseas in recent years despite returning from short abusive stints expressed the hope that they would find a good sponsor because they believed that there were good sponsors. Their belief was held together by what they knew of the experiences of other workers. Nageswari, for instance, described her employer in the following terms. 'In that house, the Madam was so good, she meant more to me that my mother and my husband... She would give me rice and roti (food that Indian MDWs are accustomed to) and ask me to eat first and only then to work. It is through the grace of Allah that I got this house. She used to listen to what I had to say' (OBC, Kadapa, Interview, November, 2013).

MDWs may choose to continue with a sponsor even in conditions of weak reciprocity. Mariyam's sponsor for the past 18 years in Saudi Arabia exploited her vulnerability. Prior to taking up this job, Mariyam had manipulated her return from Qatar by letting the police apprehend her because she could not cope with the workload in her sponsor's house. This was her first overseas job. When she was on vacation her sponsor dismissed her two co-workers expecting her to do all the work. Mariyam had responsibilities as a single parent with four daughters and a son, and prospects for work were bleak in her Malappuram village, where agriculture and the fishing trade could provide only irregular work.

In Saudi Arabia, her salary was a moderate 600 Riyals (Rs. 10,000) in 2013 up from 400 Riyals when she started working there in 1996. The sponsor was averse to letting her go. 'At first even if my salary was in arrears, they would pay when I left for home but later even that was not done. Then I would go back because they owed me money... If they pay the full amount they know we will not return. They will not let you go when they find you suitable. They will keep you there. Now when I came last they owed me eight months salary' (Malappuram, Interview, November 2013). Mariyam was under pressure to continue in such conditions. "After the marriage (of one of her four daughters) there was a lot of debt here. So I held on and stayed there. I came back now after nine years." In 18 years she visited home only three times. Push factors at home and weak regulation in the destination could condition MDW to accept jobs with minimum assurances such as payment of salaries and personal safety.

ii. *Precarious Employment with Sponsors*

The journeys of a segment of workers traversed several countries rarely out of deliberate intention but because, lacking personal connections in any destination, they source visas successively through informal recruiters. Periodic truncation of employment prevents MDWs from establishing patronage ties. They take up these jobs because overseas employment, considered more remunerative than work available at home, is easy to access through informal recruiters. Florence, an MDW from East Godavari with no previous experience of employment, obtained visas from informal recruiters at least half a dozen times. Her experience illustrates how repeated dependence on informal recruitment reinforces the instability of employment and draws attention, by default, to why MDWs may prefer to work within a framework of patronage relations with sponsors or to seek informal employment.

Between 1985 and 2013, Florence spent a little more than a decade working in five countries in the Middle East. Her husband's ill health shifted the entire burden of provisioning the family on to her shoulder and she needed to finance his medical treatment. Her overseas tenure was in two phases. Between 1985 and 1991, she worked for a total of five years in Qatar, Kuwait and Dubai, returning home when her husband's health got worse and going overseas when she ran out of money. On her return from Dubai in 1991, she decided not to go back but was compelled to go in 2004 to pay for her daughter's higher education.

Between 2004 and 2013, she worked in Kuwait, Saudi Arabia, the UAE and Oman. She forfeited a relatively stable job in Kuwait, where she worked with her sponsor's family for three years and with his son's family for two years, because she needed to stay at home for a year as her husband underwent a major surgery. In 2010, she returned from Saudi Arabia after barely three months because she was unable to cope as the sole domestic in a household with 15 members. She travelled to the UAE in January 2012 and was placed as the sole domestic worker in a large house. Unable to cope with the work she returned to the agency "office" in Al Ain and waited for two months to find work. Meanwhile the agent in Al Ain, a Telugu woman, left the place.

Insecure about what lay ahead and under immense pressure to find work, Florence agreed to go across the border with a sponsor from Oman. Florence was expected to do the housework and take care of an infant. Her relations with the sponsor soured because the sponsor failed to pay her salary regularly but matters came to a head eight months later when the employer, enraged that her child was hurt, charged Florence with negligence. In the altercation that ensued, the employer brandished a knife and threatened to kill Florence. Florence fled to the Indian Embassy but returned to the sponsor after the embassy mediated a rapprochement between them. It was Ramzan, a month of intensive work for domestics. When the sponsor refused to pay her salary at the end of the month she escaped again and was repatriated through the embassy.

Florence underlines the harsh conditions of employment that prompt MDWs to change jobs. She says of a job in the earlier phase in which she received her salary regularly and the sponsor was keen to have her back: "My hands were wounded because of the work. They asked me to stay but due to heavy work (in the sponsor's household, she was unable to cope hence) I assured them that I would come back (to work for them). I returned home and cancelled the visa. In that house there were four people but my madam had cats to feed... I had to look after all the twenty cats as well as the family members. How could I do all that?" (East Godavari, Interview, June, 2013).

Florence's experience in 2012–2013 emphasizes the perils of the informal recruitment process. Florence travelled to the UAE on a visit visa obtained through an informal recruiting network that sourced workers through irregular processes. Dependent on this network to find a sponsor, she felt compelled to accept a job in Oman. Her sponsor, who gave her a fresh visa, told Florence that he would send her home if she paid him the 500 Riyals she had cost him for the visa and the commission to her agent, when Florence too had paid the agent for the visa and travel charges. Each time an MDW takes up a new job, she must negotiate afresh the tensions arising from the fact that both the sponsor and she invest in visa charges and emigration expenses, the profits of which are absorbed by the recruiting industry.

iii. *Informal Employment on Private Visas*

In contrast to employment with the sponsor, informal employment on private visas is based on fairly robust contractual ties. MDWs in this category are well positioned to exploit the opportunities on the informal market because a private visa, which introduces a clear distinction between the sponsor and the employer, gives them space to manoeuvre. In particular, their ability to exit jobs and find new ones enhances their bargaining power in employment relationships. MDWs usually associate informal employment with higher returns. When I asked Florence whether she had worked "outside", a reference to informal employment, she retorted: 'would I be in this state if I had', referring to her house which had work in progress and a 28 year old unmarried daughter at home. Workers may negotiate part-time or full-time live-in work arrangements. In part-time work, payment is based on time spent on work and irregular assignments are task specific.

Lateefa had 27 years of experience as an MDW in the Middle East. She worked in Saudi Arabia, for five years with a sponsor full-time and in a hospital as a cleaning supervisor for three years before shifting to the UAE. When she arrived in the UAE she could speak Arabic fluently. I use her experience to probe the terms on which MDWs are successful on the informal market. Prior to her return, in 2013, Lateefa combined regular part-time assignments and irregular work on a private visa in Sharjah and earned at least Rs. 40,000 a month. She received 20 Dirhams per hour on regular part-time jobs and had four to five regular part-time commitments that fetched her approximately 300 Dirhams per household. When irregular work was particularly heavy, when there were parties in Arab or English speaking households usually on weekends and cleaning up on the following morning, Lateefa had earned up to Rs. 50,000 a month. Private visas are expensive and MDWs who live in rented accommodation incur additional expenses. Lateefa pays 7,000 Dirhams, more than a lakh of rupees to renew her visa every two years. In the last eight months, because her husband had returned home, she shared a room with another woman which cost her about Rs. 5,000 a month.

In 1992, when she arrived in Abu Dhabi, Lateefa's agency placed her with a large Arab household.

> There were eight children, the mother, a married daughter, her husband and two children. Cooking, cleaning, ironing, washing, I had to do everything. I was not able to, so three months later, I went back to the office that placed me there… They sent me back, but again I went to the office. Then the officer asked me "Here, free visas are made available. Do you have anyone to help you?" I knew a young man from Vembayam small town in Trivandrum… It cost me some money, because he contacted another Malayalee and that Malayalee contacted another. In this way, for various things I incurred 15,000 Dirhams. That is for me to obtain a release from Abu Dhabi and to get to Sharjah. The Arabi also was paid the money he had spent.

Her contact helped her raise the money on interest from various sources and found her a full-time job in Sharjah. She befriended two Malayalee shop assistants in the neighborhood who helped her to repay her debt. She also met a Sri Lankan woman who worked part-time, and within a month moved in with her and started working part-time. A divorcee, Lateefa married a watchman at an apartment complex, who had helped her get jobs and moved in with him. Over the years, she nurtured a network of friends and employers, and used her connections with Arab sponsors to source visas for her relatives and acquaintances. Lateefa's transition to the informal market and her success on it underlines the importance of individual resources. Dependence on informal networks is not without peril. Lateefa pointed out that one of the intermediaries who facilitated her job in Sharjah expected her to have sexual relations with him.

MDWs on private visas may choose full-time live-in employment, which is considered comparatively more protected because they are shielded from being out in the public. Despite a formal resemblance to employment with sponsors, these workers exude a sense of independence. Sita, an upper caste woman from East Godavari, who had spent over 20 years overseas, earned over Rs. 20,000 a month in a full-time job with an Arab family in Oman. When I asked whether her employer abused her, she had retorted saying, how can she when I am on my own visa?

Informal workers on private visas may not perceive a constant threat of detection even when they lived in rented accommodation, except when there is a targeted drive by the state to expose and deport illegal workers. Jumaila said she was surprised by the vehemence of the vigilance drive in Kuwait in early 2013 because "usually it is only people without *iqamas* (residence permits) who are rounded up. Most people here are on free visas and have *iqamas*". Thus, in 'normal' times, the entrenched institutional character of informality and workers' possession of documents may enable them to contain vulnerability.

Informal jobs, particularly when they are part-time, give workers the flexibility and freedom. The freedom they enjoy and their close association with informal networks in the destination, however subjects them to suspicion of illicit sexual activities. Thus, MDW women were reluctant to speak openly about building up an independent career. Typically, they speak of their transition to informal employment when male family members join them in the destination because this choice is underpinned by the economics of shared accommodation and reinforced by the perception that the presence of male members offers protection in the dual sense of negotiating the public space in the Middle East and in smothering rumours of illicit sexual activities that accompany informal employment. Women in informal jobs who live in shared accommodation that is not with family or their kin group are less willing to speak about it.

iv. *Precarious Informal Employment*

MDWs are most vulnerable when they are forced on to the informal market because they are unable to cope with the demands of employment with a sponsor. Informal support networks are crucial to survive in these circumstances. A bare sketch of the experience of an MDW from East Godavari, who died in Bahrain in 2007, brings into sharp focus the conditions in which MDWs are rendered undocumented and their vulnerability on the informal market.[16] When her sponsor showed his displeasure towards her because not knowing the language she could not communicate with the family, Mariamma feared the worst because she had been sent back home from her first overseas job in Qatar after barely three months as the sponsor was dissatisfied with her. In her first job, she received no salary and her family, left with a debt of Rs. 40,000 from that journey, borrowed another Rs. 50,000 to source a visa to Bahrain. With the debt mounting at home, Mariamma was desperate to stay in Bahrain. She ran away from the household and survived for three years as an undocumented worker, sending money home, but her luck ran out. Without a job and forced to vacate the shared rental accommodation she

[16]The Hindu, on February 20, 2011.

occupied, according to the report, she was found wandering about in a demented state. She died in a hospital.

Undocumented workers negotiate risks through their informal support networks, which not only enable them to search for employment on the informal market and to find a place to stay, but also to survive in times of distress. Mariamma's tragic end signals her inability to mobilize adequate support. Undocumented workers had survived on informal employment and returned during the amnesty — a period when absconding workers are pardoned and allowed to leave the country. Due to past experience workers expect that governments will declare amnesty periodically. Even so, workers are exposed to the risk of detection. During her 13 years as an MDW, Shally, had negotiated undocumented status twice. She overstayed her visa in Abu Dhabi in the mid-2000s, earning about 800 Dirhams a month in part-time jobs for Malayalee families and returned during an amnesty. In Kuwait, she was arrested and lost her savings.

> You need an identity card to buy gold or to send money through the bank. Because this was not possible, so that my money was not simply kept like that I put it in a chitty (informal savings). I thought that when it is over or when I go home, I can take the amount or maybe then I can buy gold. In the end three months before the chitty was over, I was caught (Trivandrum, Interview, November 2012).

Undocumented workers who have relatively stable jobs may be vulnerable because they may be unable to access public services that are premised on legal documents. Manjari, for instance, worked for seven years in several part-time jobs as an undocumented worker in Kuwait. She ran away from her sponsor of eight years because the latter refused to increase her salary and she was aware that she could earn significantly higher on the informal market. She gave herself up to the police because she developed severe diabetics and was unable to seek medical treatment (ST, Kadapa, Interview, November 2013). The uncertainties of surviving on the informal market may induce MDWs to tolerate exploitative sponsors or when their hands are forced by abusive sponsors, they may seek full-time live-in employment as a relatively safer option.

6 Conclusion: How Appropriate is Indian Policy?

Indian policy assumes that the emigration clearance system can filter through domestic service jobs that offer the basis of protection from those that do not, by using the minimum age prescription of 30 years, Indian embassy attested work contracts and visas obtained directly from sponsors. The 30-year minimum age speaks directly to a heightened social concern over the mobility of unmarried young women. It assumes that women below that age lack the social and sexual maturity required for overseas employment (Kodoth and Varghese, 2013). As women in India are likely to be married long before they are 30 years, it also signals censure of the migration of women with young children.

The aspirations of women in the sending regions and a proactive informal recruiting industry have rendered the prescribed minimum age ineffective, suggesting that MDWs do not consider it beneficial. Even the conservative argument of the social costs of women's migration when they have small children fails to justify the specification of 30 years as the minimum age. In our sample, 82% of MDW were married by 21 years and the youngest child of half the emigrants was over five years when they first migrated. MDWs with infant children justified their resort to migration in terms of the need to earn a decent livelihood.

A restrictive policy has had disempowering effects for Indian MDWs as a group on the Middle Eastern labor markets, because it increases the cost of migration and lowers the returns to MDW, it discourages aspirants from investing in skills and diminishes their labor market prospects (Kodoth, forthcoming). Sending country policies and actions are inhibited by the difficulties of intervening in the domestic sector in another country owing to differences in legal frameworks and the hurdles in putting together evidence. Nevertheless, countries like the Philippines have been proactive in protecting the interests of their MDWs. The diplomatic missions of the Philippines in the Middle East mediate in disputes, refer cases to the courts, bear the expenses of litigation and enable workers to stay on in the destination till the case is over (Oishi, 2005). In association with recruiting agencies, they also attempt to find new employers for workers (HRW 2008; IHRC, 2013). It should be relatively easy for India to enforce support structures compared to smaller states like the Philippines but also it should be easier for India to enforce supportive measures in the destination than to enforce restrictions at home.

Mariyam's words mock the emigration clearance system for its irrelevance once an MDW is in the Middle East. 'There are people who lock you up. If there is someone going that way, a written appeal may be thrown out of the window. I hear things like this. Maybe you can escape like that. Otherwise I don't know how it is possible to escape.' These are conditions in which even proactively supportive policies may fall short, but Indian policy, with its rhetoric of protectionism, merely deflects attention for the responsibility of the Indian state to support MDWs in the destination.

As the regulatory system in the Middle East structures highly precarious conditions of employment for MDW, support from sending countries could be crucial. By failing to extend support to them in the destination, Indian protectionism reinforces the vulnerability of MDWs even when they adhere to regulation.

Mariyam was well over 30 years when she took up her first job in Qatar. She received the visa through a close relative and worked in the household of the son of her relative's sponsor. When her relations with the sponsor became strained, she fled. "I ran away to the police station. They would not let me go. Had I failed or stayed a month longer, I would have died from suffering. I returned in these circumstances." Embassy officials visited Mariyam in jail and facilitated her return, but did not assist her to recover her dues nor was she aware of the possibility of pursuing a case. Chastened by this experience she chose to persist in employment with a sponsor in Saudi Arabia despite failing patronage.

MDWs report that when approached to mediate disputes, embassy officials support their sponsors. Florence had an ECNR endorsed passport and was legally employed in Oman when she approached the Indian embassy in difficult circumstances. Running away heightens tensions between MDWs and their sponsors but embassy officials sent Florence back on the word of the sponsor that she would not be ill treated. When the sponsor failed to pay her salary after another month she managed to escape again. Florence was grateful to the embassy for facilitating her return but she did not receive support to recover her dues from the sponsor nor to pursue a case against abusive treatment. Further, our respondents pointed out that Filipina and Sri Lankan MDWs were able to use the support of their embassies to bargain with their employers.

We can only speculate on why Mariamma did not approach the Indian embassy in Bahrain. A section of our respondents were unaware of the Indian embassy, but the actions of MDWs who are aware of the embassy are shaped in accordance with widespread perception that the Indian state is hostile to them. Indian officials claim that Indian MDWs end up in distress because they flout Indian regulations and support could only encourage them to resort to illegality. Contrast to this, with the law in the Philippines which mandates coordinated efforts by the state, diplomatic missions and NGOs to protect migrant workers and requires its diplomatic missions to assist migrants even if they were undocumented (IHRC, 2013).

The dearth of support from the Indian state bolsters the incentive that MDWs may have to resort to illegality. Though separated by starkly different experiences, Mariamma and Lateefa stepped into the informal market in order to avoid having to return home, the inevitable outcome if they had approached the Indian embassy. The attractions of the informal market are a fallout of the regulatory framework in the Middle East but success is subject to individual resources and access to informal support networks. In conditions of distress intermediaries extract a heavy price from MDWs for support in financial and other terms.

Restrictive Indian regulation fails to afford protection to MDWs even when they abide by it and has motivated them to resort to illegal means in order to remain in the Middle East and make good their investment in the emigration process. In this context, strong support in destination countries rather than barriers to movement from India is critical not only for the safe return of MDWs but also to enable them to tap better opportunities overseas.

Interviews cited:

Beena, Trivandrum, OBC, Latin Catholic, Kuwait
Nageshwari, Kadapa, OBC, Hindu, Kuwait
Mariyam, Malappuram, OBC, Muslim, Qatar, Saudi Arabia
Florence, East Godavari, SC, Qatar, Kuwait, UAE, Saudi Arabia, Oman
Lateefa, Trivandrum, OBC, Muslim, Saudi Arabia, UAE
Sita, East Godavari, Upper caste, Qatar, Oman
Jumaila, Trivandrum, OBC, Muslim, Saudi Arabia, Kuwait
Shally, Trivandrum, OBC, Latin Catholic, Qatar, Kuwait, UAE, Oman
Manjari, Kadapa, ST, Kuwait
POE, Hyderabad, February 2013

References

Adapa, S. (2002), 'Birds of Passage': Migration of South Indian Labourers to South East Asia. *Critical Asian Studies*, 34(1), 84–115.

al-Najjar, S. (2004), 'Women Migrant Domestic Workers in Bahrain,' in Simel, E. and M. Smith (Ed.): *Gender and Migration in the Arab States: The case of Domestic workers*, International Labour Organisation, Beirut: Regional Office of the Arab States.

Baldwin-Edwards, M. (2011), 'Labour Immigration and Labour Markets in the GCC Countries: National Patterns and Trend', Kuwait Programme on Development, Governance and Globalisation in the Gulf States, Paper No. 15, London: London School of Economics.

Breslin, J. and T. Jones (2010), '*Qatar*' in Kelly, S. and B. Julia (Ed.): *Women's Rights in the Middle East and North Africa-Progress amid Resistance*, 397–425, Plymouth, United Kingdom: Rowman and Littlefield Publishers, Inc., 397–425.

Chammartin, G.M-F. (2005), '*Domestic Workers: Little Protection for the Underpaid'*, Migration Information Source. Available from: http://www.migrationpolicy.org/article/domestic-workers-little-protection-underpaid.

Deffner, V. and C. Pfaffenbach (2011), Zones of contact and spaces of negotiation: The Indian diaspora in Muscat (Sultanate of Oman), International RC21 conference, "The struggle to belong Dealing with diversity in 21st century urban settings, Amsterdam. Available from: http://www.rc21.org/conferences/amsterdam2011/edocs/Session%2028/28-DP-Deffner.pdf.

Gardner, A.M. (2010), Engulfed: Indian Guest Workers, Bahraini Citizens and the Structural Violence of the Kafala System, in De Genova, N. and N. Mae Peutz (Eds.).

The Deportation Regime: Sovereignty, Space, and the Freedom of Movement. Durham, NC: Duke University Press.

Godfrey, M., M. Ruhs, N. Shah and M. Smith (2004), 'Migrant Domestic Workers in Kuwait: Findings based on a field survey and additional research' in Simel, E. and M. Smith (Ed.): *Gender and Migration in the Arab States*: *The Case of Domestic Workers*, International Labour Organisation, Beirut: Regional Office of the Arab States.

Human Rights Watch (2014), *'I already bought you': Abuse and Exploitation of female domestic workers in the United Arab Emirates*. Available from: https://www.hrw.org/report/2014/10/22/i-already-bought-you/abuse-and-exploitation-female-migrant-domestic-workers-united

Human Rights Watch (2008), *As If I am Not Human: Abuses against Asian Domestic Workers in Saudi Arabia*.

Human Rights Watch (2012), *World Report*. Available from: http://www.hrw.org/world-report-2012#countries.

International Human Rights Clinic (2013), The Protection of the rights of Migrant Domestic Workers in a Country of Origin and a Country of Destination, Case Studies of the Philippines and Kuwait, John Hopkins School of Advanced International Studies, International Law and Organization Program, The Protection Project.

International Labour Organization (2013), *Domestic Workers across the World: Global and Regional Statistics and the extent of Legal Protection*. Geneva: ILO Office.

Kodoth, P. (Forthcoming), Structural Violence against Emigrant Domestic Workers and Survival in the Middle East: The Effects of Indian Emigration Policy. *Journal of Interdisciplinary Economics*.

Kodoth, P. (2014), Who Goes? Failures of Marital Provisioning, Agency and Migration of Less skilled Women Workers from Kerala. *CDS Working Paper No. 456*, Trivandrum: Centre for Development Studies.

Kodoth, P. and V.J. Varghese (2012), Protecting Women or Endangering the Emigration Process: Gender and India's Migration Policy. *Economic and Political Weekly*, 47(43), 56–63.

Manseau, G.S. (2007), Contractual Solutions for Migrant Labourers: The Case of Domestic Workers in the Middle East. Human Rights Law Commentry. Available from: https://www.nottingham.ac.uk/shared/shared_hrlcpub/HRLC_Commentary_2006/manseau.pdf.

MOIA (2001), High Level Committee on the Indian Diaspora. Report (Online). Available from: http://www.indiandiaspora.nic.in/ contents. htm.

Oishi, N. (2005), *Women in Motion: Globalization, State Policies and Labor Migration in Asia*. Stanford University Press, Stanford.

Pradhan, S. (2009), India's Economic and Political Presence in the Gulf: A Gulf Perspective, in *India's Growing Role in the Gulf: Implications for the Region and the United States*, Monograph. Washington DC: The Gulf Research Centre, Dubai and The Nixon Centre.

Sabban, R. (2004), Women migrant domestic workers in the United Arab Emirates, in Simel, E. and M. Smith (Eds.): *Gender and Migration in the Arab States: The Case of Domestic Workers*. International Labour Organisation, Beirut: Regional Office of the Arab States.

Simel, E. and C. Kerbage (2011), The Situation of Migrant Domestic Workers in Arab States: A Legislative Overview, Available from: http://www.academia.edu/1006359/The_Situation_of_Migrant_Domestic_Workers_in_Arab_States_A_Legislative_Overview.

Shah, N.M. (2009), *The Management of Irregular Migration and Its Consequences for Development: Gulf Cooperation Council*, Bangkok: Working Paper No. 19, ILO.

Index